Mystical
Rites and Rituals

Mystical Rites and Rituals

*Initiation
and Fertility Rites,
Sacrifice and Burial Customs,
Incantation and
Ritual Magic*

Contents

Rituals 11

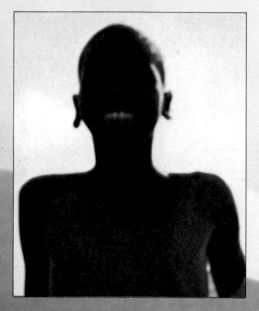

Rites of Passage 19

The Rhythm of Life 43

First published 1975 by
Octopus Books Limited
59 Grosvenor Street, London W.1.

ISBN 0 7064 0449 1

© 1970-1971 BPC Publishing Ltd.
© 1975 BPC Publishing Ltd. This
book has been produced by Phoebus
Publishing Company in cooperation with
Octopus Books Limited.

Produced by Mandarin Publishers Limited
22a Westlands Road, Quarry Bay, Hong Kong

Printed in Hong Kong

Ritual

The Origins

Many different kinds of phenomena have been described as ritual. The term has been applied, for example, to the mating habits of birds and animals, such as the dance on the water of the crested grebe; by psychoanalysts to the obsessive behaviour of neurotics, as when a man persistently checks whether he has turned off a tap, only to check anew after each check; and by anthropologists and sociologists to the established forms of behaviour of devotees of cults and religions. But while it is important to try to establish common explanations for the phenomena thus categorized, it is essential to grasp that there are fundamental differences between them and also between modes of interpreting them.

Freud himself argued that there were marked similarities between the obsessive 'rituals' of neurotics and psychotics, and the 'rituals' of what he called primitive society. Indeed, he postulated in *Totem and Tabu* (1913) from his theory of the development of the Oedipus complex (a theory derived from depth analyses of his patients), that the origin of sacrifice and religion in general was to be derived from a primordial killing and devouring of a patriarchal male. Freud conceived of human society as originally comprising a 'primitive horde', ruled over and controlled by a father who kept all the females for himself and repelled his growing sons. The sons, who both hated and admired their father, finally united in killing and eating him, to absorb his strength and virility. Then, stricken with a sense of guilt, they invented rites of expiation, which involved totemism, taboo and all the other institutions of primitive society. This presentation of the Oedipus complex as the source or cause of religion had the support of no archeological or anthropological evidence, but it excited much interest and won great

Left The Bapende tribe in ritual costume.

Right Mandan braves of North America enduring voluntary torture at the conclusion of a buffalo dance, part of the great annual ceremony called the Okipa: the dances lasted for many days and the myths of the origins of things were re-told; by George Catlin, 19th century.

Su Gooders/Royal Anthropological Institute

Procession of penitents in Venice, a painting by Gentile Bellini: the rite is both a formal expression of repentance for sin and a way of arousing the emotion of repentance in the participants and spectators.

publicity. If it be taken as what the anthropologist A. Kroeber called a 'Just-so Story' (that is, a story which explains the origin of some well-known phenomenon), then there is no evidence for it, and more recent studies of the social life of the apes make it highly improbable. On the other hand, Kroeber allowed that it might represent a psychological process which most human males undergo, in symbolical form, in the course of their development. Then it might well be

one of the springs of emotion which feed into social rituals. Even so, sociologists and anthropologists would argue that Freud's theory cannot be used to explain the development, and the complexity, of the social and cultural relationships involved in rituals.

Variations in Response

Similarly, anthropologists would reject any claim by psychoanalysts that, for example, circumcision ceremonies of boys near puberty can be 'explained' by saying that they create castration-anxiety and fix the incest taboo firmly in the boys' minds. While the above is the standard psychoanalytical explanation of circumcision, one psycho-

analyst, B. Bettelheim, has argued from a study of four schizoid children who developed their own initiation ceremonies, that the practice of circumcision arises among males through envy of the productive wombs of females.

Anthropologists would concede that particular persons, passing through circumcision ceremonies, may feel castration-anxiety or womb-envy; but that this would have to be demonstrated by appropriate methods of research, and that the structure of the personalities of the persons enforcing, or undergoing, such ceremonial operations should be taken into account. It may well be that in all men and women, at very deep levels of the psyche, similar syndromes of

Scala

feeling are to be found; but psychoanalysis itself shows that people vary in their degree of adjustment to those syndromes, in their more conscious feelings and their actions. Thus there is a considerable degree of variation in both the type and the intensity of individuals' reaction to participation in the same ritual.

Examples of this were noted by the present writer at circumcision ceremonies held among certain African tribes. At the ritual circumcision each candidate (aged from seven to 15), while being operated on, should be supported by his father, who is supposed to hold his son's penis and help the circumciser, a ritual adept, turn back the foreskin. On one occasion, the hands of the

first father shook so much that it was impossible for the circumciser to act; and the father was replaced by his brother-in-law, the boy's mother's brother, who strictly was not appropriate. The hands of the second father were very steady, and he watched the operation steadily. The hands of the third father were steady, but he could not watch the operation and turned his head away to look over his shoulder. One must draw the conclusion that the circumcision of each boy meant something quite different to each father, in terms of present relationships, of what each had felt and suffered when he himself as a boy underwent the operation, of the psychological syndromes established in each during infancy, and so on. Hence it

seems that psychological analysis can only be effective if it is applied to bring out the significance of a particular ritual, or part of a ritual, for particular individuals, each with his own history of psychological development and his own established personality.

Swazi Songs of Hate

The Swazi of southern Africa, at the ripening of the first fruits, stage elaborate national ceremonies, at certain phases of which they are required to hurl insults at their king, who is the central figure of the rituals, and to sing sacred national songs stating how much the king is hated by his subjects. In social-anthropological analysis these rites have been successfully related to the low density

The Indian peoples of Brazil have some of the most complex and mysterious rituals on earth: Kamaiura Indian seen praying for the rains to stop so that the fishing season can begin. The wooden flute is the instrument through which he speaks to the gods. Among many Indians the sacred flutes represent the ancestors of the tribe, and it is death for a woman or a boy who has not yet been initiated to see them. At one time, so the story says, the women had charge of the flutes and so were able to rule the men, but the men rebelled and seized the flutes.

sion, or as the transference of stifled feelings of aggression on to scapegoats, or as simply and directly strengthening social sentiments. In the Swazi ceremony summarily analysed above, it is justified to say that the rites are calculated to arouse the sentiments that support national solidarity. Since we know that acting an emotion is likely to produce feelings of that emotion, it is probable that occasions of group celebration will arouse the sentiments which are appropriate to group solidarity and which support adherence to certain group values and morals, in most participants at least.

But we know equally well that the most complex and intensive reaction to a religious ceremony may come from the sinners in the congregation: they may be most deeply moved by emotions evoked by ritual, particularly ritual in which they have participated as children and as adolescents, and they may then feel determined during the ritual to sin no more. Their intensive emotional reaction may well be provoked by strong feelings of guilt and unworthiness. On the other hand, the man who conforms in his daily life with the precepts of religion and morality is likely to worship with a much more restrained and consistent devotion, while those who are betwixt and between will respond in moderate degree. So in the Swazi ritual cited above, loyal men may have their sentiments of patriotism evoked less strongly than the potential traitors.

Milk Tree Society

A much more complicated theory to relate rituals to emotional predispositions is therefore required, and the best as yet advanced is that of Victor W. Turner, in a series of analyses of the significance of ritual symbols. His highly complex argument can be summarized as follows. Information on the meaning of ritual symbols can be collected from participants, who will give interpretations of various degrees of complexity, depending on whether they are ritual adepts or not. In general, explanations of this kind stress the harmonious, socially valuable attributes of the symbol. Thus, when the Ndembu of Zambia, whom Turner studied, are initiating a nubile girl into womanood, the key symbol is a tree which exudes a white substance, like milk. The Ndembu specifically compare the white sap of the 'milk tree' with mother's milk, and state that it represents the tie between mother and child: it thus represents the tie between the girl being initiated and her own mother, and her future, nurturing tie with the children whom it is hoped she will produce.

Further, since the Ndembu are a matrilineal society (reckoning descent and suc-

of population as a result of the simple system of husbandry; the low variation in standards of living; and the delegation of authority from the king to subordinates ruling numbers of men who, because of the simplicity of weapons, are all warriors, constituting a private army which can help its leader in attempts to gain power. These leaders are of royal blood and may organize rebellions aimed at the kingship. There is therefore present in the national ceremony a symbolic representation of political processes within the nation, riven by civil wars.

The rites emphasize that while the kingship itself is sacred and is 'strengthened' in the rites, the king is beset by internal enemies on whose loyalty he cannot rely. But this does not mean that each warrior who

insults the king or who sings the songs of hatred against him must necessarily have sentiments of disloyalty awakened, or go through a severe crisis of loyalty. For one warrior, though he may feel the sacredness of the occasion, it may be in some ways like a fete, a kind of carnival when licence is allowed. At the other extreme, other warriors may go through an emotional turmoil in which strong resentments against authority are awakened, and perhaps a reliving of childhood difficulties in their relationships with their fathers. Again, analysis of individual, possibly variable, reactions to ritual is required.

One must similarly reject any simple direct explanation of ritual as the expression of tension, of despair, of anxiety or aggres-

Times Newspapers

Federico and Aldo Patellani

cession and inheritance from brother to sister's son), they are organized in groups of kinsfolk related to one another by descent through females. The milk tree therefore represents these groups, technically called matrilineages. As the matrilineages are the persisting groups of Ndembu society, and villages are to some extent combinations of matrilineages, the matrilineal principle in the abstract is vertebral to Ndembu society, and the milk tree symbolizes this, and symbolizes both the continuity of the society and its whole culture, its customs and its laws. In a graphic comparison, one of the Ndembu compared it with the Union Jack flying over the administrative headquarters of the district, then under British rule. He described the milk tree as 'our flag'.

But Turner showed that if one examined actions around the milk tree, in the ritual itself, these were not altogether harmonious, and did not reflect a continual state of harmony in accordance with the values stressed in the Ndembu's own account of the ritual. In practice, there was considerable competition and 'strife' among the people.

Duty Made Desirable

Turner shows that all the dominant ritual symbols of Ndembu society can be similarly analysed. His thesis is that two sharply different poles of reference for the symbols – the sensory and the ideological – must be distinguished. At the sensory pole are clustered meanings which refer to physiological facts and processes, such as mother's

Armed with weapons and dressed to kill, the Watusi of the former Ruanda province dance themselves to a frenzied pitch of excitement before going to war.

milk, blood, blood of menstruation and birth, semen, genitalia, copulation, excreta, death, and so on. While at the ideological pole are clustered social values and allegiances: conformity with law, morality and custom; motherhood as a nurturing relationship; the established relationships between women and men, married women and girls, membership of matrilineages and villages, and so on. Symbols cover these diverse meanings because they can condense many meanings, can unify disparate meanings and can polarize meanings.

Musée de l'Homme

The Mansell Collection

Turner argues that in the course of ritual, marked by feasting, drinking, dancing and music – all physiologically stimulating – as well as by fellowship, strong and varied emotions are evoked in response both to the feasting, drinking and so on, and to the sensory associations of the rites and symbols. The energy thus aroused is then transferred to, and fixed upon, the values evoked at the ideological pole. Thus there occurs a process in which the obligatory is felt also to be desirable.

Clearly this theory involves a much more complex approach to the relation between emotions evoked and forms of ritual, than the notions briefly criticized above. We can appreciate why it is that singing songs of hate and hurling insults at the king may act to strengthen, at least temporarily, sentiments of loyalty to him. Moreover, it is a theory which is in accord with the psycho-analytic theory of the sublimation of instinctual drives and demands towards socially approved ends.

If the step from psychological interpretation of ritual to understanding of its sociological functioning is so complicated, it is even more mistaken to relate ritual directly to the behaviour of animals, in mating dances, display and the like.

Ritual from Relationships

Turner's theory was worked out on tribal rituals, but it seems that it could equally be applied to the ritual symbols of the great religions. These types of rituals, however, differ markedly from each other. Sociolo-gists who have written on the general evolution of human society have all stressed that this development, associated with more complex technology and a greater division of labour, is marked by an increasing obsolescence of ritual and its replacement by what have been called universal religions, such as Christianity, Islam and Buddhism, which any person can join as a convert, and in which any adherent can join any congregation assembled to worship. The examples above, of the Swazi first fruits rites and the Ndembu nubility ritual, show that in tribal society rituals are constituted to specific social relationships according to the domestic, kinship, sexual, local or political affiliations of the members of the cult. Only persons occupying specific positions in those relationships can participate, and they do so in terms of the specific ways in which they are related to one another. Moreover, in the ritual, apart from using special symbols (in the form of things, words or actions), they act their specific roles in secular life, either directly, or sometimes invertedly (as in transvestism, by women dressing as men and men as women), or in some particular symbolic form. Hence an analysis of tribal rituals leads one into a detailed analysis of secular relationships because these are of the fabric of the ritual, and because it is believed that the symbolic representation of those relationships in some hidden, occult way creates and directs occult power in such a way as to bless, purify, protect, strengthen, make fruitful and otherwise successful, the persons who happen to be involved in those particular types of relationships.

This type of analysis has shown that in some of the rituals the enactment of secular relationships involves a statement, in an exaggerated form, not only of the harmonious and unifying aspects of the relationships, but also of the conflicts which reside in them. This is one of the main means by which emotion is aroused, which is then fixed on socially approved values: out of the very conflicts which exist in normal life, on special occasions the value of an ideal of life without conflict is emotionally and intellectually established.

It has therefore been argued that ritual, occult beliefs and practices will tend to occur in crisis situations in which the discrepant principles out of which social organization is formed, principles which are in conflict, produce actual or potential disputes which cannot be settled by judicial and other purely intellectual procedures. Ritual then may operate where there are fundamental disharmonies which occur within the theoretically stable harmony of a social system.

This theory is based on the perception that in human, as against animal, society, there is a consistent tendency to exaggerate the differences between categories of persons. Thus belief in the occult contaminating effect of menstrual blood and its threat to things virile exaggerates the biological difference between women and men. There are other beliefs, and associated practices, of this kind, based on distinctions of age, the

Far left A witch doctor from Kisangani: with so many ghosts and spirits to contend with it is natural that the pagan Negro should turn for help to experts in the supernatural. Zairois witch-doctors, called *Mganga* or *Mfumu* are a combination of soothsayer, herbalist, philosopher and psychiatrist.

Left The belief that monarchs inherited the magical power to cure scrofula, the King's Evil, by touching was widespread from the 11th to the 18th centuries. Edward the Confessor, the first monarch to show healing powers, curing a leper. Charles II is believed to have 'touched' more than 92,000 people.

Right Foetuses of dogs and llamas on sale in Bolivia: they bring good luck if they are buried under the foundations of a new building. This belief is probably a survival of the earlier ritual killing of an animal or human being in order to ensure the arrival of a spirit guardian for the building. Today, exorcism constitutes possibly the last surviving magico-religious ceremony associated with the house. It appears that there are certain wanton household spirits who do not submit as readily as ghosts to the commands of the exorcist. These are the poltergeists whose activities are closely bound up with the family. The poltergeist has much in common with the old kobold, of whom it is doubtless a direct descendant, being capricious, troublesome and occasionally violent, hurling stones and wrenching bed clothes off people who are sleeping, and occasionally setting a house alight.

facts of locality, different kinds of relationship through birth and kinship, the relationship of ruler and subject, and so forth. This tendency is more marked in tribal society than in complex industrial societies where peoples' roles, the material things which they handle, the places they work and worship and play in, are much more clearly differentiated and defined.

This may explain why in tribal society we find a 'ritualization' of secular roles, while as society develops a more complex technology on which is based a more complex division of labour, there is a movement towards universal religions.

E. R. Leach and other anthropologists have argued from studies of tribal rituals that ritual is only a symbolic statement of status. This is undoubtedly one of the aspects of ritual, as has been shown. Others assert that rituals mainly manifest competition for power. This too is present in tribal rituals, and is also to be found within the congregations of universal religions. But there is clearly much more to ritual than these two aspects.

Complex problems are involved in the question of when actions referring to beliefs in occult power occur, and how they operate, It therefore seems advisable to use a more complicated vocabulary in discussing these problems. The term *ceremonial* may be used to describe all actions which involve symbolic statements of social status (for instance, All Saints' Day and the October Revolution parade).

The coronation of King Arthur, from a 15th century MS: one aspect of ritual is as a symbolic statement of status and, although the kingship itself never dies, a new ruler is not felt to be fully a king until the correct ritual of coronation has been performed.

As a further distinction, the word *ceremoniousness* could be used to describe ceremonial where the practitioners have no idea of occult powers being involved (such as standing when *God Save the Queen* is played). Ritual describes ceremonial where ideas of occult power are present. Within the field of ritual in this sense, there is in tribal society a *ritualization* of secular social roles, of domestic places, and so forth. As this ritualization decreases with advancing civilization, some religions will be austere, while others will be marked by a high *ritualism*, symbolic itself, drawing on the same complex of emotions maybe, but not involving the enacting of everyday roles.

Rites of Passage

Transitions

A Flemish anthropologist working at the Sorbonne, A. van Gennep, was the first person to distinguish rites of passage as a distinct category of ritual, in his book *Les Rites de Passage*, published in 1909. His work immediately made a great impression on all scholars working on the interpretation of the rituals of what were then called primitive and are here called tribal societies, though many of the rituals considered by van Gennep were ancient Roman, Greek or Near Eastern, and Hebraic, Christian and Islamic. Van Gennep pointed out that many of these rituals showed a 'passage' in location or in time, and he showed conclusively that the rituals could be broken into three phases: first, a 'preliminal' phase in which the persons or groups who were the subjects of the ritual were *separated* from their previous social condition; secondly, a 'liminal' phase in which they were in a *marginal* situation; and finally a third 'postliminal' phase in which they were *reaggregated* to their previous social condition or *aggregated* to a new social condition, sometimes in the idea of resurrection. He stressed that these three phases, found in similar form in many societies, correspond to underlying necessities of social life: all social life involves movement in space, in time, and in social situation, and certain of these movements are marked by ritual transitions.

Van Gennep began his analysis by pointing to the high significance in many cultures of the threshold of a house, and the care with which this is built with ritual or magical accompaniments, or marked by religious protection, notably in the concept of the Roman god Janus, who looked both ways; while Orthodox Jews still fix to their doorways the *mezuzah*, a small case containing religious texts, sometimes even putting one on the doorway of each room. The doorway to a house marked a transition from one world of relationships to another: from this developed ritual that marked crossing the threshold (Lat. *limen*, hence 'limnal').

Van Gennep then proceeded to look at a whole series of characteristic rituals present in situations which involve changes in social conditions: erection of houses, commencement of agricultural activities, the gathering of first fruits and harvest, birth, marriage, funerals, ordination, and the initiation of youths or girls into manhood and womanhood. These are but a few examples from the multitude of occasions which van Gennep showed to be marked by separation, marginal and aggregatory rites.

It may easily be seen how the analysis of these rites was related to his starting point, the building of the house. From our own customs we know of the symbolic carrying of a bride by her husband across the threshold of their new home, a liminal rite which marks her movement after the wedding ceremony from her residence in her natal home to her residence in her conjugal home, with all which that movement marks in the alteration of her roles. Similarly, in some cultures a corpse cannot be carried out of a house over the sacred threshold but has to be taken out through a window, or through an opening broken in the wall.

Van Gennep's theory immediately made a profound impression on scholars studying ritual. In fact his phrase, *rites de passage*, passed in its French form into all anthropological literature. The subjects dealt with most commonly under this heading were rites of birth, puberty, initiation into manhood and womanhood (which van Gennep carefully pointed out did not necessarily correspond with puberty), and burial.

Cutting of Apron Strings

The nature of these rites can be briefly illustrated with examples: the rites, for example, surrounding the circumcision of boys of southern African tribes on their initiation into manhood. They first undergo separation rites, such as jumping over fire or water, which exhibit clearly the main purpose of the ritual – to separate them symbolically from the ignorance of boyhood and from the company of their mothers. These initial rites culminate in circumcision at a spot in the bush, on which no woman must look. The boys are then segregated during a marginal period, while the circumcision wounds heal, in a lodge of brushwood built out of sight of the women. There they learn special actions, songs and

formulas, often meaningless (though said to be in an ancient language), and wear special costumes marked by special colours.

Early records stated that this symbolic cutting of the apron strings holding a boy to his mother was complete: more recent research has shown that the boys' mothers must collaborate in some of the rites of this marginal period, because they have a duty to assist their husbands in altering the tie of sons with mothers, so that the sons can grow up to be independent men. Thus in some rites, men and boys sing songs through the cold of the winter night; and the women have to huddle in the open, on the edge of the village, around inadequate fires, ready to respond with ululations to the ending of each song. This response is said to be essential to help the boys to grow up.

When the circumcision wounds have healed, the boys are finely dressed and are allowed to appear to their mothers: these strain to get at their sons, but are driven off, often with real struggles, by the men. In some tribes the menfolk are assisted by masked and clothed figures who represent ancestral spirits. This temporary aggregation of the initiates, when their mothers can see them but not touch them, is succeeded by a less restricted marginal phase when they can be seen by the women at a distance, and even visited by their pre-nubile sisters. Finally in a great celebration the boys are brought in smart new clothes, to dance in the village and to be surrounded by their mothers, who can now scoff at the previously feared masked figures. Whatever their actual age, the boys emerge socially as men, who may begin sexual relationships, are forbidden to sleep in a hut with their mothers, and are allowed to sit with the men.

Time in Limbo

A second example of a rite of passage is the funeral. This often consists of an elaborate complex of rites, broken into three distinct phases. After the burial, both the mourners and the dead person's spirit enter a marginal phase. The mourners' behaviour is marked by many taboos and special modes of behaviour, dress and adornment or lack of adornment. At this time, the spirit of the deceased may be believed to be making an arduous journey to the 'world of spirits', or else, in societies where there is a cult of ancestral worship, it may be conceived to

Marriage ceremonies frequently follow the same basic pattern as other rites of passage: a young couple are purified from all evil influences by pouring the blood of a sacrificed chicken over their heads; part of a ceremony among the Land Dyaks of the Sadong River in Sarawak.

Professor W. R. Geddes

Birth

To the present-day western city-dweller, childbirth is associated primarily with the antiseptic atmosphere of the maternity ward. The sense of being at the mercy of powers beyond ourselves has been almost abolished. But this very recent emancipation has separated us not only from our ancestors but from the great majority of mankind, for whom childbirth is still one of the great crises of life and, above all, a mystery.

Among the first works of art to emerge from the mists of prehistory are the so-called 'Venuses'. They are squat, ugly female figurines, only a few inches high, carved between 10,000 and 40,000 years ago. As figurative art, they are rudimentary. But they are unmistakably pregnant.

The crisis of childbirth begins with conception. In many primitive societies, however, the immediate cause of conception remains a mystery. A woman could, it seems, become pregnant by eating almost anything, animal, vegetable or mineral; by drinking one liquid or another; or merely by visiting a certain powerful place. The role of the husband might be recognized, but the ultimate source of power lay outside him.

Failure to conceive might be cured by a variety of means. In the Indian state of Gujarat, for example, a barren woman might swallow the umbilical cord of a newborn child, or eat a mixture of seeds and spices, while seated on the cot of a woman in child-bed. The power to conceive might be transferred in some way: in the Indian Deccan it was held that a barren woman who touched another woman suckling her child would become pregnant; but the child would die.

Once pregnant, a woman was usually separated from her family and tribe, at least as the time of her delivery approached. Certain foods would be prohibited. She would be secluded in a special hut or in a special part of her house, in order not to endanger either herself or anyone else. For a woman in childbirth was ritually unclean. In fact, the pollution incurred by contact with such a woman was considered even worse than that connected with death and the dead.

The real source of this pollution was, of course, the copious flow of blood – always and in all situations a source of the deepest impurity. In the Old Testament (in Leviticus, chapter 12) we read that a woman giving birth to a boy is unclean for seven days, as at the time of menstruation: blood being the common factor. For the birth of a girl the period of impurity was two weeks longer. Anything the mother touched, or anyone who touched her, would become similarly impure by contagion: hence her isolation, otherwise the religious and social life of the group could not proceed.

At the confinement, elaborate precautions were taken, aimed at making the delivery easier and at protecting the mother and her infant. In the former category would

be wandering loose, homeless and restless. Finally, after this marginal period, aggregation rites are held, either to mark the entry of the spirit to the world of spirits, or else to institute the spirit among the company of the ancestors.

The 'passage' theme is evident in wedding rites, as it is in such ceremonies as initiation to special societies, or the ordination of a priest or consecration of a church, even though in our own culture such rites are often much attenuated. It appears also in seasonal festivals such as the celebration of the New Year, the gathering of first fruits and Harvest Festivals. At the festival of first fruits the whole of a classical or tribal society might perform rituals which marked the separation of the people – often represented by their leaders – from their normal way of life and their entry into a marginal period when they had to observe many taboos, such as not eating particular foods and not speaking loudly save in the performance of special rites. In this marginal phase normal rules might be suspended until it was completed.

Great festivities, dancing and drinking, mark the aggregation into the New Year. Sometimes, in societies without well-organized government, these are the oc-

casions when normally highly independent sections of society, potentially hostile to each other, show their unity in great festivals.

Van Gennep was correct in pointing out that rites of this kind fall into disuse with the technical and economic development of society, though some remain. To refer this change to a decreasing interest in the sacred, and its separation from the profane, seems inadequate. The present writer has suggested an alternative explanation, that in tribal and other simple societies individuals perform their various roles (filial, parental, political, economic, religious, educational, and so on) in the same places with largely the same material belongings in relationships with largely the same set of other persons. These societies are marked by a high ceremoniousness or even ritualization of behaviour, which marks the special relationships in terms of which a person is acting, or the role he is performing, in a particular place at a particular time. The ritualization is achieved by attaching occult power to the acting – directly, or invertedly, or symbolically – of specific secular roles. The ceremoniousness serves symbolically to segregate roles and relationships where this cannot be done materially. In an industrialized society, on the other hand, people commonly interact in their various activities with a wide range of individuals, in many different buildings using different material goods: roles and relationships are materially and not ceremoniously or ritually segregated, and for this reason there is no ritualization of secular roles.

come the careful untying of all knots in the house, to help the woman to relax; in the latter, the bolting and barring of all doors and windows, to keep evil spirits out. An additional precaution taken in parts of India was to secrete a knife or other weapon under the bed, again for protection against spirits. In Greece, it was believed that women in childbirth were especially susceptible to the Evil Eye; therefore all mirrors were removed from the room, since it was possible to put the Evil Eye on oneself. Nor, after the birth, might the woman go out at night, because she would be in danger from the malignant stars. So she shut herself up after dark with doors and windows closed, at least until after the child had been baptized and she herself had been churched.

The death of a woman in childbirth was the gravest of all calamities, since in popular belief the ghost of such a woman was peculiarly malevolent. In the north-west of India, for example, it was held that a woman dying within 10 days of childbirth or during menstruation became an evil spirit, called *Hadal* or *Hedali*. If her corpse was cremated, mustard seeds were strewn on the road behind the bier, since it was believed that the ghost could return home only if she could collect all the seeds along the way. If the corpse was buried, four iron nails were fixed at the four corners of the grave.

Similarly, precautions had to be taken on the death of a child, whether still-born or (in Christian countries) unbaptized. In the north of England it was believed until quite recently that it was unlucky to tread on the grave of such a child. In Northumberland an unbaptized child would often be buried in the same grave as some other adult, for protection and care in the life beyond.

But assuming that the delivery had gone well, there were other rites to be performed. Even in Christian countries, the child and its mother had, as it were, to be 'introduced' to the household deities. The practice of 'saining' (blessing) was observed in Scotland during the last century. A fir-candle was lighted and carried three times round the bed. Then a Bible and a morsel of food were placed under the pillow, with the words, 'May the Almichty debar a' ill frae this 'uman, an' be aboot her, an' bless her an' her bairn.' Or the child might be put on a cloth spread over a basket of provisions and carried three times round the crook of the chimney, for the hearth was the abode of the 'little people'.

Other necessary rites in primitive societies concerned the disposal of the afterbirth, the placenta and the umbilical cord which, having been part of the living child, were sometimes believed to be the seat of the 'free-soul' (the soul which wanders in dreams, and which finally departs at death). At all costs these relics must be prevented from falling into the hands of ill-disposed persons, who might use them for magical

Prehistoric 'Venuses', small, squat female figurines dating from between 10,000 and 40,000 years ago, are among the earliest works of art to have survived. Unmistakably pregnant, they reveal man's intense concern with birth and fertility: the *Venus of Willendorf*, Natural History Museum, Vienna.

purposes. We have already seen that they could be used as cures for barrenness. But the usual practice was either to give them to a relative to care for, or to make positive magical use of them. So, for instance, the Kwakiutl Indians of British Columbia threw a boy's placenta to the ravens, believing that this would give him power to see into the future; a girl's placenta would be buried at high-water mark, to make her a good clam-digger.

Churching of Women

Once the danger period for mother and child had come to an end, when the flow of blood

ceased and the umbilicus healed, both had to be received into society – the child by circumcision (after eight days in Judaism), naming or baptism; the mother by offering the appropriate sacrifices and receiving a renewed blessing. The period of purification could be as long as 80 days on the birth of a daughter. In Hinduism the period of impurity varies with the caste of the woman concerned, from 10 days for a high-born Brahmin to 30 days for a low caste Sudra.

The Christian practice of 'churching' women originally had this same function, of purification and reintegration into the worshipping community. Until this rite had been carried out, the woman was a danger to her neighbours. In Scotland she was not permitted to enter any other house.

Tlazolteotl, the Aztec goddess of sexual love, depicted in the act of giving birth.

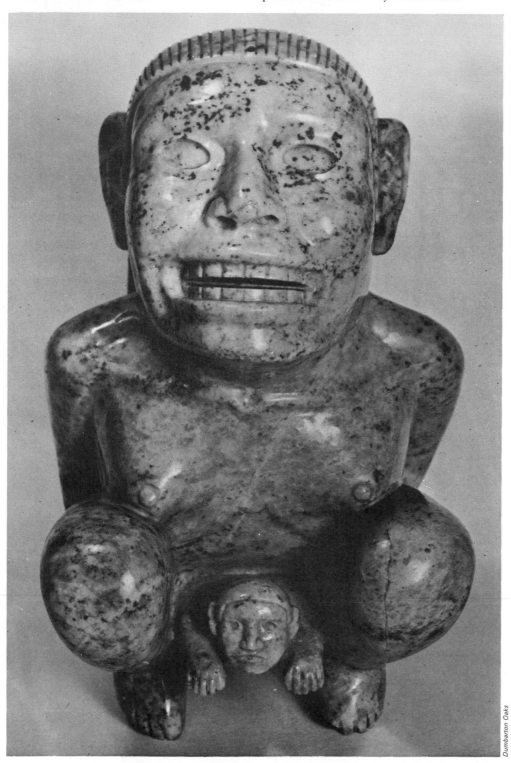

Dumbarton Oaks

Initiation

In every initiation ceremony there is some idea of a new birth as part of the process of assuming full status in the group. 'Except a man be born again' is the Christian phrasing for a process which in many ceremonies involves acting out a return to a symbolic womb. Part of the ritual of the Kunapipi, an Australian aboriginal group, involves the initiates being brought into the sacred ground 'to enter the Mother; they go into her uterus, the ring place, as happened in the beginning.' In acting out the ritual they are covered over with bark and hung from a pole. 'They are', as Mircea Eliade shows, 'in the womb, and they will emerge reborn – "their spirit comes out new".'

The theme of rebirth is paralleled by the equally important recurring theme of death. Both are closely linked structurally in the whole process of initiation. The new life cannot start until the old has been disposed of. Ritual death to the old life, the former sinful, corrupt condition, is expressed in the elaborate mythology surrounding most puberty rites. In the Congo on the Loango coast boys between ten and twelve years old have a ritual death in the village when they are given a potion to make them unconscious as a prelude. Now 'dead', they are taken into the jungle, circumcised, buried in the fetish house and painted white, a sign that they are ghosts of their former existence.

Rebirth may be similarly expressed by the infantile behaviour of the initiates when they return. They may appear helpless, like babies. The stay in the bush serves the important function of signifying the death of the previous relationship between a son and his mother. Initiation ceremonies serve several functions in relation to the social structure but they also emphasize the deeper belief system. The newly initiated have a special status because they have learned the mysteries, survived the ordeals; having escaped the belly of whale or serpent or whatever other experience may be central to the creation myth of the group.

Initiation into secret societies, shamanic or other groups of priests, witches or warriors, follows a similar pattern but with a more elaborate and distinctive indoctrination of the individual. In these ceremonies the demonstration of some magical, divine or shamanic power by the initiate is looked for as a sign that he has attained the appropriate characteristics of a god, animal or spirit. A transcendent existence, and the powers that go with it, replace the mere human condition. In most hero legends the young warrior characteristically undergoes an experience of a sacred, mystical kind which gives him superhuman powers or magical elements which he can use in his ordeal. The tasks which are set to those who hope to win the hand of the beautiful princess in the classical fairy tales depend on more than normal attributes in the performer. The hero becomes seized with power, he becomes heated, baptized with fire. Eliade describes how in Germanic secret societies the young man became a berserker in a frenzy of fury. 'He became "heated" to an extreme degree, flooded by a mysterious, non-human and irresistible force.' The initiation of the Kwakiutl Indian warrior in British Columbia involves a similar frenzy of possession and heating and the same thing is recorded in the Irish hero legends of Cu Chulainn or the Greek and Indo-European initiations of cultural hero figures.

Rebirth Through Pain

Trials of strength and endurance, as tests of fitness to share the sacred membership with the ancestors of folk heroes, are common to all initiations. Formal learning and preparation for the new status in the 'initiation school' is only part of the experience which is bound up with a complex of fear, awe and dread in face of the mysteries. The adult must be brave in the face of danger and must be steadfast in the face of pain. Consequently the novice is subjected to the fearful noise of the Melanesian bullroarer – a wooden instrument which makes a booming sound – or to the beating with stinging nettles and the dropping of hornets on to their backs which the Naudi adolescents in East Africa experience.

The common experience of fear and pain provides an important social bond between the novices who have survived the experience. They are incorporated into a group distinguished sharply from outsiders who have not shared in the ordeal. By having passed through the sacred experience they have attained a new status prescribed by tradition. Their circumcision, the decoration of their skin by cuts, their ordeals in the initiation school, their skill as warriors, show that they are boys no longer but men ready to take a full part in the life of the community.

One Melanesian experience described by R. M. Berndt includes a progressive series of nose bleedings caused by slivers of bamboo which are covered with salt and then twirled in the nostrils. The tongue is also cut and the penis rubbed with rough, abrasive leaves. By the time he is 18 or 20 years old the young man is introduced to penis bleeding caused by progressively larger objects pushed into the urethra and twirled. Some of the puberty rites for girls include similar insertions into the vagina to cause bleeding. These rites demonstrate strength (if a man's penis is strong his arrows will be also) while blood has importance both as a symbolic representation of menstruation and of the religious and magical qualities associated with sexual elements.

Ritual Rapes and Panty Raids

The ritual rapes of Kikuyu warrior bands following circumcision have attracted a certain amount of notoriety, particularly when English women living in the Kenya

Puberty rites, frequently involving circumcision of boys and artifically induced vaginal bleeding in girls, are an initiation into adulthood, connected with the religious and magical qualities associated with sex: puberty rites among Brazilian Indians.

highlands were the victims. The explanation for the ceremonial rape lies in the need of the young men to purify themselves after the initiation rites. This could be achieved by passing on the 'contagion' to a woman through intercourse before they could return to the group to claim a wife of their own. Often a band of young men wandered the countryside far away from their homes until they found a woman who was of married status and a stranger to them.

Something very similar is to be found in some of the ceremonies and 'dares' demanded of newcomers to the armed forces and in particular those aspiring to membership of male fraternities in American colleges and universities. These may range from the 'panty raid' on the women students' resi-

dence (ritual rapes) to tasks requiring the initiates to collect some prized possession which signify their manliness and daring – bringing back G-strings from night clubs or placing chamber pots on Oxford spires. Various forms of the 'chicken' game, especially when played with cars or motorcycles, are of the same order.

Such activities may be part of the official conditions of membership of the group but often they represent an unofficial response by the existing members to the newcomer. Apart from tests of skill and daring, initiates are often subjected to debasing ceremonies of an equivalent kind. Initiates of one fraternity must wear an iron ball and chain padlocked to their ankles for a week, others must wear women's or children's clothing

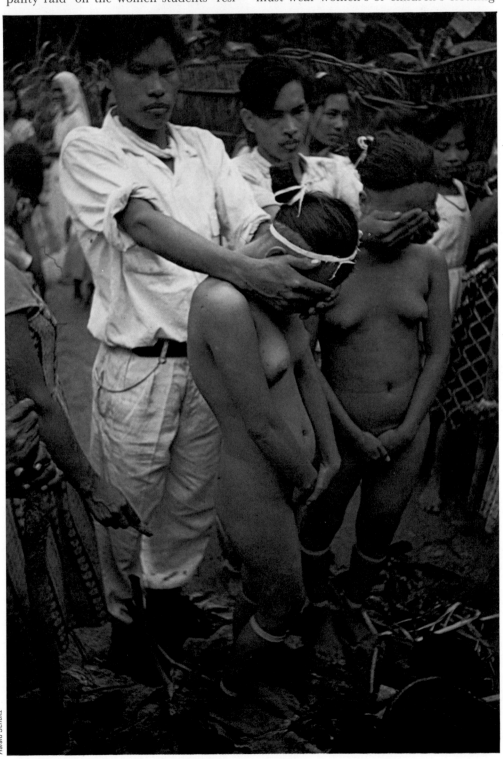

Harald Schultz

Harald Schultz

Masked and robed figures representing dangerous spirits, emerging from the forest to attend the initiation of young girls, among the Tikuna Indians of the Upper Solimoes River.

or have their hair cut in a special way. Another quite common practice involved an initiate being taken to a deserted spot often at a considerable distance and there left without clothing or money (or with a minimum of each) to see if he could get back.

Similar, less formal initiation rites are conducted in most social groupings to emphasize the common and shared trials through which members have passed and on which their solidarity is based. A recent newspaper report (*Daily Telegraph*, 21 April, 1970) describes the bullying of a 16-year-old garage hand on his first day at work. After a certain amount of general ragging of the 'new boy' he was tied up and petrol was sprinkled round him and set alight. In this case he was badly burned but it was noted in the court hearing that he had submitted willingly – recognizing that this kind of initiation ritual was a condition of his acceptance by his workmates.

Tests of endurance, strength, ridicule and fear are used in the more elaborate initiation 'schools' as a means of emphasizing and disciplining the novice as he learns the cultic knowledge and mysteries of the group. An important feature of many initiation ceremonies, especially in the secret preparation period or 'school', involves the use of figurines symbolizing traditional magical or religious characters, ancestors, or elements in the total knowledge and moral structure

of the society. These figurines are often carefully guarded by the members of a particular group and are not allowed to be seen by those who have not been initiated. They have spiritual significance and consequently are carefully guarded from enemies. The special rituals appropriate to each are similarly reserved for fear that the sacred objects might be angered or polluted by those who had no right to see them, or did not know 'how to behave' in their presence. The sacraments are similarly reserved in the Christian Church for those who have become full members.

Lessons in Sex
Initiation figurines are either kept as part of a store of sacred objects or are fashioned anew for each group of novices. Examples from East Africa include instructive, cautionary and punitive figures. They are all associated with songs, proverbs or riddles which the novice must learn. One example of a simple and obvious kind is the model of a hare used by the Sambaa as part of the rites for boys. The teaching that is depicted is that it is foolish to be quarrelsome and the associated words state that the hare is cleverer than most animals but he is never anxious to start a fight. A large majority of the figurines are used to convey lessons about sexual behaviour or morality and here again proverbs are taught to the initiates to define correct behaviour. A good example of such a riddle is shown in the female figurine used by the Zigua with a riddle which runs: 'There is only one person who laughs when she should mourn and who rejoices in her

loss', to which the answer is 'A girl on her wedding night'. As well as being used in puberty ceremonies, these figurines are used in the entry rites to secret societies and associations. Clay or wooden figures are handled ritually and associated with a fixed form of words sung or recited. Again the objects depict familiar social roles, or common objects as well as highly stylized art with a very complex symbolism. The figures and the form of words are treated as sacred and are kept secret from the uninitiated.

The initiation schools and the lengthy process of disciplined teaching of the lessons associated with the puberty rituals in tribal societies have inevitably been affected by social change. Often lack of time and the constraints of formal education or occupation have meant that both the ceremonies and the training period of the initiation must be curtailed. Where figurines are used the number may be limited or the verses only will be learned. These effects of social change only serve to emphasize the important and complex function served by the initiation of adolescents in tribal society. They ensured that each individual was fully educated in the central belief system, moral codes and normative standards of the society and was intellectually as well as emotionally prepared for an adult role in the community.

One particular set of initiation ceremonies involves the installation of new incumbents into various offices. Kings, chiefs, presidents, professors are all expected to observe formal ritual procedures and take part in ceremonies connected with their assumption of the prerogatives of office.

Coronation ceremonies are an elaborate example of the combination of rituals designed to acknowledge formally and acclaim publicly and anoint the one chosen for the office. Part of the ceremony usually involves admission to a ritually appointed place or locus of office. The professor has no actual 'chair' but a bishop has a cathedral throne and knights of orders of chivalry are ceremonially led to their stalls in the chapel of their orders. Similarly with a mayor or president the office holder is sanctified with the symbolic elements of authority: orb and sceptre, crown and sword, seal or gavel. These objects signify that the incumbent has been properly chosen, indoctrinated and acquainted with the mysteries that surround the office. The laying on of hands, the anointment, represents the conferring of divine or magical power which alone sets the initiated incumbent of office 'apart'. Where the succession to office is hereditary, or where the successor is selected in childhood (as in the case of the Dalai Lama before the Chinese invasion of Tibet), the whole process of growing up forms an overall initiation which points toward the eventual attainment of office.

Humiliation and Abuse

Much of the ritual surrounding the initiation of new holders of office shares the characteristics that have been noted in the rites surrounding puberty. The symbolic death of the old and rebirth to the new condition and status is represented in the divesting of original clothing, and the profane objects of life. The new ruler, as in the coronation ceremony of the British monarch, assumes a new royal robe as well as other symbols of office: orb or sceptre, crown and sword.

Some of the ceremonies are dignified and formal, enshrined with pomp and circumstance, but it is significant that even the most solemn occasions also have a festive and irreverent side in which 'the gods are mocked'. The chancellors of Scottish universities, elected by the students, however honoured and dignified, endure a bombardment of flour, missiles and abuse as part of their inaugural ceremony, and it is customary for the professors at some American universities to be subjected to similar horseplay. These examples show clearly the conflicting and complementary elements of debasement and honouring that characterize the initiation process. Just as we have seen with puberty rites, the candidate must be 'cut down to size' and divested of his former status before he can assume the new. The experience of the army recruit is no different once he joins up. The admonition 'Get your hair cut – you're in the Army now' demonstrates the removal of the civilian

status and the assumption of the new status of 'soldier' with uniform, dress, style, regulations and equipment just as clearly.

Modern examples of initiation rituals abound and demonstrate many of the features already noted. In some cases the ceremonies are merely vestigial remnants of earlier, more elaborate and public rituals, involving the whole community. Infant baptism 'casts out the devil' and 'makes new' and the baptismal water is an indication of the washing away of sin. Adult initiations in some churches often involve baptisms by total immersion and 'speaking in tongues', spiritual trance and 'possession' in the new member. The transcendental religious or magical recognition of the new member both fortifies the faith of the group and signifies that the initiation procedure was correctly performed.

Symbolic Social Statement

Just as in the initiation ceremonies of secret societies, in simpler societies membership represents a distinct and far-reaching social statement about the individual. Being adult or being a Mason or being a Baptist or a witch represent far more than the mere labels. They are involved statements about the whole society and the place and significance of different groups within the society; statements which have significance in all those aspects of the social structure in which particular kinds of belonging can be a means of articulating social relations. The questions of whom you may marry, where you can live or whom you may work with are not idle when belonging to the Roman Catholic Church or the Loyal Orange Order, probably the prime defining characteristics of life in Northern Ireland; or being a Jew or an Arab define sharply the possible relationships in a situation of conflict in the Middle East. Where 'belonging' in this sense is open to the individual the significance of the transition from one condition to another is very apparent. Those who have 'passed' from Negro culture to white in the United States or those who have succeeded in the world of espionage, are acutely conscious of the dimensions and social significance of the new roles they have chosen to adopt. But even in these rather mundane examples the questions are not simply social in the sense of setting out rules of behaviour. They are symbolic, as all

Chris Barker

British Travel Authority

The transition from youth to adulthood, acceptance into an order or into a trade, are important turning points in a person's life and are marked with appropriate ceremony.

Above Barmitzvah cakes are presented to Jewish children as part of the celebrations marking their coming-of-age.

Right A cooper apprentice is initiated by being rolled in a tar barrel.

Tate Gallery

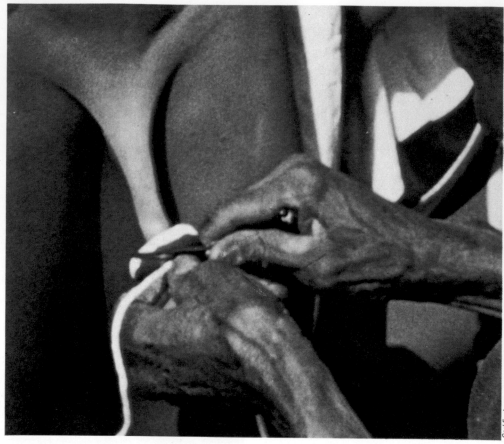

Carl Fuchs

social statements are inevitably symbolic, because they are statements about man, the world, the cosmos and the possibilities of human existence, as well as statements about life and death. It is precisely in those areas where the maintenance of distinct boundaries is most important to the people in a particular society that one finds a particular emphasis on their maintenance and on the proper observation of the boundary-crossing rituals of initiation.

In some societies age distinctions may be pivotal, in most societies sex differences, and in many societies differences of race or ethnic origin or language may serve to demarcate structurally the bounds of social relationships. In many societies the division between male and female is sharply observed in territorial definitions of space in the settlement or living quarters. Male and female areas for eating, washing and defecation are reserved and this latter distinction can be seen also in contemporary Western societies. A good example is the division by sex of public lavatories and the recognition that for very small children the rigid differences generally observed are considered unimportant. In the Southern United States the problem was multiplied in some areas by the belief that it is necessary to provide facilities for white and coloured as well as for male and female: four separate spaces to fulfil one natural function. The point of importance is that these particular divisions are pivotal for the world view of these particular societies. It is not surprising that one finds fraternities of men or sororities of woman's groups of one kind or another which as distinct sex groups serve the important function of emphasizing and symbolizing these distinctions which their

own initiation into the particular group at the same time recognizes and supports.

All religious groups, cults and societies develop a conscious boundary between those who have membership and those who do not. Fear of malevolent or benevolent spirits or beings often characterize the concern with which it is felt necessary to observe the proper 'passage' ceremonies which connect these two states. Quite apart from the examples of initation that we have already discussed, birth and death are surrounded by similar ritual observations designed to placate various forces which may have an influence on the destiny of the child or the dead person. Even in tribal societies no necessary claim will be made for these rites as essential and empirical measures which will bring the desired result. But man is not only a practical being and even in contemporary societies initiation ceremonies convey the mixture of beliefs at a variety of levels – mystical, magical, metaphysical and religious, as well as scientific – which can co-exist without difficulty in the same individual and group.

Initiation rituals surrounding death are often elaborate, both at the level of preparation and in the way in which the dead are treated. There are numerous examples in the rites of burial of the placing of money in the hand or mouth to secure the passage of the dead across the Styx which illustrate that the characteristics of initiation are found here as well. Burial in the foetal position also symbolizes the recognition of rebirth following death.

Death and rebirth indeed characterize the features of all initation rites. We have seen this illustrated in boys' puberty initiation schools and it is found equally in the

Above left A squire keeps an all-night vigil in church to dedicate himself before receiving his arms and being initiated into knighthood.

Above right One of the most ancient forms of mutilation, circumcision is part of the initiation rites of primitive societies all over the world; the deliberate infliction of pain is thought to appease the gods and spirits, and to inure young men to the dangers that lie ahead of them: youth of the Omar tribe in the Sudan undergoes circumcision during his initiation.

Right The common experience of fear and pain promotes a social bond, distinguishing the initiated from the outsiders: in Chad, cicatrization or the decoration of the skin by painful cuts, indicates the fully fledged member of the community.

often less developed puberty rites for girls. Girls' ceremonies tend to involve a less intentional process than those of boys which represent a more deliberate introduction to a world of spirit and culture. For girls, as Eliade points out 'initiation involves a series of revelations concerning the secret meaning of a phenomenon that is apparently natural – the visible sign of their sexual maturity.'

This does not preclude considerable emphasis being given to some female puberty rites in certain societies. The Dyaks exemplify this in the separation and isolation of girls for a whole year in a white cabin, dressed in white and only eating white foods. This separation – the wilderness experience – recognizes the fact that during this period the initiate is 'nothing', neither man nor woman, asexual. Together with other separations – Christ's 'forty days in the wilderness' – it is a condition of the attainment of spirituality. The emerging initiate is reborn in a symbolic and spiritual way. The return announces that the mystery of

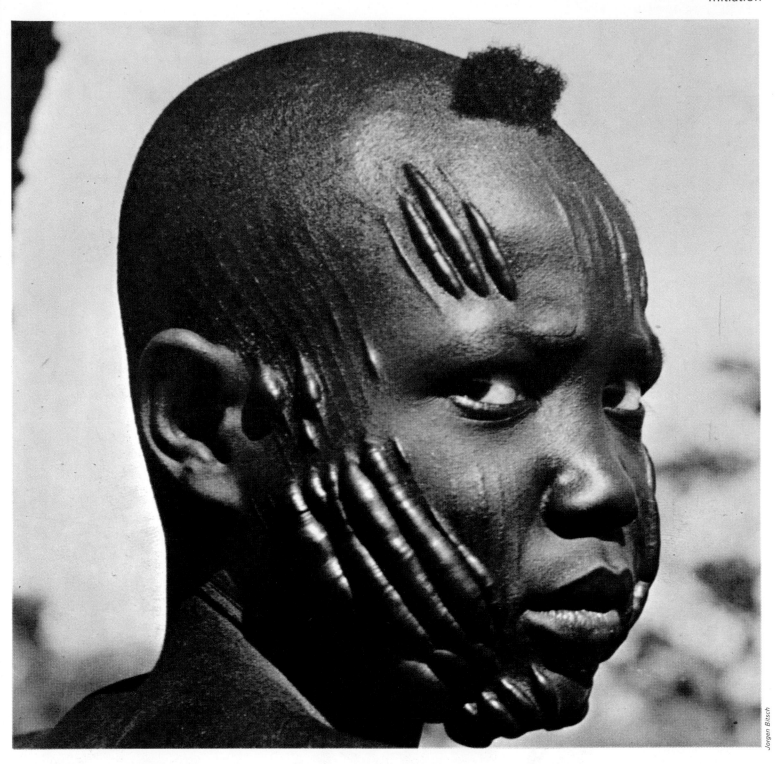

Jorgen Bitsch

rebirth has been accomplished. Eliade gives the example of the Kavirondo Bantu to illustrate a characteristic imagery found also in Brahmanic initiation in India and the recognition of the double character of birth in the egg from which the chick emerges when the shell breaks. It is said of the Kavirondo initiates when they complete their ritual: 'The white chick is now creeping out of the egg, we are like newly fired pots.'

One final example will serve to illustrate something of the elaborate character of initiation mythology. An ascetic period of isolation is characteristic of many North American Indian initiations. The novice leaves the community in order to obtain those dreams and visions which will identify for him a particular spirit with which he will then continue to be associated. He will fast and exhaust himself until the spirit appears to him, usually in animal form. Once he has achieved this personal sacred experience he can return to the tribe, having died to be reborn with his guiding spirit.

The Dancing Societies of the Kwakiutl Indians studied by F. Boas show a more elaborate version of the same isolating and sacralizing experience. The ritual commences with the initiate falling into a trance to signify his death to the profane world. He is then carried off to be initiated by the spirits. He may be taken to a cave or to a special hut in which the spirit lives. An extreme example is that of the Cannibal Society where as part of the initiation the candidate is served by a woman while he is secluded in the forest. He is identified with the god and demonstrates this by swallowing strips of a corpse which she prepares for him. His cannibalism is a reversal of the horror of the Kwakiutl for human flesh. To overcome this revulsion he must indeed be divine and the similar acts of frenzy in which he engages on his return serve also to demonstrate this possession by the god.

In the final ceremony he acts like a beast of prey attacking all he can reach, biting their arms. He is almost impossible to restrain but finally is subdued after the woman who served him in the wilderness dances naked before him with a corpse in her arms. His frenzy is finally subdued by repeated immersions in salt water and his new personality and identity is achieved.

27

Betrothal and Marriage

Although betrothal, the binding promise of marriage, has little significance for us today, it was at one time an occasion for considerable ceremony. In Greek Macedonia, for example, it was conducted with prayers and exchange of rings, in the presence of a matchmaker, the priest, family and friends. The bride offered her married relatives the traditional formal refreshments – jam, coffee, alcohol – and presented the groom's parents and the matchmaker with socks she had knitted herself. They thanked her with the customary greeting: 'Mayest thou enjoy the kerchief in good health.' During Cheese Week, which immediately preceded Lent, the young man sent his betrothed sweet cakes, and on the eve of Easter she received gifts of a coloured candle and Easter eggs.

The nomadic Vlachs, a people scattered through the Balkans, arranged for a group of friends and relations, acting on behalf of the groom, to call at the home of the bride. There they found a low table covered with fine cloth and laid with three soup plates. Two of these contained sweets. The third, which was empty, had to be filled with gold, sometimes made into a necklace. It is still a common Balkan custom for a woman to wear her betrothal gift in this fashion. When the groom's party returned, they threw flour over him, wishing him a long life with the words: 'May you grow white like this flour.'

Meanwhile, the same custom was performed for the bride, by her family.

In 17th century Holland the betrothed couple were required to sit together on a bed and kiss each other in the presence of both families; the ceremony was ratified by exchange of rings. These were very big, sometimes engraved with suitable pictures, and sometimes, like the English gemmel ring, formed of two parallel circles. The halves, separated between the partners at the betrothal, were joined together as a wedding ring for the marriage ceremony. To pledge fidelity, the couple would cut themselves and drink each other's blood; or they might use the blood to make a written declaration. In England, halving a coin was a popular custom. A character in a play called *The Country Wake* (1696) says: 'I ask't her the question last Lammas, and at Allhallow's-tide we broke a piece of money.' The straw true-lover's knot was another token of fidelity, in use within living memory. A young man prepared two, one for himself and one for his sweetheart. If she pinned hers over her heart, this meant she had chosen him, and the couple wore the knots until their wedding day. The girl might also be presented with a sprig of the plant Lad's Love; if she threw it away, her lover had been rejected, but to smell it was a sign of acceptance.

A young man from the fens would present a fur tippet to his sweetheart. This was a narrow fur stole, prepared by the lover from animal skins, which he had obtained and cured himself. The couple stitched the hide to a silk lining, stuffed it with sheep's wool, and inside each end placed a sachet containing a little pubic hair: the man's on the right, the woman's on the left. When worn, the criss-cross ends covered the woman's heart, and the little packets inside ensured a happy married life.

Bundling and Handfasting

Anticipation of the intimacies of marriage was not so frowned upon in the past as one might suppose, since betrothal was often considered to be nearly as binding as marriage. The early 17th century Puritan settlers of New England practised bundling, a custom known variously in England, Scotland, Ireland and Wales, as well as Holland, Norway and probably elsewhere. The parents of a New England girl who was courting permitted the couple to spend the night together in her bedroom. The pair who were expected to behave with reasonable propriety, wore all their clothes and were occasionally separated by additional layers of bedding. This custom, which seems

A bridegroom or his kin may give presents to the bride's family to compensate them for the loss of her services. Conversely, a bride may be given a dowry which she brings to her husband: brideprice of feathers and money in New Guinea.

Axel Poignant

Marriage means the transfer of one of the couple from one kin-group to another, and many marriage and betrothal customs are connected with this. In New Guinea (*top*) women of the bride's group stage a mock fight to prevent her from leaving. Elsewhere, the bride may be led to her wedding in brand new clothes and in ceremonial procession, as at this village in Cyprus (*centre*). *Below* At Dunmow, in Essex, a side of bacon is awarded to a married couple who can swear that they have not regretted their marriage for a year and a day.

to have begun dying out in America during the 18th century, was still common within living memory in England in Cambridgeshire, where it was introduced by Irish labourers.

In 17th century Holland bundling was known as *queesten*. Suitors on Texel Island traditionally arrived through the window and, since this necessitated smashing the pane, few houses had all their windows unbroken. Although couples met in the girl's bed, it was again intended that propriety should be observed. The girl lay on the sheet, the boy between sheet and cover. Nearby an iron vessel and a pair of fire tongs were ready for her to sound the alarm if the young man became too bold. Parents usually approved of the custom since it was thought an honour for their daughter to receive these visits. The call might last all night, and if a pregnancy resulted the baby was taken along to its parents' wedding, concealed beneath the mother's cloak, though clearly visible for everyone to see. Today, in the Calvinist village of Staphorst, trial marriage is still practised and custom decrees that a couple marry only when there is evidence of a pregnancy.

The Scottish custom of 'handfasting' also provided a testing period. Young men and women chose a companion at a fair held annually in Dumfriesshire, and lived together as man and wife until the following year. If the experiment was a success, they married; if not, they were free to take another partner. A priest nicknamed Book-in-the-Bosom, perhaps because he carried a marriage register, arrived periodically to solemnize these weddings.

There is usually no difficulty about arranging marriage for an attractive girl or man, but it may be a problem in cases of deformity or physical defect. In Poland such a man was betrothed to a relative and the banns read out in church, not with any real intention of marriage, but simply to make it known that he was eligible.

In Scotland and the North of England a 'Bride-wain' was arranged. This meant that carts and horses were taken round the houses of friends and relatives, who gave sacks of corn, meal, wool, and anything else they could spare. Sometimes there was a ceremonial procession from the bride's old home to the new one. A waggon, loaded with household articles and furniture, set out and, as it passed by, friends threw gifts upon the load. In Lancashire, among the very poor, everyone gathered together on the day of the wedding and built the young couple a house of clay and wood, which was known as the 'clay bigging'.

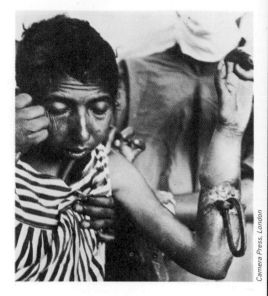

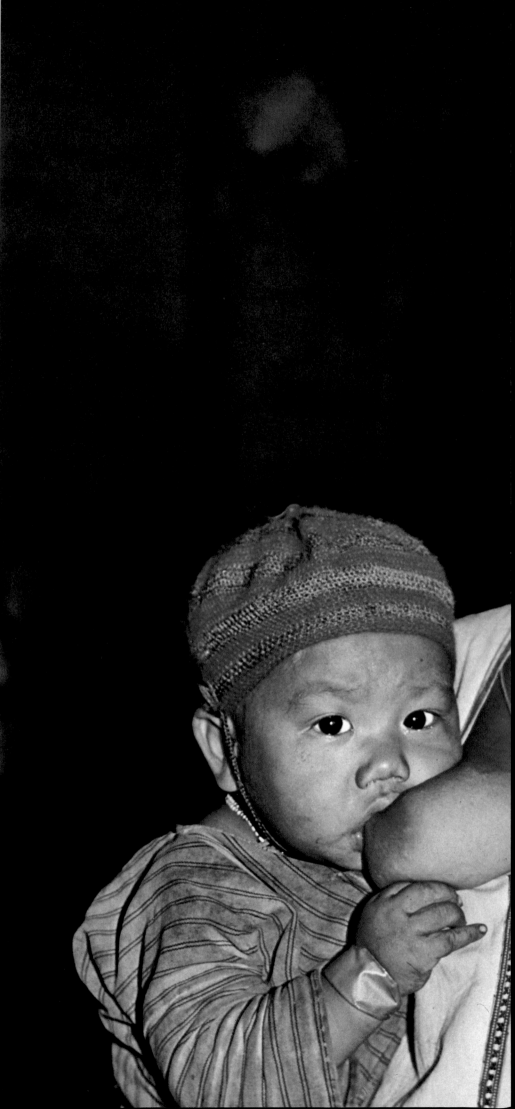

Above In many societies to this day, a woman may be severely punished for infidelity, desertion or breaking up a marriage. This Yemeni woman claimed that an iron ring had been driven through her forearm as a punishment for deserting her husband.

Right Spiral brass collars worn by adult women of the Padaung people in Northern Burma, are removed, perhaps causing serious injury, if a married woman complains of her husband.

If a husband was wealthy, but nonetheless did not wish to inherit any earlier debts from his wife, there was a traditional remedy. Until about 100 years ago in England, it was commonly believed that if a bride arrived at her wedding dressed in nothing but a shift, her husband would be freed from any such obligation. Again, if the bride walked stark naked from her house to her future husband's, the same purpose would be served. During the last century a woman tried to do this at Kirton-in-Lindsey in Lincolnshire. She had intended starting out down a ladder from her bedroom window, but her courage failed her; she partially dressed while still standing at the top.

The idea of approaching one's wedding in a state of nakedness is echoed in the custom of removing old clothes and putting on a completely new set. A Vlach bridegroom would stand in a flat metal dish and strip, preparatory to donning his pristine wedding clothes. English brides too were freshly dressed from head to foot, though the requirements of the old rhyme: 'Something old, something new, something borrowed, and something blue' were carefully observed. Today the luckiest colours for a bridal dress are white, pink and blue. Green is thought to be especially unlucky and in parts of Scotland even green table decorations and vegetables were omitted from the bridal meal.

Food is an important feature of any wedding celebration, and certain items are essentially symbolic. Formerly in the Netherlands the bridal couple were offered salted cream sprinkled with sugar, a confection representative of the bitter and the sweet sides of married life. English wedding-cake with its icing sugar and bitter almonds is said to possess the same significance. The rich mixture traditionally used in its prep-

Camera Press, London

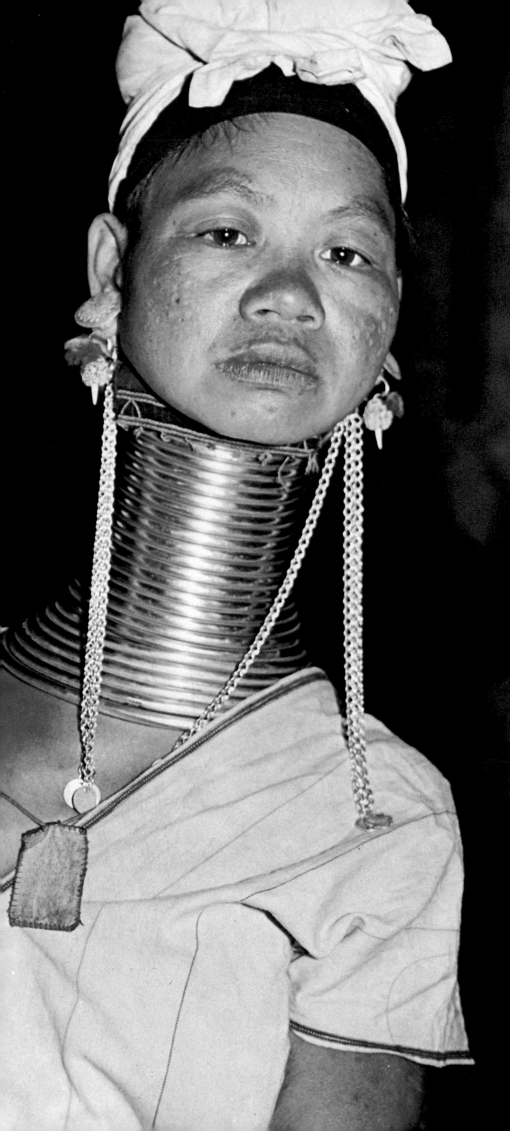
University Films

aration stands for fertility and abundance. Every guest must eat some and unmarried girls are supposed to sleep with a slice beneath their pillow in order to dream of their husbands-to-be. Yorkshire folk called this 'dreaming bread'. A sliver of cake used formerly to be passed nine times through a wedding ring to achieve the same result. This form of wedding divination has always been popular. Indeed as early as 1279 the Church in Poland was obliged to issue a decree forbidding its practice.

When people were very poor, as in Ireland during the last century, the food for a wedding simply consisted of what was available; in this case, bruised potatoes, flour, oatbread and butter. More often it was representative of fertility and abundance. For this reason, on entering her new home, a Greek bride crushed a pomegranate – a popular symbol of fruitfulness in the East – and marked the doorpost with a butter cross. The couple ascended the stairs beneath a shower of sweets, coins, barley, chick-peas and rice. These ideas are present in our own wedding ceremonies.

The symbolism of the cereals in wedding ceremonies arises from the fact that they are basic foods in the countries where they are used. At a Polish wedding feast a flat, plaited wheaten loaf called *kolacze*, which has been blessed in church, represents all bread. Good solid food is served: a traditional mixture of lentils and barley called *kasha*, peas, gravy, a bird, and *borscht*, soup made from beetroot or cabbage. Everyone cries 'The soup is bitter' until bride and groom have kissed each other. Since the wedding feast is said to represent the couple's future married life, there is always plenty of food. For the same reason, the fiddlers are fed by the bridesmaids so that they will not stop playing.

It was commonly believed that the success of a marriage would depend upon the time at which it was celebrated. We know that the ancient Romans avoided May weddings because the month was a time of purification. The *Lemuria*, or Feast of the Unhappy Dead, was celebrated on the 9th, 11th and 13th of that month, and the poet Ovid says those who married in May would soon die.

There is a curious association of death and marriage in Jewish custom, perhaps explained by the tragedies of their history. The couple must be reminded of sorrow in the midst of joy and hence a glass is broken. The pieces used sometimes to be carefully saved and used to weigh down their eyelids in death. Numerous examples from different cultures of the ceremonial smashing of certain Jewish wedding customs, particularly among the Ashkenazim, were not dissimilar from those known elsewhere. Bride and groom were escorted separately to the synagogue in a gay procession, and on arrival were showered with wheat or barley. To make the significance of this ritual quite clear, the celebrants called out three times to the bridal pair: 'Be fruitful and multiply', while a wedding canopy, the *chuppah*, set out of doors, signified God's promise to Abraham: 'Thus shall thy children be, like the stars of heaven.'

31

Death and Burial

In the Guattari Cave on Monte Circeo, on the Italian coast north of Naples, there was found in 1939 a solitary skull, lying on a platform of earth and stones. Round the skull was a circle of stones, and strewn about the floor were the bones of deer, buffalo and horses, and also the lower jaw of another human being. The skull belonged to a man aged 40 or 50, who had been killed by a blow on the right temple with a sharp weapon. There were indications that the brain had been extracted, perhaps to be eaten. The skull may originally have been set up on a stake, the ring of stones suggests a magic circle and the animal bones may be the remains of offerings to the skull or of meals eaten in its presence.

Since prehistoric men left no written explanation of themselves, much of what can be said of them is highly speculative but it looks as if this skull was worshipped in some fashion, though it is not certain that its owner was murdered: he may have been killed in battle or by accident. What is certain is that one of the most striking differences between men and other animals is that animals ignore their dead and men do not. Men treat their dead with love, hatred, awe, sorrow, or even with appetite, but rarely with casual disregard.

Lying behind this is an even more important distinction. Unlike the other animals, a man is aware that he himself will eventually die. The effects of this realization on human behaviour have been incalculably great. It is the root of the hope for a life beyond death and it is probably one of the roots of belief in supernatural beings which do not die, which create and maintain the order of Nature, on which each man depends for his brief earthly existence.

The Origins of Burial
The deliberate burial of the dead is one of

man's earliest cultural achievements. It was first associated with the culture of Neanderthal man, towards the close of the Middle Stone Age. In the later Stone Age when present-day man made his appearance, some 40,000 years ago, there was a great outburst of magical, artistic activity, evidence of which can be found in the cave art of southern France. At the same time, there was a greater elaboration both of graves and grave goods; objects were placed beside the corpse and the bones of the dead were sometimes coloured with red ochre. In living cultures, where it is possible to establish the meanings of such customs, the red of the ochre is often associated with blood, a basic element in life itself. In these same societies the burial of the grave goods implies their continued use by the dead though in a different form from life on earth. It therefore seems probable that by the time of the Upper Paleolithic Age, the period of cave art, man had some idea of continuity after death, of another world, a land of the dead, of which the Christian heaven and hell is but a dualistic expression.

The basic logical requirement of such a conception is the development of a dualistic view of man's nature, which is seen as split into flesh and spirit, mind and matter, body and soul. Of these two elements, one dies with the body, one lives on after death. So that life and death are not two completely opposed states: the spirit interpenetrates death and peoples the otherworld with the living dead.

The significance of the appearance of elaborate burial customs and artistic achievements in the Upper Paleolithic Age is greater than at first appears. For their existence suggests that by this time man had developed a means of elaborating concepts and ideas, a language such as we know today. The development of language from a more elementary sign system, such as animals possess, was undoubtedly the greatest technological advance in the history of man. It is the feature that most clearly separates contemporary man from the apes.

Thinking is not confined to the users of language, but there can be no doubt that the development of thought and its use as a major instrument of human growth is dependent upon the invention of a communication system of this kind. One of the first signs of this advance in the technology of communications is the appearance of burial customs which suggests that man had developed a set of ideas which divided his nature into body and soul, and his universe into earth and heaven, or this world and the next. The belief in immortality, as the

Man, in contrast to other animals, treats his dead with love, hatred, awe or sorrow: he rarely ignores them completely. Behind this is the hope that they live on after death, and very often the belief that they will help those who survive.

Left Papuan natives blow through tubes into figures which represent their ancestors, perhaps to keep them alive with breath.

Right Among the Kraho Indians of Brazil women weep for their dead relatives by the special logs made to receive the souls of the dead.

famous anthropologist Malinowski pointed out, is one of the principal sources of religious inspiration.

A Cemetery in the Belly

The burial customs we know from direct observation and written record, rather than from digging into the past, display a number of striking similarities, as well as a wide range of variation in other respects. The variations are in specific customs such as methods of disposal. Burial in the earth (inhumation) is only one such method. Other forms include burial in caves and in mounds or tumuli, obvious forerunners of the Egyptian pyramids and the mausoleums of Europe, by which the important dead are singled out for exceptional treatment. Water burial is practised by seafaring peoples not only out of necessity but also as a way of honouring the great. In Scandinavian legend the corpse of the slain Balder, with his wife and horse, and the gift of Odin's ring Draupnir, was laid in his ship upon a funeral pyre and launched blazing out to sea. Elsewhere, as among the LoDagaa of northern Ghana, burial in a river or its bank is a method of cleansing the community of someone who has died a 'bad death'.

The placing of the dead in trees or on scaffolds is found in many parts of the world and is especially associated with the Zoroastrian religion, practised by the Parsee community of Bombay. Their holy book, the *Zend-Avesta*, proclaims a punishment of a thousand stripes for a person who shall

bury in the earth the corpse of dog or man, and not disinter it before the end of the second year. For only such a treatment can secure the proper ascent of the dead to the other world.

Cannibalism, in those relatively rare parts of the world where it was practised, was sometimes a recognized means of disposing of the dead and was an obligation on the surviving relatives. The meat of the funeral feast is 'nothing less than the corpse of the departed kinsman'. Of inhabitants of the eastern highlands of New Guinea it has been remarked that 'their cemeteries are their bellies'. Certainly this mode of disposal of the dead, the consumption of one generation by the next, is a striking way of conquering death.

Methods of disposing of the dead vary from people to people. But they may also vary within a particular group. We have already seen how important leaders may be accorded special treatment; 'sinners' or despised categories of persons may be differentiated in the same way, especially those who have died a 'bad death'; for example, suicides, witches and those killed by drowning or by lightning, young children who have not yet been fully incorporated into the society and, in Africa, women who have died in childbirth. In each of these cases, whether intentionally or unintentionally, something is wrong.

In Europe, until recent times, certain Christian sects refused to bury unbaptized children and suicides in 'holy ground', while the blood-guilty were interred at a

Harald Schultz

Camera Press London

Above Shrines, portraits, images and graves are important because they provide a point of contact between the living and the dead. Ancestor worship is still a powerful force in China; in Hong Kong joss sticks and candles are burnt, with prayers for the spirits of the dead. *A Chinese girl goes to the grave of her mother:* . . . I would return to this place, this being the eighth year of her tenancy, and draw her forth. With a Taoist priest of Macau I would come, which would pay tribute to my mother, and a labourer. I would expose the coffin and lift the lid. One by one I would take out her bones, first hiding the skull under my coat away from eyes. Then I would polish the bones with sand, the little bones of her feet I would polish first and place them at the bottom of the Canton urn. Next the leg bones I would take, and these I would perfume, and lay them next in the urn, then the rib cage, the arms, the tiny bones of the fingers – all these I would place most carefully in the urn lest I bring her lopsided into Paradise. On these, amid the incantations of the priest, I would lay the skull and cover the mouth of the urn away from flies.

Alexander Cordell
The Bright Cantonese

Left Skulls of monks sharing a single anonymous grave, as they shared all things during life. Down the centuries the remains of monks have been preserved in the monastery garden on Mt Sinai. *Above left* Mourners pay their respects by the deceased's open coffin. *Above right* The Karaja Indians of Brazil leave food on the top of ceramic urns, containing the remains of the dead, to sustain them in the afterworld.

crossroads with a stake in the heart. The last crossroads burial in England took place outside Lord's cricket ground in 1823. And in 1811, in the neighbourhood of Shoreditch, a corpse was arrested for debt, a survival of the procedure whereby the body of a debtor could be legally deprived of a proper burial until his creditors had been repaid.

Love and Fear

The dead are treated in different ways not only for reasons of status, but also as a sanction upon those who remain behind. The earthly system of rewards and punishments is often projected onto the dead, and their destination after death may depend on the way in which they are buried. Only a full burial will ensure proper despatch to the other world; a partial performance may mean that the dead man becomes not a sanctified ancestor but an unsanctified ghost hanging around his earthly dwelling, haunting those who survive in an attempt to get his grievances put right.

The attempt to put oneself at a distance from the ghost is a constant theme of funeral customs everywhere. It is the task of the living to set the dead on the path to the other world, the last journey from which there is no return. For this purpose, the dead may be provided (as in rural Greece) with a coin for the ferryman who rows them across the river of death, with food to sustain them on the way, and with property to use when they get there. This property may include slaves, slaughtered on the tomb, or wives, burnt on the funeral

pyre, or the more humble possessions of the deceased, his clothes, his weapons or his drinking vessels.

The general trend towards actions of this kind, which are implicit in the body-soul division, is illustrated by a report from Lincolnshire at the turn of the century. A widow had placed her husband's mug and jug on his grave, having first broken them both. Explaining her actions to the rector, she said, 'I was that moidered with crying that I clean forgot to put 'em in t'coffin . . . So I goes and does t'next best. I deads 'em both over his grave, and says I to mysen, my old man, he set a vast of store, he did, by yon mug and jug, and when their ghoastes gets over on yon side he'll holler out, "Yon's mine, hand 'em over to me," and I'd like to see them as would stop him a-having of them an' all.'

In simpler hunting societies such as those of North America, where the social investment in property was small, a man's possessions were usually destroyed after his death. As the accumulation of capital goods becomes a more prominent feature of society, so grave goods become more nominal, tokens and toys being substituted for the real thing. Eventually expenditure on the dead is seen as neglect of the living, and strong efforts are made to cut down on such 'unnecessary' expenses.

The destruction of a man's property provides a clear instance of the double attitude that lies behind many aspects of funeral ceremonies. Sidney Hartland commented (in his article on 'Death and Disposal of

Axel Poignant

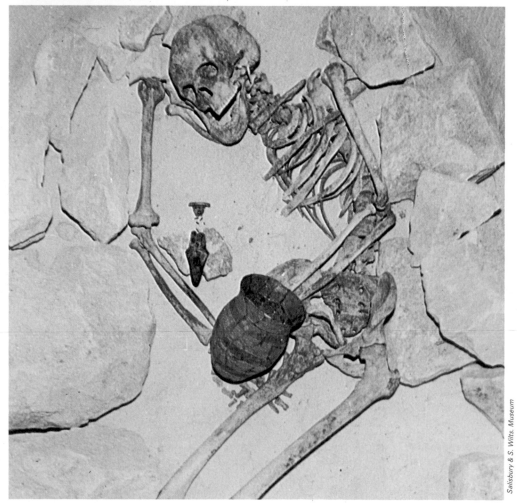

Salisbury & S. Wilts. Museum

Other people's methods of disposing of their dead usually seem bizarre: *Above* In Sicily corpses were placed on shelves in the catacombs; a similar method is used in some of the modern American mausoleums. *Above right* In Nigeria the bodies of criminals are denied proper tribal burial and are thrown onto a platform and left to disintegrate. *Above far right* In the East Indies a widow might be buried alive with her dead husband, to accompany him in the otherworld: an 18th century engraving.

Left Two opposite motives lie behind burial customs all through history: one is affection for the dead and the other is fear of them. Fear causes burial in a sealed container, a coffin six feet underground, a mound or a jar. Affection provides something red, to give blood and so 'new life' to the corpse, or food and useful articles for the dead man to use in the afterlife, like the beaker in this reconstruction of a prehistoric burial at Shrewton in Wiltshire.

the Dead' in *Hasting's Encyclopedia of Religion and Ethics*): 'Throughout the rites and observances attendant on death, two motives – two principles – are found struggling for the mastery. On the one hand, there is the fear of death and of the dead, which produces the horror of the corpse, the fear of defilement, and the overlapping desire to ban the ghost. On the other hand, there is the affection, real or simulated, for the deceased, which bewails his departure and is unwilling to let him go.' The corpse is thus both loved and feared by his kin in the course of these ceremonies, since they are the ones who have most to gain (and most to lose) from his death.

Mansell Collection

Radio Times Hulton Picture Library

The funeral ceremony is not only a matter of disposing of the dead and despatching him to the other world, but also of filling his place in the land of the living and redistributing his rights and duties over people and property. The transition from life to death is the major 'rite of passage' through which all must go, and the great change in status from living to dead cannot be performed just with a nod of the head. The process has to be a gradual one and the burial service is customarily followed, at a suitably discreet interval, by a second funeral, an obituary service, in which the close kin are released from mourning, the dead despatched to their final abode, and their life on earth summed up in the equivalent of a funeral oration.

The expression of this change often takes the concrete form of rituals of reversal, indicating the shift from life to death and the opposition between the two. In this country arms are still reversed at military funerals; the drill command is 'Rest on your arms reversed' and the rifle is turned upside down with the muzzle placed on the soldier's toe-cap. In the domestic context, until recently, clocks were stopped, mirrors turned to the wall, water-vessels emptied and windows flung open; these, besides being acts of reversal, enabled the spirit of the person who had died to quit the presence of the living.

Reaction to death mellows in the course of the funeral and one of the functions of such ceremonies is to relieve the bereaved of anxiety and grief, as well as to reconcile the community to the loss of one of their number, for death constitutes a distinct threat to those who remain behind. But such a threat can never be totally set aside. The idea of continuity after death is itself an aspect of the refusal to accept the reality of death. So too perhaps is the idea that death, except for the old, is 'unnatural'. In most pre-industrial societies a specific supernatural cause was assigned for every event. Hence the frequent ordeals, centring upon the corpse, that occurred during the funerals, in an attempt to find out who killed the dead man. In one form or another, accusations of witchcraft or of sins against the supernatural powers were a constant accompaniment to funerals.

One striking illustration of this attempt to reject its inevitability is to be found in the tales of the origin of death. The biblical story of Adam, Eve and the apple has its parallels in other stories that attribute the coming of death to man's disobedience. But often what is remarkable is the triviality of the offence man has committed. Another set of stories, found in all parts of the world, contrasts the mortality of man and the waxing and waning of the moon. In one version God sends messengers to convey the news of immortality to man, and of death to the moon; the message to man gets delayed or reversed, with the result that he loses the gift of eternal life. But the manner in which this was lost is almost accidental. It is as if the chance introduction of death left open the possibility that the present state of affairs could be reversed.

The Trappings of Fear

Over thousands of years, the world's customs have become such a tangle of facts, faiths, superstitions and rationalizations that it is hard to be sure of the real meaning of any particular custom. However, the customs themselves, all rooted in the ancient and continuing hopes and fears, follow a consistent pattern. We have a common daydream of sudden wealth: 'What would you do if you won the Pools?' We would be reborn, of course, a trip round the world, everything new, a new life. Usually, as losers, we make do with an occasional new suitcase, but our clothes are clean and we have a new face-flannel for a holiday. Similarly with the dead, the body is washed, straightened and wrapped in new cloth for its new state, and it probably goes in a new box, in a new hole, six feet deep.

With all this there will be prayers to help the spirit leave the body and to comfort it in the afterlife; some religions, including Christianity, pass the responsibility on to God, and neither tell the dead what to do nor give him ghostly possessions. But the love-hate ambivalence of all family relationships persists in death; gold, blood, hair, memorial plaques, flowers, ashes in a debased baroque urn on the mantelshelf – whichever we use, our motives are obscure and dark, coloured by superstition in the most rational of us, twitched back from the edge of common sense by a little nudge of fear. Hygiene and honour may seem to compel us, but the washing, anointing, parcelling-up, shutting in a box, burying

Marking the resting place of the dead with imperishable stone, as a perpetual memorial and a symbol of eternal life, occurs in burials ancient and modern: Prehistoric dolmen or 'chamber tomb' in Ireland, probably once wholly or partly covered with earth.

the undertaker's men lay it out and take it straight back to his shop, where there are special rooms for visiting if required.

The coffin is made of wood. Most undertakers now sell caskets as well as coffins, an American fashion for a rectangular box instead of the traditional tapered shape.

Notices of the funeral are sent out privately and to the newspapers, and as soon as the arrangements can be made and the family gathered, the corpse is buried. The hearse is a powerful, black car like an estate-wagon, much more expensive than most people have in life, and either it is driven to the house with the coffin already in it, or it arrives empty and the undertaker's bearers carry the coffin out, on their shoulders in the south, down at arm's length by the handles in the north. All over the coffin and on the roof of the hearse (and sometimes in a special car as well) are the flowers, often made up into wreaths and crosses as in the 19th century, but mostly now in sheaves, large flat arrangements tied with bows and bagged in cellophane. The hearse drives very slowly to the church or the cemetery chapel, followed by the matching cars of the undertaker's fleet, containing the mourners.

When they arrive at the church, the coffin is carried in and set on draped trestles before the altar for the burial service. Then it is taken to the grave, already dug, and lowered in. The words of committal are read by the priest, and the mourners may throw a little earth onto the coffin before they leave. Later the grave is filled by the cemetery staff, and then the mourners' flowers are arranged on top of it.

Some months later, there may be a memorial service which strangers can attend if the family feels the dead to have been very loved or distinguished, and in any case when the grave has settled a memorial stone, slab ('mousetrap' in the trade), or curb may be put up with name, dates of birth and death, and a remembering or loving message. In the last century, these stones were often large and fanciful; now the authorities in charge have clamped down on size and style, and also encourage lawn cemeteries, plain fields with little bronze plaques let flat into the ground so that the grass can easily be cut with a motor-mower. Graves may be visited, and flowers placed or planted, but not many people visit their family graves regularly.

deep and pinning down with a heavy stone may also be seen to come from fright.

The Business of Burial

A state funeral in England or America still has much pageantry; troops slow-marching with reversed rifles to bands playing the Dead March in *Saul*, black crepe muffling the drums, the coffin on a horse-drawn gun carriage, and the mournful notes of the 'Last Post'; but state funerals are rare.

When the average Englishman dies at home, the funeral is organized by an undertaker, who is called in as soon as possible. Some people still keep the body in the house, and then one of the family, or a nurse, may lay it out before he comes. The corpse is stripped, straightened, washed, and dressed in clean or new nightdress or pyjamas, the eyes and mouth are closed, the hands folded on the breast, the hair brushed and combed, and a clean sheet is put over the body, turned down to show the face. If the undertaker's assistant comes to do the laying-out, he will also pin on a square like a nappy after the washing, shave a noticeable beard, and arrange the corpse, using bandages for arms and legs, to look as if it is asleep with the head a little on one side. He has been taught to step back at intervals to see that the effect is 'natural'. (If there is a delay before the funeral in hot weather, the corpse may be embalmed. It is not eviscerated; the blood is simply drawn off through a vein in the armpit and replaced with a formalin-based embalming fluid.) The corpse is then put into the coffin and covered with a shroud to match the pillow and lining, if the family prefers this to ordinary clothes.

In some parts of Britain, relatives and close friends traditionally came to see the corpse and at night one of the family would sit up with it, with candles at head and feet, but this is now rare, and viewing is becoming rare too. More and more people prefer not to keep the body in the house at all, but have

Cosmetics for the Corpse

During the 19th century, funerals were much more complicated than this, and hung over the family for at least a year, during which it was almost compulsory to wear black. The periods of mourning for different degrees of blood relationship were exactly laid down and exactly followed; a widow might wear black for the rest of her life. Now, some old-fashioned people wear dark clothes for the funeral, and men may wear a black tie or an armband for a little while, but that is all. The English see less and less necessity for 'a good funeral' and for the outward rites of grief and mourning.

In the United States of America, however, where funerals were once deliberately simple, the undertakers, who call themselves 'funeral directors' with more conviction than they do in England, have steadily increased the possibilities of big spending on funerals, both as status symbols and as 'grief-therapy', and though mourning clothes are as unfashionable as they are in England, everything else is more elaborate. The undertaker plays a more prominent part throughout. The corpse is almost always embalmed, the face and hands are carefully painted, hair tinted and waved, and spectacles set in place. A complete new outfit (dress or suit, underclothing, hose, shoes) is put on, though nothing shows below the waist, and an artistic arrangement made in a rich wooden or metal casket, lined with ruched and tucked velvet. It is set up in a bower of flowers in an interior-decorated reposing room at the funeral home, where friends often visit the glamorous corpse for several days before the funeral.

The emphasis, exactly as in Ancient Egypt, is on eternal preservation. No 'grave goods' are supplied, but the undertaker does everything he can to foster the belief that the incomplete embalming, the forever metal casket, and the concrete vault that may be bought to enclose it, will prevent decomposition.

Transworld Features

Black Crepe and Plumes
The Roman Catholic countries of Europe and South America have neither simplified their burial customs, as in England, nor changed their slant as in the United States, but rather cling to the old black-and-baroque fashions of the 18th and 19th centuries. Mourning is still extensively worn, and there are sometimes horse-drawn hearses with black plumes and velvet caparisons. The motor-hearses have richly carved and gilded decorations, and there are longer processions and more flowers. Graves are still regularly visited.

Roman Catholics also preserve the custom of having a portrait of the dead person at the tomb, an ancient and widespread practice that produced superb portraits and ancestor figures. Some of the most interesting were carried on royal coffins in medieval England and France. The corpse was formerly carried exposed on top of the coffin so that all might see that the king was dead, but later it was put inside and was replaced by a portrait statue, robed and crowned. The few which survive may be seen in Westminster Abbey. The modern pictures for the average man are a very dim reminder, small sepia photographs set in the tombstone.

Primitive man lived in tiny communities in an enormous world with long hours of darkness. There is less room for fear in our shrunken, bright, and crowded world. Millions of us are hardly conscious of night at all, the unknown is receding into space, and our funeral customs, already diluted from primitive rituals, are going the way of

No moment in most people's lives attracts the ceremonial with which they are honoured after death. Roman Catholic countries have retained elaborate funeral customs, including the solemn and sinister horse-drawn hearse.

all religious ceremony, becoming more and more alike, less and less urgent.

The Disposal of the Dead
Very few people want to die. Very few admit that they will, and almost everyone everywhere has hoped that survival can somehow be contrived if enough trouble is taken. The trouble can be taken by the hoper himself, behaving well enough in life to earn immortality; or even, if he is lucky in his religion, by repentance on his deathbed. Or his survivors may propitiate someone or something on his behalf.

Life after death can also be thought of in two ways. The spirit may survive, bodiless, or reborn in a new human, a tree, an animal, or an ancestor figure. Or the body itself may be resurrected in the flesh for the spirit to inhabit. Most funeral customs are the result of one of these two ways of thinking, and the most elaborate rites have come from the conviction that the reborn spirit will need in its future life all that it had on earth, so that if it is to settle comfortably it must be as rich as possible, often at great cost to the living.

Not all customs have been elaborate, but all successful religions have included in their rituals the means for ensuring some form of life beyond death. On the other hand, no

religion has managed to demonstrate what *does* happen after death, and so there are also rituals to protect the living if anything goes wrong, preventing the furious ghost, unable to find a new body or paradise or whatever, from haunting his careless kin. Terror of the unsettled spirits of the dead dies very hard; food may be put out for them, or their names made taboo so that they are not inadvertently summoned. Graveyards are still shunned at night, fingers are crossed, and very few people are prepared to deny the existence of ghosts with complete confidence.

The Shrines of Ancestors
At death the dead make their journey to the other world. But communication with them has to continue from this world. Even the memorialization of the dead inevitably tends to take on material forms; the appropriate behaviour is directed towards and focused upon a grave, or an object associated with the dead man or an effigy, such as a statue or painting. In this context, great stress is placed upon the actual burial, the actual dwelling-place, the actual representation of the dead. It has been argued that drama began with the acts and scenes of burial ceremonies, which incorporated drama and mime. However this may be, many forms of representative art are rooted in ancestor worship and memorialization of the dead. For the living individual, the portrait on the walls of the ancestral home ensures one's survival after death: and the greater the artist, the greater the hope of

In Bali, the body of a king is placed on a tower together with effigies of bulls and a dragon, and burnt: cremation of Chokorda Sukawati, the last king of Bali.

symbol of authority. The Ashanti believe that at the birth of their nation a golden stool descended from the heavens and became the most valued part of their regalia, the symbol of their new-found unity, the 'soul of the nation'. In 1900 when the British Governor of the Gold Coast, Sir Frederick Hodgson, tried to take possession of it in the name of Queen Victoria, the result was insurrection.

The stool represents not only the spirit of the nation, but also the spirit of the individual. At death a man's stool is seized and the white wood blackened with soot. It is then placed in the 'stool-house' of the lineage to which the dead man belonged, normally just a room in the elder's compound. Here it rests among the shrines of earlier dead, receiving offerings of food and flesh from the living members of the lineage.

Shrines and memorials may be collective or individual, the former tending to be abstract, the latter representational. Among the Ashanti only the stools of important members of the lineage are placed in the shrine-room. To the north, in the savannah lands of Ghana, each individual Tallensi has a shrine, but only when he has been survived by two generations of descendants and therefore established his own 'house'. Among the nearby LoDagaa every man who leaves behind him a son (or whose widow produces a son to his name by marrying his brother) has an ancestor shrine carved for him during the long course of the various funeral ceremonies.

Few systems of ancestor worship are as elaborate or as specific as these, nor yet so closely linked with organizing the relationships between living men; for to sacrifice together to common ancestors is clearly a unifying bond of the greatest importance. In most societies, it is the more immediate dead that are man's primary concern. But here too the tombs, relics and shrines, both abstract and representational, provide a thread of continuity between the living and the dead.

Food for the Dead

Ancestor worship is simply a form of communication between the living and the dead. The forms of the communication vary, though all fall within the range of normal human intercourse. There are verbal forms – prayer, oaths, written formulae. There are visual forms – gesture (usually gestures of obeisance), painting, sculpture, the temple itself, then dance and more extensive types of movement such as the procession and the pilgrimage. Finally there are the offerings of flesh and food which form so important a part of ancestor worship. The worshippers pay homage to a 'divinity' that was once a man, a 'god' who was once a producer and consumer, and in many cases owner of the very means by which the living continue to produce – the land, the oxen or the plough-

immortality. For the survivors, the creation of an image provides a point of contact, a living and enduring memorial.

Such memorials and shrines range from the abstract to the representational, these different forms often being found side by side in the same region, though in general it is true that the simpler the society the more abstract the style. In West Africa, the poorer agriculturalists have shrines of mud mounds or earthenware pots, or even of selected stones. Among the Ashanti, with their elaborate state system and richer resources, the ancestor shrine is a carved stool, which is blackened on a man's death.

The Ashanti stool is an example of the complexity of such ancestral shrines. In the first place, it is an outward and visible sign

of an individual's status. A child will be presented with a small stool when, after seven days, he goes through the 'outdooring' ceremony and acquires a real human personality. Different chiefships and different clans have their own stools, carved in a traditional way and often illustrating some appropriate proverb.

On such a stool only the office-holder himself may sit; when he rises it is placed on its side. For someone else to sit there would be a direct challenge, not only to a man's office but to his very existence. For so closely is the stool identified with the individual, impregnated as it is with the 'dirt' of his body, that his life itself is threatened by such an act.

The stool is at once chair and throne, the

share. So the dead continue to be offered the basic food and drink of the country, the bread and the wine, the yam and palm sap, the porridge and the beer.

But service to the dead cannot be the simple duplication of service to the living; the things of this world have a different meaning for those who can no longer enjoy them in the same way. With food the ancestors receive only a part of the whole; with livestock, the whole is offered in sacrifice, but the biggest portion is in fact consumed by those who remain behind. As far as the ancestors are concerned, a major element in the transaction would seem to be not so much giving as repaying; one is in perpetual debt to the forefathers, just as one is to parents who have raised one from infancy; one can repay this debt only by continual piety in the shape of sacrifice.

Human Sacrifice

Sacrifice is of two general kinds. The regular offerings to the dead are made on festivals like the three day period (the period of the moon's rebirth, the period of Christ's resurrection) of Hallowe'en, All Saints and All Souls. Then there are the occasional sacrifices made at times of affliction, when one's child is ill and a diviner has pointed to an ancestor as the cause. For the dead, while beneficent to their descendants, can also punish. Indeed recent ghosts and others who have not been properly settled in the land of the true dead, are often plain vindictive, sometimes so that the living will be forced to undertake the correct rituals on their behalf, or to right a wrong that has been done them. Whereas the regular transactions approximate to the payment of debt, to the fulfilment of an obligation, the latter smack more of a gift that tries to repair some damage done. But often the damage has itself been caused by failing to give the ancestors their due, thereby incurring their wrath.

Sacrifice is not, of course, confined to the ancestors: it is a way of communicating with supernatural agencies of all kinds. But there is one kind of offering of living beings that is often directed towards the dead – human sacrifice. The ritual immolation of human beings was widely practised; it was found among practically all the Indo-European peoples; in early Israel, Samuel 'hewed Agag in pieces before the Lord'; it occurred in India and Japan, among the Aztecs of Central America and in the forest states of West Africa. Like many other peoples, the Germanic tribes slaughtered captives to honour Odin, the god of war, of battles and of death; they carried out sacrifices on the beaches to appease the gods of the sea and killed other humans on the foundations of new buildings, all with a view to protecting the lives of the sacrificers and keeping malignant demons at bay.

In many cultures burning the body of a dead hero or warrior was thought to be a fitting and spectacular way of speeding him on his journey to the otherworld, a romantic belief that retained its appeal even when cremation was rejected by the Christian Church: illustration from a 16th century manuscript.

Cremation

The Christian religion objected to burning the dead because it seemed to violate and invalidate the doctrine of the resurrection of the body. This clerical objection, however, was countered by the philanthropist Lord Shaftesbury who declared that if burning prevented resurrection, 'What would, in such a case, become of the blessed martyrs?' In Christian countries cremation was forbidden for centuries although in the 19th century even clergymen began to argue in its favour.

Support from Science

The main argument for cremation came from those who were horrified by the insanitary conditions caused in towns by the custom of burial. The problems caused by drainage from churchyards and cemeteries and the waste of land in and around towns and villages were set out in a book by Edwin Chadwick, *A Special Inquiry into the Practice of Interment in Towns*, published in 1843. In the second half of the 19th century many physicians and chemists, especially in Italy and Switzerland, recommended the adoption of cremation. A congress at Milan in 1874 petitioned the Chamber of Deputies for a clause permitting cremation. In the same year the Cremation Society of England was founded to promote the practice of cremation. 'We disapprove of the present custom of burying the dead,' it declared, 'and desire to substitute some mode which shall rapidly resolve the body into its component elements by a process which cannot offend the living, and shall render the remains absolutely innocuous. Until some better method is devised, we desire to adopt that usually known as cremation.'

Great difficulties were placed in the way of all who wanted to bring back the ancient rite of burning the dead. The Council of the Cremation Society of England was unable to purchase a freehold until 1878, when an acre of land was obtained at Woking not far from the cemetery there. In 1885, the first publicly organized and controlled cremation in Britain took place.

There was much opposition and prejudice in the early days and police protection was required at some cremations. Now all this has changed. Today 51% of those who die in Britain are cremated, and there are already more than 200 crematoria in the country. The ban on Roman Catholic cremations was lifted in 1964. Orthodox Jews, however, still continue to object to cremation. In America, high pressure funeral salesmanship combines with organized religion to keep the figures down, but cremation is growing more popular every year.

The ashes from cremated bodies are disposed of in various ways. The remains of a Hindu funeral pyre are put in the river – usually the sacred river Ganges. The Digger Indians smear the ashes with gum onto the heads of the mourners. In Europe and America the ashes are stored in urns, buried in the earth or in graves inside a church, thrown to the winds, or scattered in a garden of remembrance. Cremation has dealt with the sanitary problem that worried the 19th century reformers; the scattering of ashes deals with the problem of storage and grave-space, but its widespread adoption brings to an end the tombs and monuments for the dead which were a feature of western European Christian civilization for so many hundreds of years.

The Rhythm of Life

Fertility

Man has always had a passionate concern with fertility: it has been a consistent feature of almost every type of human society, and particularly, agricultural society. Consequently, scholars have often seized upon the ideas of, and the rituals connected with fertility, as a key with which to attempt to decipher the mysteries of primitive religion and magic.

Ripeness Is All

The obsession itself is not difficult to account for. Man's knowledge of the biological and physiological processes controlling fertility is of very recent date, and human life-expectancy only a century or so ago was assured only on condition of frequent reproduction, for as long as the female of the human species remained capable of bearing children. Death was perhaps a calamity; but not so great a calamity as barrenness. Human life depended, too, upon the fertility of the fields which man tilled, the fruit which he gathered, the animals which he ate, milked, or hunted. It is only in the technological societies of the West that man has become to some extent liberated from a life-and-death struggle for existence, in which the need to reproduce his kind, and to see his crops growing and his animals bearing young, has been paramount. Elsewhere in the world, and at almost any other point in human history than the 20th century, failure of fertility, whether of man, animal, or field, has meant simply and starkly death. Small wonder, then, that the idea of fertility has loomed so large in his thinking and feeling.

Man's constant attempts to promote fertility are equally easy to explain, at least

In India the male and female elements in the universe were personified as Shiva and Shakti, whose generative powers cross and recross to form the basis of the entire cosmos.
Left Ithyphallic figure of Shiva in his creative aspect.

Primitive man often made images with exaggerated sexual features, hoping by magic to appropriate some of their fertility powers.
Right The crudely erotic figures on a hut in Chad.

Jörgen Bitsch

43

Left The magic rituals associated with the divine king and the dying god were designed to secure the primary wants of man – order, peace and plenty: Rameses VI and his wife: Egyptian pharaohs were identified with the god Horus in life and with Osiris in death. At the Sed festival they were ritually rejuvenated to prevent their ageing bringing famine and decay.

Below left The Wakamba fertility dance is frequently performed in many parts of Kenya. While the women stand in a circle and play on whistles, the men drum, dance and display their physical prowess by performing gymnastic feats, gradually working their way towards the women.

Right May Day celebrations begin with the gathering of flowers and branches and 'bringing home the May', or bringing the new life of spring, into the village. A maypole is erected and festooned, and young girls perform a dance around this phallic symbol.

the Sky Father had impregnated the Earth Mother and caused her to bring forth. If a child died, it was not through disease or malnutrition, but because an evil spirit had stolen away the child's soul.

To archaic man then, the world appeared to be governed by its own immutable laws: not the biological laws we think we know so well, but the laws of universal cause and effect, of giving and withholding, of correspondence and adjustment. And fertility – which is, after all, only a convenient Western abstraction – was completely subject to this pattern.

Rhythm of the Seasons

The first characteristic of the pattern of fertility, as man has experienced it for the greater part of history, is its cyclical character. In the temperate zones the rhythm of the seasons, on which so much depended, was utterly reliable and could without difficulty be regarded as a divine ordinance, as in the ancient Hebrew tradition: 'While the earth remains, seedtime and harvest, cold and heat, summer and winter, day and night, shall not cease' (Genesis 8.22).

In parts of the world where the seasons were less well defined, other patterns took their place – patterns dominated by the alternation of wet and dry periods, by the phases of the moon, and the like. To the seasons corresponded the stages in the growth of the crops, and the mating habits of animals. Crops, animals and humans had their appropriate gestation periods. The menstrual cycle of women was seen to correspond with the phases of the moon. All this adds up to a conception of time, not as an ordinary linear progression from point A to point B, but as an infinitely repeated series of cycles, in which growth succeeds birth, maturity succeeds growth, and death succeeds maturity. But even death was not the end, for spring came to drive out winter, and the annual miracle of the rebirth of the crops served to remind man that life was always latent in death.

It is easy thus to characterize the fertility cycle as a series of 'natural' phenomena; but archaic man did not think of it in that way. The power of life was not an impersonal entity, which merely needed to be left

on one level. We know that in the past, the world has not as a rule been particularly amenable to man's efforts to control it. But despite this, the human animal has obstinately refused to give in. We must not fall into the trap of supposing that archaic man's attitude to the world in which he lived was one of dull resignation. Where archaic and primitive man differs from modern man is that whereas modern man strives to master certain fields of knowledge and influence, and acts accordingly, archaic man was convinced that ultimate power was never in his own hands. There were sources of power, but these lay without exception in the spirit world – the unseen, supernatural world of gods, spirits, demons and ghosts. What man had to do was to establish contact and rapport with the unseen world, with a view to channelling and applying its power. For power was a property of spirit;

and thus the spirit world had to be approached, and if possible controlled, if man was to have a share in its blessings. Equally, since that power could (and frequently did) work in ways inimical to man, it had to be propitiated and kept friendly, lest it should simply sweep him, his children, his cattle and his crops away.

Fertility was entirely subject to the power and control of the spirit world, whose greatest gift was the gift of life. When life came into being, it was because the spirits had made it so; when life ebbed and disappeared, or was withheld, this too was the work of spirits. In this most vital area of human experience, there was no effect without its spiritual cause. If a woman conceived, it was not because she had intercourse with her husband, but because the spirits had put a child into her womb. If the corn sprouted in due season, it was because to its own devices. Accordingly we may say that its second characteristic was its personal, 'hierarchical' nature. Personal not necessarily because it was regarded altogether in human terms, but because it was able to be approached by humans, with whom it had some features in common, and could be, in some cases, communicated with. Hierarchical because it was thought of as a graded hierarchy of spiritual beings, from the mighty gods of the sky to minor demons.

Whether the various deities and spirits that went to make up the supernatural chain of beings were intrinsically benevolent or malevolent is an open question. Many could be either or both, according to their moods and to the extent to which they had been acknowledged and propitiated. Perhaps it would be safe to say that any one of them *could* be dangerous, especially if slighted or ignored.

Art and Magic

The third characteristic of the fertility pattern, depended on the first two. The various cycles of fertility were thought to depend for their continuance upon the activity of the supernatural powers: the great cycles upon the great powers; the lesser cycles on lesser powers. In other words fertility, at whatever level, is always caused; it never just happens. Once the dependent nature of fertility in the thought of the greater part of mankind is recognized, it becomes clear firstly, that should the supernaturals choose for any reason to withhold the gift of life, this is a sufficient explanation for famine, failure in hunting, miscarriage and barrenness. And secondly, that the nucleus of primitive and archaic religion and magic alike concerns man's attempts to reconcile and appropriate the power, or life-force, that the supernaturals wield. Therefore man does what he can to ensure that the gods and spirits remain friendly. This may involve playing off one against another – a greater power against a lesser, or a benevolent spirit against a malevolent. In so far as man is consciously attempting to manipulate the powers, this is magic, and not religion; but the dividing line between the two is indistinct, and the same action or rite may have elements of both in it.

An example of this attempt to control Nature is the celebrated cave art of south-western France and the Pyrenees. It has been supposed by some authorities that their main purpose was magical: to ensure a supply of game animals, and success in hunting them. It has also been noted that the more dangerous the animal, the more often it occurs in the paintings, and the more seldom its bones appear in prehistoric kitchen refuse heaps. Scenes in which a bison, for example, is shown transfixed by spears or arrows, as well as recording an actual successful event may well have been intended to ensure repeated success. To this extent the purpose of the paintings appears entirely magical. But the underlying attitude, which saw the prey which a hunter hoped to catch as controlled by forces outside man's control, verges upon the religious; it presupposes the existence of a supernatural world, and the need for man

to take that world into consideration.

Analogies from more recent pre-literate peoples may only be of limited value, but the various hunting tribes of the northern hemisphere (America, Europe and Asia) appear to exhibit a similar mixture of motives. North American Indian tribes, for instance, combine 'magical' rituals, designed to ensure the increase of the species, with a firm belief in the 'Owner of the Animals', who owns and rules the particular species in the same way as the Supreme Being rules over the universe and the world of men. The bear, which was always held in especial reverence, was hunted; but the killing was done with apologies and with as little blood as possible, and after death honour was paid to the skull. Doubtless the motive was in this case one of sharing in the great power of the bear; but in the case of the Ainu of Sakhalin Island in Japan, when

a bear was killed, it was despatched with ceremony and sent home to its Owner, to tell of the good treatment it had received and to ask that more game be released. Should the Owner be offended, on the other hand, bear cubs would not be born and the bear could not be hunted.

Festivals to Ensure Fertility

In agriculture, the great fertility cycle is that of the seasons of the year, and in agricultural communities, two major events – the sowing of the seed and the harvest – were frequently the occasion for particular celebrations or festivals. Lesser festivals, though with virtually the same significance, took place at midsummer and midwinter. Traces of all these festivals survive to this day in the West, sometimes changed out of all recognition, sometimes – as in the case of the Scandinavian *Jul* (Yuletide or

Christmas) – retaining enough of the original symbolism to demonstrate its origins.

In all such cases, the objective was the continuation of the seasonal pattern, and the ensuring of a good and fertile year. The High Gods of the sky were the protectors of the cosmic order and the great givers of fertility, and so the festivals were centred, explicitly or implicitly, around the mighty deeds of these gods. A further feature which must be borne in mind is that the annual renewal of fertility was in very many cases seen as a repetition of an original act of creation, in which order triumphed for the first time over chaos, fertility over barrenness; accordingly, the festival itself was a magico-religious renewal of creation.

In the Babylonian *Akitu* (New Year) festival, the great epic of creation was recited, celebrating the victory of the god Marduk over the dragon of chaos. In addition there was a pattern of ritual, to which the myth served as a type of libretto. Centring on the figure of the king as the representative of the High God, this took the form of a symbolical dramatic confrontation between the god and the powers of chaos: chaos wins a temporary victory, law and order is forgotten for a time, the king is divested of his symbols of office; but then order is restored, rejoicing breaks out, the king is enthroned anew, and celebrates a 'sacred marriage' with a chosen priestess. New Year festivals of this type ensured the fertility of the land for another cycle. Since the power of fertility was in the hands of the High God, who stood at (or near) the head of the pantheon, only the king, as the head of the human hierarchy, could take it upon himself to approach the god and appropriate this power on behalf of his people.

The sacred marriage could be repeated on all levels of the hierarchy. Here, as elsewhere, we are confronted with an elaborate correspondence of man with the cosmos. The intercourse of the king and the priestess might be believed to further the fertility of the fields. References are scattered through the literature of popular religion and folklore to this practice.

The Killing of the King

Sir James Frazer found that the Shilluk of the White Nile starved (or later strangled) their king to death when he showed signs of old age or disease, and that they also allowed any of the king's sons to attack him and fight him to the death for the crown. He found traces of the same customs in many other parts of the world, and he connected the killing of the king with the dying and rising gods of the eastern Mediterranean area – Osiris, Adonis, Attis, Tammuz.

All this suggested the conclusion that at a certain stage in the evolution of human societies it was the custom to kill the king, either at regular intervals or when he began to grow old. He was killed because his life was bound up with the fertility and prosperity of his land and people. If he grew old and weak, the crops would fail, women and beasts would be barren. In many cases, like the King of the Wood, the king had to fight a challenger. If he won, his victory showed that he was still strong and virile. If he was killed, the challenger ruled in his place.

In course of time this primitive custom was modified. The king was killed in mimicry, not in reality. Or instead of the real king being sacrificed, a substitute was chosen, treated as king for a few days and then slaughtered. Eventually the rite died out altogether, leaving tell-tale traces behind it in custom, folklore and legend.

The king who was sacrificed was a god. He was the visible manifestation of the dying and rising god, the lover of the mother or earth goddess. He was the god who is the growing crops which must die so that their seeds fall into the earth-mother, who gives birth to the crops of the following harvest.

This correspondence of function extends to the person of the woman and the 'person' of the earth. In mother goddess symbolism, the earth is regarded as a woman; conversely the woman may be regarded as a ploughed field, and the male organ as the plough. Regard for the sacredness of the 'body' of the earth has, however, been known to give rise to a refusal to cultivate it. A North American chief is recorded as having said: 'You ask me to plough the ground! Shall I take a knife and tear my mother's bosom? Then when I die she will not take me to her bosom to rest. You ask me to dig for a stone! Shall I dig under her skin for bones? Then when I die, I cannot enter her body to be born again. You ask me to cut grass and make hay and sell it, and be rich like white men! But how dare I cut off my mother's hair?'

The Coming of Spring

The celebration of returning fertility along with the magical stimulation of fertility form the basis for all ancient spring rituals and festivals, and so through them for most modern ones.

Drinking, dancing, feasting, noisemaking and love-making have been the usual ways in which men have celebrated occasions of communal happiness; the winning of a war, for instance, or an election, the birth of a royal heir or the death of a tyrant. But ever since prehistoric times man has reserved special celebratory energies for the turning of the seasons, and has reacted with perhaps the strongest surge of emotion to spring, the time when the earth is freed from the shackles of winter.

This emotion was expressed in the form of religious rites, mainly because for ancient man no aspect of life could be kept apart from religion. Modern commentators have seen in the Paleolithic cave paintings of dancing figures in animal masks or disguises a form of hunting magic that itself was probably seasonal; but later ages brought agriculture to mankind, and the seasonal rites became of crucial importance.

Something of their essence can be seen in the ancient spring customs of Mesopotamia in which the Babylonians performed ritual re-enactments of a Creation myth, reflecting the re-creation of spring. And they staged the sacred intercourse of the king and a priestess in a room set aside for the rite and decorated with leaves and flowers.

Sex and drama also occur in the rituals of the Greeks, a festive people who took every opportunity available for some sort of celebration. And the eastern cults that were introduced during later centuries offered many opportunities. Before that the early Greeks held a spring Festival of Flowers to praise fertility and the god Dionysus, with plenty of sacrificing, feasting and drinking. There was also some placation of the community's dead, the ancestral ghosts, a practice adopted by many later traditions.

In March, the Great Dionysia was celebrated, which by the 6th century BC had come to be a time not only for general revels of a wildly unrestrained nature, but also for the presentation of drama in Athens. Evolved from older choric hymns and rites of Dionysus, the tragedies of Aeschylus, Sophocles and Euripides developed first, but comedy followed fast. And the latter retained explicit aspects of its fertility rite origins, as in the traditional flaunting of over-sized phalluses.

Rome's spring festivals took up many of these older threads and entwined them with new ones. In early Republican days there were minor festivities such as the dancing and processions of the *Salii*, in March, or the uninhibited merrymaking of the April *Parilia*, originally a shepherd's rite. Also in April was a movable feast, the beautiful *Floralia*, which in the true primitive tradition combined vegetation magic and ritual sexuality.

Below The celebration of fertility, and its magical stimulation, form the basis for spring rituals all over the world. Drinking, dancing, feasting and love-making are frequent methods of celebration: fertility dance, in a village on the Ivory Coast.

Uniphoto

In Christian Europe, and later in North and South America, the first celebrations of spring were also in the nature of a 'last fling' before the strict fasting of Lent. *Below and left* Scenes from the Mardi Gras held annually in New Orleans; this celebration was originally brought to Louisiana by French settlers, and it has now developed into a major tourist attraction.

Barnaby's Picture Library

Above Masks are always part of the festivities, possibly recalling the primitive belief that they keep evil spirits at bay: masks for sale in Rio de Janeiro which is the scene of the most famous carnival in South America. *Above right* Effigy used in celebrations held in May in Portugal.

The better known ceremonies of the *Lemuria* in May recall the Greek festival that paid homage to the dead: for the Romans it was also a time for laying restless ancestral spirits, and preventing them from wreaking harm. Something of the same intention functioned in another well-known late Roman festive occasion, the *Lupercalia*, which was held in February, at the very start of the Roman spring. It involved sacrifices, offerings of the first fruits of the previous harvest, and the other usual basic enjoyments. But it also required some ritual flagellation of people, most usually of barren women, to stimulate their fertility and perhaps to drive off whatever evil baulked that fertility. The priests also 'beat the bounds' of the communities, or of the fields, again to set up magical protection against evil for the year to come.

The declining Empire came to know many new cults and their festivals (apart from the novel worship of Christianity). One was the *Bacchanalia*, the frenzied Roman version of the Greek Dionysia, but another more austere festival developed with the cult worship of Attis. This was the March celebration called *Hilaria*. It involved processions and sacrifices, followed by abstention from meat, and general restrictions, to accompany the ritual mourning of the god's death. The god's eventual resur-

rection was followed by ritual joy and festivity. Christians will find the pattern not unfamiliar.

First and Last Flings
From the earliest Christian times, the celebration of spring tended to begin on or shortly after Twelfth Night, but to come to a head especially in the few days before Ash Wednesday and the austerites of Lent. Many pre-Christian festivals were held at this time, and again this is an example of Christianity superimposing itself onto paganism. In fact, the folk festivals, as opposed to the liturgical ones, always tended towards the secular, not to say the profane. Nevertheless, the Church's terminology took over: the final day of the festivals is invariably Shrove Tuesday, presumably so called because it was a day for priests to shrive folk in preparation for Lent. Yet, although the festivals may appear to be in the nature of 'last flings' before Lenten asceticism, they were, and are, also 'first flings', expressing universal joy at the spring renewal. The pre-Lenten festivals were not the sole spring festivities, but for Christian Europe and the Americas, they were the first.

Some motifs are found in most of these early spring celebrations. Feasting is always important, especially for Christians who had to give up meat and any kind of rich delicacy in Lent; but sometimes the feasting is merely symbolized by the eating of some special Shrovetide food. Dancing invariably takes place, as always at times of communal joy; some special dances may be mimetic and dramatic, concerning some suitable spring-

time theme, while others might be processional, the ancestors of later parades. The modern idea of parades with great decorated 'floats' was foreshadowed in the Germanic rite praising the goddess Nerthus, which involved processions with sacred objects borne on a strange 'boat-on-wheels'.

Masks and costumes are always part of the festivities, perhaps recalling the prehistoric dancers in animal head-dresses, and the primitive belief that fearful masks provided a way of keeping evil spirits at bay. But in more modern times the costumes are worn largely for the sake of competitive splendour, and the masks have always helped the celebrants to shed their inhibitions in relative safety.

The motif of warding off or driving off evil crops up in many places in forms other than masking. Sometimes it is a magical ritual to protect the crops, at other times it appears as a magical destruction or exorcism of the demonic winter or some other appropriate symbol of evil. Noise plays a large part in the expulsion, as it does in many primitive rites; often an effigy figure is burned or suitably destroyed.

Mock battles of one kind or another occur frequently, and are probably linked with the motif of driving off evil. For while they may have taken on special colourations, such as re-enactments of historical combats, or riotous sport, their presence in a spring festival links them with more ancient ritual battles symbolizing the conflict of winter and summer.

Spring festivals all naturally incorporate some form of sexuality – not only private sex activity, which has always accompanied drinking, feasting and dancing, but also ritual sex that long antedates the Christian traditions. Some traditions incorporate variants of the sacred marriage; others merely bring in rude songs, the coarse antics of clowns, and earthy folk drama.

Drama, on any level, is a spring motif of its own. The incomparable Greek drama grew from much older, primitive rites; and the high traditions of English drama had their roots in choric liturgical rites of the Church at Easter which gave rise to later mystery and miracle plays, and the folk dances, mimes and mummery of the people, performed at Shrovetide, which developed the morality thread of the English tradition. Many lands still have special folk dramas and masques which are performed before Lent as they have been for centuries.

The sexual and dramatic aspects of the revelry sometimes overlap with another common motif, in which the normal order of things is overturned. Servants or fools become rulers, Lords of Misrule dominate the festivities of many countries, men dress as women.

Driving off demons also seems all-important in Teutonic traditions, especially in the great *Fastnacht* celebrations of Germany, known as *Fasching* in Austria. The Austrian *Schemen*, a wild assortment of masked demonic dancers, which form the centrepiece of the Innsbruck festival the week before Ash Wednesday, are especially notable. Cologne's revelry features a Prince of Fastnacht with a court of fools, while Saxony was given to staging a mock battle between the forces of winter and summer. Munich's gorgeous pageantry is world-famous, but seems to dwell more on the city's medieval history than on folk custom or ancient rite; the German-speaking Swiss of Zurich have a tradition of killing an effigy of winter in their spring festivities.

British customs generally seem to have missed out the parades and pageantry so favoured in other lands, but some of the old spring motifs make their appearance. Shrove Tuesday is still Pancake Day in Britain, symbolic of the coming abstention from meat. But apart from this special food, Shrovetide for Britons once meant a time for rough games and hooliganism. In the past apprentices were given a holiday on the Tuesday, and showed their appreciation by all kinds of happy rowdiness. A special sort of Shrovetide football was played in many towns and rural villages. The sexuality theme seems to be lacking in the British Shrovetide, though the traditional post-Easter fun, and especially the Maytime delights of the past, tended to make up for this lack.

Farther south in Europe, terms meaning 'Shrovetide' are replaced by the word carnival, which has come to mean un-

Intended to promote fertility and reinvigorate the year, the *Holi* is celebrated in northern India when the crops of the spring harvest are almost ripe; festivities include ritual dramas in which women battle with the men, and generally culminate in a procession; on the second day dust and coloured water are flung over the spectators: Dyes for use in the celebrations, for sale in an Indian market place.

Brian Mondine

49

restrained festive gaiety. Italy sometimes begins its *carnevale* in mid-January or earlier, and keeps up the feasting and dancing and pageantry until Shrove Tuesday. Venice crowns an overweight effigy, the spirit of fleshy indulgence, as King of Carnival and ritually burns him to bring in Ash Wednesday. Florence, among other centres, is noted for the delightful rudeness of traditional carnival songs.

The Spanish carnival spirit produces most of the usual traditions, especially public dancing and masked processions. In northern Spain, a stuffed effigy again acts as the emblem of carnival licence; it rides in a cart decorated with greenery, reflecting the ancient belief in vegetation magic, and is duly burned. Elsewhere in Spain an effigy representing the King of Evil is ritually buried; and the spring *fiesta* also includes many folk dramas on sacred marriage or Resurrection themes, or on the symbolic battle theme, which is sometimes in the form of dramatic dance battles between Moors and Christians.

The Spanish concepts of pre-Lent fiesta were widely adopted in Latin and South America, and there too the motif of the mock battle seems to be strong. A Mexican drama ritually depicts the capture of a famous bandit by soldiers, while in southeast Mexico a mock battle dance concerns 'priests' and 'devils'. Throughout Latin America maskers represent devils and the dead, signifying the supernatural forces that are to be warded off.

But the Spanish ex-colonies take fiesta to its heights in their immense variety of special dances, such as the quadrille-type dance of central Mexico, for instance, in which participants wear medieval garb. Many of the dances incorporate elements of pre-Columbian Indian dances and rites. In Mexico, for instance, the time that is now carnival was once given to revelry in praise of the Aztec god of agriculture.

'Fat Tuesday'

The French have always enjoyed many different kinds of carnival, including a now extinct festival of butchers in Paris, which featured Le Boeuf Gras, a fattened ox decorated with ribbons, which was probably another emblem of the indulgence to be forsworn in Lent. But the chief festival is the carnival of Nice, with glorious parades and pageants, dominated by King Carnival and his court of clowns and harlequins, embodying the free wild spirit of the season. This spirit flourished especially in the French colony which is now the American state of Louisiana. There the significant French name for Shrove Tuesday took on new meaning as the general term for the whole festive time – Mardi Gras.

Mardi Gras traditions date from the mid-18th century, in New Orleans, when private masquerade balls often exploded onto the streets to become public, sometimes violent, merrymaking. By the early 19th century the city's revellers had taken to parading through the streets on horseback or in carriages to display their finery; and tableaux, masques and similar light dramas had become a part of the occasion.

Keystone Press

Midsummer's Eve

Since our ancestors relied upon the sun for warmth and light, the arrival of Midsummer inevitably brought a reminder of approaching darkness and cold. It was a time of uncertainty when, so it was once believed, poisonous dragons thronged the air. Excited by the heat of summer, they copulated, and their emission fell upon the earth, polluting the drinking water: 'There was soo greate hete the which causid that dragons to go togyther in tokenynge that Johan dyed in brennynge love and charyte to God and man.'

This curious reconciliation of early myth and Christian tradition explains the transfer of pagan usage from the solstice, 21 June, to a celebration three days later. This was the Nativity of John the Baptist; but some churchmen voiced their objections. An entry in the Register of the Synod of Caithness and Orkney for 21 June 1708 reads: 'Johnmas fires which are commonly observed sometimes in this month are very common in many paroches. Therefor recommends to the several ministers where this or the like superstitious custome is to deall with persons and to bring them to a sense of yr sin and that they continue to rebuke the same from yr pulpits.'

Bonfires, supposedly honouring St John, are still lit in Cornwall; at one time they blazed all over Europe, to strengthen the

Druids at Stonehenge on Midsummer Day, one of the principal stages in the 'life-cycle' of the sun, and so of life on earth.

weakening sun and keep evil creatures at bay. The vigour and extent of the crops were believed to be governed by the distance from which the fires were visible, and the height which people reached by jumping over them. Leaping of this kind was once a common folk custom, intended to stimulate the crops by sympathy. Burning torches were carried through the fields to guard against mishaps, and fires were lit to the windward so that their smoke would blow over the grain. A piece of blazing turf was thrown in the growing corn or carried round the cattle, and wheels covered with burning straw were rolled downhill to imitate the sun's descending course.

The bonfires were often a social occasion. An old account records: 'For making the king's bonefuyr, 10s'. One was lit at Augsburg in 1497 in the presence of Emperor Maximilian, and Philip the Handsome led the first ring dance around it. Louis XIV, crowned with roses, is known to have kindled the flames himself, and he also joined in the dancing. The custom was practised of burning live animals in the fire; usually foxes or cats, probably because witches were thought to assume these forms.

Harvest

It is difficult for us to realize nowadays, with tins and frozen foods available throughout the year, and imported tropical fruits on our tables even in the middle of winter, the anxiety which our ancestors felt as they waited for the annual harvest. When man first progressed from the primitive stage of gathering wild foodstuffs to cultivation of the soil, the procession of the seasons became increasingly important. In an agricultural economy his very life depended on the success or failure of the crops, and enormous efforts were made to ensure a fruitful harvest.

The Jews still celebrate Succoth – the Feast of Booths or Tabernacles – as they have done since the time of the command in Deuteronomy (chapter 16), 'You shall keep the feast of booths seven days, when you make your ingathering from your threshing floor and your wine press; you shall rejoice in your feast.' Citron, palm, myrtle and willow (the 'four kinds') are carried in procession during the synagogue service, and each family builds a booth before the festival begins. As a rule it is set up in the garden if there is one, or if not, on the flat roof. The top of the booth is covered with green boughs, arranged in such a way that the starlight can shine through. This is to remind the Jews of the time of the Exodus, when they were nomads in the wilderness. Inside are gay decorations taken from the season's produce – apples, grapes, pomegranates and brightly coloured Indian corn.

The Harvest Supper

Churchgoers today send vegetables, fruit and flowers to the Harvest Festival service, a popular occasion followed by the traditional Harvest Supper. Best known as Harvest Home, it had many dialect names, like Kern, Mell and Horkey Supper.

On the evening of the day when the last load had been brought in, the farmer and his wife would traditionally provide a good meal for the reapers. As a rule it was served in the barn, which had been specially decorated with garlands and branches. In Lincolnshire the Old Sow often put in an appearance. This was two men disguised with sacking and wearing a head stuffed with furze, which they used for pricking the others.

Frumenty sometimes used to be served, a milk pudding made from wheat boiled in milk with raisins and currants, and flavoured with spices and sugar. More often there would be a round of beef, followed by plum pudding and served with plenty of beer.

Probably it was the memory of suppers such as these that the Pilgrim Fathers carried with them from England to America. During the autumn of 1621, settlers in Plymouth Colony gathered to give thanks for the harvest after their first difficult year in the New World. This was America's first Thanksgiving. The exact date of this first celebration has never been established (it has even been said that it was in February). But in 1864 President Lincoln set aside the last Thursday in November as the appointed day. (Canadians hold Thanksgiving earlier, in October.)

Left The harvest pillar remains the focal point of the Cannstatt festival held each September at Stuttgart; begun in 1818, this great harvest festival now includes a funfair and cattle market, and goes on for 12 days.

Below Font in a Somerset church decorated with field and garden produce: the practice of holding a Harvest Festival Service, established in the 19th century, has ousted the Harvest Home.

Verfehrsamt

Barnaby's Picture Library

Today Thanksgiving Day is an important family occasion, with a traditional meal that includes roast turkey, corn on the cob, and pumpkin pie, in honour of the Pilgrims' typical fare. The day is also rich in special leisure activities, among them important football games. Interestingly, the ancient Mayans held an annual harvest celebration each autumn, on a particular day, which also featured turkey on the festive menu and ritual ball games. And many forest Indians of the American South, such as the Natchez, celebrated the harvest with a feast of specially grown corn and their own forms of ball games.

The English ancestors of the Pilgrim Fathers traditionally brought in their harvest with great style. The last load, decorated with branches and garlands, was taken triumphantly through the village. Handbells were rung, everyone cheered and shouted, and children who helped were presented with slices of plum cake. At some stage people hiding in the bushes threw buckets of water over the cart; the custom was rooted in imitative magic, being designated to ensure rain for the nourishment of next year's crop.

Seated on top of the load, and probably drenched to the skin, were the Lord of the Harvest and his Lady. Before the coming of mechanization farmers were obliged to engage extra hands to assist with the harvest. The men appointed one of their number to negotiate with the farmer and take the lead in the scything: he was called Lord of the Harvest. The second reaper, a man dressed as a woman who replaced the Lord in his absence, was known as the Harvest Lady. If anyone swore or told a lie in front of the Lord of the Harvest, he was obliged to pay a fine. In Cambridgeshire each new workman was 'shoed' by the Lord of the Harvest, who tapped the soles of his shoes in return for a shilling.

Mechanized farming eliminated the Lord and Lady of the Harvest. Gone too are the elaborate rituals surrounding the cutting of the last sheaf, in which it was supposed that the power of the harvest resided. In some countries a few ears of corn were left standing in the field because people were afraid of exhausting the strength of the crop. They were said to be an offering for Odin's horses, or those who dwell under the earth. However, cutting the last sheaf was a more usual ceremony. This could be a great honour, but it also seems to have been regarded as a disagreeable duty. In England the men sometimes used to throw their sickles at it in turn, as if they were anxious that the responsibility should be shared. Behind this custom lay the old belief that the spirit of the corn had taken refuge in the last sheaf.

Crying the Mare

Sometimes it was carried in triumph to the farmhouse but often it was dumped on a neighbour's land to get rid of it, in case it brought bad luck. Around Herefordshire and Shropshire the final handful of corn was grasped and tied together. The men flung their sickles towards it and whoever was successful cried:

'I have her!'

A brief ritual exhange followed:

'What have you?'
'A mare, a mare, a mare!'

This was called Crying the Mare. An old Devonshire custom known as Crying the Neck suggests, on the contrary, that the final sheaf was thought to bring good luck. While the reapers were finishing, an old harvester went round, selecting all the best ears he could find. These were gathered into a bundle, known as the neck, which he plaited and arranged as attractively as possible. When the work of harvesting was done, everyone formed a circle and the man who had made the neck stood in the centre, holding it firmly with both hands. He stooped, lowering the neck down to the ground, and all the men took off their hats; they too bent low, hats in hand. Then slowly standing upright, they raised their hats above their heads, and the man with the neck held it high in the air. Everyone cried 'the neck', and the whole ceremony was repeated three times over. There was a great deal of cheering and, during the mêlée which followed, someone seized the neck and ran with it to the farmhouse. A maid was waiting, ready at the door with a bucket of water. If the man could get past her, or enter the house by any other route, he was allowed to kiss her. But if he failed she soaked him thoroughly with water from her bucket.

Harvest competitions of this kind used to be very popular. In Scotland and the north of England, groups of three or four men each took a ridge of grain and raced to see who would finish reaping first. But there used to be a day when 'kemping' as this was called, and indeed all harvesting, was forbidden. As John Brand, the Newcastle antiquary, tells us: 'There is one day in harvest on which the vulgar abstain from work, because of an ancient and foolish tradition, that if they do their work the ridges will bleed.'

A version of this strange belief turns up in the Shetlands. Swinaness, on the Island of Unst, was traditionally thought too sacred for cultivation because, so it was said, the sea kings had fought many furious battles there. One man ignored the prohibition and planted some seeds of corn but when the time for harvesting came, to his horror the ears dripped, not dew, but salty tears and the stalks were filled with blood.

This suggests that there was thought to be some connection between the harvest and the realm of the dead – 'those who dwell underneath the earth'. In Germany peasants used to break the first straws of hay brought into the barns, saying, 'This is food for the dead'. Many peoples throughout the world hold annual festivals honouring the departed. The time of year chosen varies according to the region but there is a tendency to associate it with harvest.

In Arabia the last sheaf is ceremonially interred in a miniature grave, specially prepared with a stone placed at the head and another at the foot. The owner of the land, announcing that the Old Man is dead, prays that Allah will send 'the wheat of the dead'.

But if the harvest fields are associated with the realm of the dead, there are probably more ways in which they are linked to fertility and new life. In some countries people used to speak as if a child had been separated from its mother by the stroke of the sickle. A Pole who reaped the last handful of corn was told: 'You have cut the navel string.' In Prussia the last sheaf was called the Bastard: a boy was concealed inside, and the woman who bound it cried out as if in labour. An old woman acted as midwife until the 'birth' took place, and the boy inside the sheaf then squalled like a baby. The sheaf was swaddled with sacking and carried into the barn.

The Baby Rice Soul

In early Egypt fertility of the crops was closely associated with human fecundity. Min, god of vegetation and sexual reproduction, is always represented with phallus erect, a flail raised in his right hand. He was honoured as Lord of the Harvest, and temple carvings show him receiving a ceremonial offering of the first sheaf. Indonesians perform a ritual marriage at the time of the rice harvest. Two sheaves are fastened together in a bundle: this is called the bridal pair. One sheaf contains a special rice, the bridegroom. The other, which contains rice of the ordinary variety, represents the bride. A magician lays them together on a bed of leaves, so that their union may increase the next yield of rice.

Elaborate rituals surround the 'birth' of the Baby Rice Soul at harvest time in Malaya. Rubbish and unpleasant smelling herbs are burnt in advance to drive away evil spirits, and a magician is employed to choose seven stalks of rice, which are cut and swaddled like an infant. The Rice Baby is carried to the farmer's house, and all the protocol surrounding a human birth is carefully observed. On each of the three days following, only one small basket of rice is allowed to be gathered. The reaper works in silence, taking care that his shadow never falls across the plants. But the real work of harvesting cannot begin until the seventh day after the birth of the Baby Rice Soul. Whatever is gathered then must be donated towards a feast held to honour the spirits of dead magicians.

Dolls Made of Corn

The power which was thought to exist in the crops was in fact often personified, not necessarily as a baby. Sometimes it took animal form – a wolf, pig, goat, hare or cock – perhaps because small creatures often took refuge in the final sheaf when the rest of the field had been scythed. In England the last sheaf was used to make an effigy which was dressed in women's clothes and carried on the Horkey Cart to the Harvest Supper, where it sat on a special chair. This puppet had many regional names: kern baby, mell doll, harvest queen and, in Kent, the ivy doll. The Yorkshire mell sheaf was made from different varieties of corn, plaited together and decorated with ribbons and flowers. It was placed in the middle of the room for people to dance round. Sometimes the kern baby was hung up in the farmhouse

To celebrate the yam harvest festival, girls in the Trobriand Islands in Melanesia wear bands of leaves round their arms, which they believe contain magical properties; they also rub their bodies with coconut oil, afterwards plastering themselves with marigold petals.

and kept through the following year to bring good luck and be a protection against witchcraft. A Lancashire farmer is said to have laid a curse on anyone damaging his puppet before the coming harvest.

In 1899 an Old Lincolnshire woman remarked that one of these dolls – made of barley straw and stuck up on a sheaf facing the gate – would ward off thunder and lightning: 'Prayers be good enough as far as they goes, but the Almighty mun be strange and throng with so much corn to look after, and in these here bad times we mustn't forget old Providence. Happen it's best to keep in with both parties.'

Rick decorating used to be quite popular in England. A corn dolly was worked into the corner of the stack to bring good luck. Some stacks in the west of Somerset still carry a little stook at each end of the ridge, and a peaked projection on some cottages in that area is called the dolly by very old people. A few farmers leave the last stook in the field to stand till it falls apart, or it may be hung in the barn. But if the farmer is questioned about this custom, he usually replies that it is intended for the birds; the meaning has been forgotten.

Harvest knots – twists of straw in attractive shapes – are still made in parts of Ireland. Girls wear them in their hair and men fasten them to their coats. At one time they were exchanged as tokens of love. In England, if an engaged girl wished to bear children from her marriage, she went secretly to the harvest fields on a Friday night. Taking a straw from the stooks for every child desired, wheat for a boy and oat for a girl, she plaited them into a garter, murmuring a charm referring to the straw on which the Christ Child lay in the manger. The garter had to be worn until the following Monday morning. If it stayed in place the omen was good, but if it broke or slipped the spell would not succeed. It was also very important that the girl's fiancé should know nothing about this. Only a virgin could use

Probably as a result of the general harshness of the season, there is a widespread belief that the world will come to an end in the middle of a terrible winter.

Left Christmas mummers.

Below The 'Wassail Bowl'; winter has always been a time for feasting and celebration, when the hostility of the elements made men conscious of their essential brotherhood; these traditional Christmas scenes reflect the pagan elements that are still an essential part of the Christian festival.

Right Mexican New Year dancers.

Human Flesh to Aid Crops

Rituals of this kind are harmless by any standards. Not so some of the customs of the past: 'The seven of them perished together. They were put to death in the first days of harvest, at the beginning of barley harvest' (2 Samuel, chapter 21). This ambiguous remark, referring to the killing of seven men in time of famine, dates from biblical times.

The Khonds, a tribe of Bengal, offered a sacrifice to assist the harvest until the middle of the 19th century. The victim, often the descendant of other victims, was called the *Meriah*. About two weeks before the sacrifice was due to be offered, his hair was all cut off, and he was taken in procession to a virgin forest and anointed with melted butter. When the moment arrived he was drugged and crushed to death, or roasted over a fire, and cut into little pieces. Representatives from many villages arrived for the occasion. Each of them was given a small portion of flesh, which was taken home and ceremonially buried in the fields. What remained, chiefly the bones and head, was buried and the ashes scattered over the farmland so that the harvest would be successful. This custom was eventually brought to an end by the British authorities.

In Tibet, to the north, the chief purpose of the Harvest Festival was to propitiate the *Zhidah*, local spirits of the mountains, so that they would send enough sun and rain to assist the crops and hold back any frost or hail. The *Yonnehcham*, Dance of the Sacrificers, was performed specially in their honour. This took place around the middle of September. For 100 days before, the priests stayed indoors to avoid accidentally stepping on any of the many worms and summer insects about at that time of year. They were forbidden to quarrel amongst themselves and anything borrowed had to be returned. It was also very important that the sky should not look upon a corpse, so anyone who chanced to die during the festival was temporarily buried in a stable. Since there was always the risk of light from moon or stars, even night burial was ruled out. Harvest was a gay occasion and large crowds came to see the dancing. They pitched tents and cooked on outdoor stoves.

Evidently the Zhidah were among those spirits well disposed towards mankind. Probably the forces appealed to by ringing church bells in England were imagined to be less benign. The purpose of this custom was to ensure the safety of the gathered crop.

'Burning the Witch', a Yorkshire custom, perhaps also derives originally from some ritual disposing of a malevolent influence. At

the charm: a girl who was not would cause harm to all her children.

In southern Europe, 15 August, the Feast of the Assumption of the Virgin Mary, is sometimes called the Feast of Our Lady in Harvest. In Italy it replaced the festival of the goddess Diana on 13 August: further north, where the harvest comes later, the crop is dedicated to the Virgin Mary on 8 September, the Feast of her Nativity.

A young virgin features in the central role of a once popular Polish custom. *Wienjec*, the harvest wreath or crown, was made from the final sheaf and prettily decorated with a variety of flowers, nuts and apples and perhaps even a gingerbread cake. It was blessed in church, usually on the Feast of the Assumption when herbs were also blessed, and worn by the chief girl harvester. It was essential that she should be chaste for,

if she were not, it was supposed that the fertility of the land would be destroyed and the harvest would be a poor one. The girl was expected to walk in procession to the farmhouse door, where she was received by the farmer who drenched her with water – a rain charm again.

This custom of throwing water on the last sheaf, or else on the person who brings it, is widespread. In the north of the Greek island of Euboea, when the corn sheaves had been stacked, the farmer's wife brought out a pitcher of water and offered it to the men for washing their hands. Each sprinkled water on the corn and on the threshing floor. The farmer's wife then held the pitcher at an angle and ran as fast as she could around the stack without spilling a drop. When this had been done she made a wish for the stack to last as long as the circle she had just made.

harvest time peas were left to dry in small piles, known locally as 'reaps'. On the last day, when the remaining corn had been cut, some of these piles were pushed together and burnt in the straw. Boys and girls ran about, blacking each other's faces with charred straw. Everyone enjoyed the peas and there was dancing and Cream Pot Supper – a dish of cream and currant cakes flavoured with caraway.

In Shetland the menu for the *Foy* was not dissimilar. This traditional party, held at the skipper's house, is interesting since it was, in effect, a Harvest Home of the sea. A favourite toast was: 'Lord! Open the mouth of the grey fish, and hold thy hand about the corn.'

Winter

In northern lands the season of cold, wet and darkness has also traditionally been the time when the freest rein is given to fantasy. It was in winter that whole families in bygone ages huddled together in smoky huts listening, as the storms raged outside, to sagas and folktales. In winter, more than any other season, ghosts stalk abroad, and in the countryside a solitary light, glimpsed in the distance by a lone wayfarer, can flood the soul with emotion. Winter has always been, too, a time for feasting and celebrating. When harsh weather made warfare and even trivial disputes between neighbours impossible, and the concerted hostility of the elements made men mindful of their own essential brotherhood, it was natural to think of winter as the season of goodwill. There was also the gloom and tedium of long nights crying out for relief, and when the days began at last to lengthen, however imperceptibly, men looked upon it as the rebirth of the sun, and celebrated the nativity of a god.

Two members of the Hasidim, a Jewish revivalist sect, wearing their traditional costume buy willows in a Jerusalem market for the New Year ceremony of shaking away their sins. The term Hasidism is derived from the Hebrew noun *hasid* which, in biblical Hebrew and especially in the Psalms, means one who is steadfast in his trust and faith in God and in his devotion to him.

The earliest of these winter festivals about which we know anything was the Sacaea in Babylon, a celebration of the New Year, lasting several days. From the third millennium down to the very end of Mesopotamian civilization, a few centuries before the Christian era, mock battles were held every year, in which the king impersonated the god Marduk, who had won a mighty victory over Tiamat, the watery goddess of chaos, on the very first New Year's day, when the world had been created. In Babylonia new temples were inaugurated only on New Year's day, and from this day a king officially dated the beginning of his reign.

According to later Greek writers, the Babylonian Sacaea was a time of sexual licence, feasting and disguising. Slaves gave orders to their masters during the days of the festival, and a criminal was chosen to have royal rights conferred upon him, only to be executed at the end of the celebrations. Whether these Greeks are reading contemporary practices in the Roman world into the Babylonian setting it is impossible to say, but if their reports are accurate, then the Babylonian festival must have been the ancestor of a number of similar celebrations in the ancient world.

The Roman Saturnalia, celebrated at the end of December, was a festival of merry-making and exchanging gifts which left its mark on our own Christmas celebrations. All work and business was suspended, originally for three days, but eventually for seven, and slaves were free to say and do

what they liked. Gambling, usually punishable with a fine fixed at four times the value of the stakes, was officially permitted on these 'best of days', as the Roman poet Catullus calls the Saturnalia. Rich men gave their 'clients' presents of silverware, and children were frequently the recipients of little wax dolls.

A Greek writer of the 4th century AD, the sophist Libanius, has left a description of the winter festival as it was celebrated in his own city of Antioch: 'There is food everywhere, heavy, rich food. And laughter. A positive urge to spend seizes on everyone, so that people who have taken pleasure in saving up the whole year now think it's a good idea to squander. The streets are full of people and coaches, staggering under the load of gifts. Children are free of the dread of their teachers, and for slaves the festival is as good as a holiday. Another good thing about it – it teaches people not to be too fond of money, but to let it circulate from hand to hand.'

Libanius was an early opponent of Christianity who nevertheless had Christians among his pupils, one of them St John Chrysostom. He is here describing pagan festivities in general, though he seems to have had the Saturnalia particularly in mind. The corresponding Greek festival, the Kronia, was celebrated at harvest time, but the Greeks had winter festivals, including the rustic Dionysia, held in December, and celebrated in villages with a burlesque procession; the Lenaea, or feast of the wine vats, celebrated in January with a proces-

sion, sacrifice and competing plays; and the Anthesteria, held during three days about the time that we call February, when the casks were opened and the new wine was tasted.

All the winter festivals were connected in some way with Dionysus, the god of wine, and the Greeks in fact divided the cult-year into two halves, the Dionysiac and the Apollonian, corresponding to winter and summer. A similar division was made by the ancient Hindus, for whom winter was the time for ancestor worship and summer for the gods of Nature. In other parts of the world, too, winter is the time for appeasing the spirits of the dead. On the third day of the Anthesteria, the celebrations were held within the family circle, with rites in appeasement of ancestors. This festival came at the end of winter in Greece – indeed, it was to celebrate the end of winter marked by the appearance of the year's first flowers – but in northern Europe the cult of the dead was celebrated either in autumn, as among the Saxons, or in early or midwinter, as among the Scandinavians and Celts. In these pre-Christian festivals, bonfires were lighted as representations of the waning and waxing of the sun.

The rites were absorbed into Christianity in the guise of All Saints' day on 1 November and All Souls' on 2 November. Winter festivals in commemoration of the dead were also celebrated in China until comparatively recent times.

The belief that dead ancestors are present in winter explains the practice of the Kwakiutl Indians of British Columbia who change their names at the beginning of winter, when the ghosts arrive, and adopt the names of their ancestors. They also form secret societies in winter, in place of their ordinary summer family life. The practice of exorcizing evil and evil spirits at either the beginning or end of winter is widespread among primitive peoples.

Porridge for the Frost Man

Frost is personified in Finnish magic songs, and Frost man appears as the brother of Mist man in a charming Japanese legend. But the frost spirits were taken most seriously by the Finnish tribes of Russia and Siberia, the Votiaks, the Cheremiss, the Mordvins and the Ostiaks. There was a 'Frost woman' as well as a 'Frost man' to whom sacrifices were made. It was the custom among the Mordvins (who live in the district lying between Nizhni Novgorod and Saratov, and who in Byzantine times scored many victories over the Russians) to place porridge for the 'Frost man' in the smoke outlet of their huts on the Thursday before Easter, in order to protect the spring sowings, for the Mordvins still clung to their ancient pagan beliefs and practices.

New Year

Rites in celebration of the New Year take place the world over, irrespective of differing system of computing time. Among many nomadic and agricultural communities it was customary to calculate the year on a lunar basis and most modern calenders continue to show this influence. Sometimes, as in the case of the Jews, New Year is a moveable feast. In ancient Babylon it was celebrated in what is now March and April, and in Egypt it was linked with the annual flooding of the Nile. In Europe the New Year was celebrated at different times varying from Christmas to March, and its official celebration on 1 January is a comparatively modern innovation. Until the introduction of the Gregorian Calendar in 1752 the official New Year in the British Isles began in March, but as far as the common people were concerned, it has always been celebrated on 1 January.

Many of the ceremonies associated with

this turning point combine the elements of a funeral ceremony and a birth, of death and sorrow on the one hand, and on the other hope and joy. The first is represented by an old man often depicted with a scythe, and the second by a male child, the symbol of the infant year. The completion of one phase of existence and its re-emergence into another has always been an occasion of ceremonial importance in human affairs, and in many ways the rites of the New Year correspond to the rites of passage of individual life. The sense of continuity is still further emphasized in the role of the Roman god Janus guardian of the gateway of the year, who faces both ways, looking backwards into the past and forwards into the future.

In keeping with the mourning element which underlies many of the rituals, obsequies for the dying year were once celebrated by English mummers who went from house to house, collecting tribute. The custom of tolling bells to mark its passing was quite literally a funeral dirge for the death of the old year. Originally, muffled bells were rung till just before midnight, and as the clock struck twelve the wrappings were removed to permit a loud clear chime.

It is the happier and more hopeful aspects, however, which predominate

throughout the world. Everywhere, East or West, the New Year is the occasion for greater rejoicing. In China the house windows are decorated with texts in honour of the most important annual festival in the Chinese calendar, a time when the gods of wealth and procreation are encouraged to visit the home, while at the same time the devils of bad luck are warned to stay away. The Japanese celebrate the day with specially baked cakes which they offer to the sun and moon. In India it is customary for new foods to be eaten and in some places for new clothes to be worn; cattle are gaily decked with flowers, and in Bengal the River Ganges is worshipped. The modern Mexican ends his five days of ritual lamentation with wild rejoicings. North American Indians at New Year extinguish the tribal fires, scatter the ashes, and then ceremoniously relight them. There are also sacrifices and offerings to the gods and sometimes water is sprinkled on the passer-by.

A very ancient custom, now almost extinct, involved the giving and receiving of New Year presents which were intended to insure that the year started on an auspicious footing. Some have ascribed this to a practice current among the Druids of distributing mistletoe to the people on this day, and gift-giving at this time was common in ancient Rome. The Puritans were inclined to regard New Year gifts with a jaundiced eye since to their eyes the custom reeked of paganism, even the innocent phrase 'Happy New Year' being frowned upon.

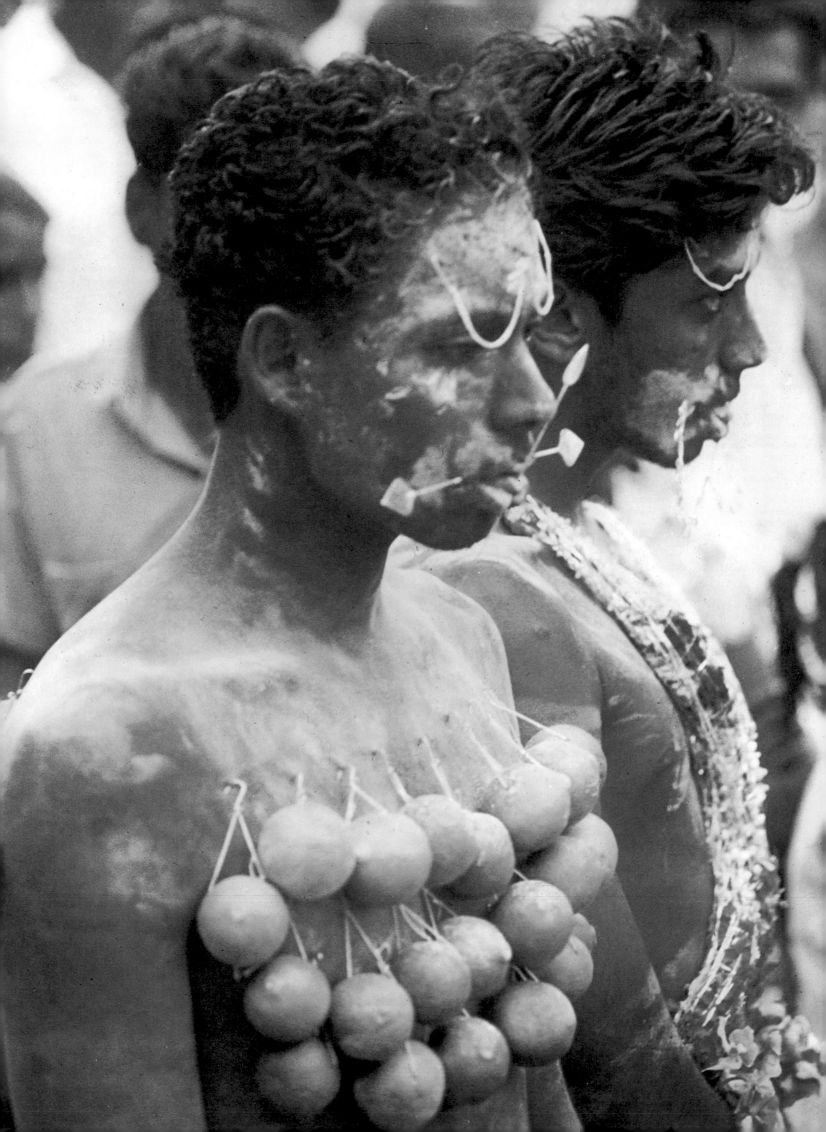

Religious Ritual

Baptism

In the creation myths of many peoples water is the substance out of which the world, or the creator of the world, originally emerged. The ancient Egyptians imagined that in the beginning there was only a featureless expanse of water, called Nun. Out of this the primeval hill first emerged, followed by the creator god Atum, who stood on it to begin the work of creating the universe. In Babylonian myth the first gods are produced by the intercourse of the salt waters (Tiamat) and the fresh waters (Apsu). Later, the Babylonian god Marduk slays Tiamat, which is conceived of as a great monster, and fashions the universe out of its body.

In these ancient traditions water was regarded as the source of life, a belief which was strengthened by the fact that man and all other living creatures need water to maintain life. The idea of water as a life-giving substance has found expression in different cultures and in many religions in the idea of a mystic 'water of life' or 'fountain of life'.

The cleansing property of water also acquired religious significance as a means or symbol of ritual and spiritual purification: thus in Psalm 51 the petition is made to God: 'Wash me thoroughly from my iniquity . . . purge me with hyssop, and I shall be clean: wash me, and I shall be whiter than snow.'

The Salvation of Pharaoh

It is not surprising, therefore, to find in the earliest religious writings so far known, the *Pyramid Texts* of Egypt, which date from about 2500 BC, that water has both a revivifying and a purifying role. These texts are concerned with the mortuary ritual practised to ensure the resurrection of the dead pharaoh to a blessed and eternal life, and

Left A penitent at the annual festival of Thaipusan in Singapore. Religious fervour has made him insensitive to pain.

Right The conversion of a person to a new religious belief is often confirmed by a ceremony after which the convert feels cleansed, purified and regenerated. Communal baptism, by Canadian Baptist missionaries, in Bolivia.

Picturepoint London

they illustrate the ideas and beliefs of the Egyptians at this time. Several of them refer to a lake in the next world in which the sun-god Re revivifies himself each morning, and in which the dead king will also bathe and be revivified. The texts also show that ritual lustrations (washing) were frequent during the ritual of embalming, their purpose being both to purify the corpse from the contamination of death and to revivify it. The ritual was patterned on the rites believed to have been performed by various deities to raise the dead god Osiris to life again. The dead pharaoh was ritually identified with Osiris, in the belief that the re-enactment of the rites would similarly resurrect him to a new life.

The ancient Egyptian evidence is especially important because it presents so graphically the two aspects of water combined in a single ritual process of salvation. The water cleanses the body of the deceased from the corruption of death and also revivifies or regenerates it for a life of eternal blessedness. This twofold process for the achievement of a blessed immortality is not found again until the emergence of Christianity. But ritual ablution as an initiatory rite or for spiritual rebirth was practised in the mystery religions of the Graeco-Roman world, and there are interesting comparisons with Christian baptism.

Washing the Pig

As a purificatory rite only, bathing in the sea was an important part of the initiatory ritual of the Eleusinian Mysteries, the oldest mystery cult of ancient Greece. On the second day of its Greater Mysteries initiates hastened down to the sea, each carrying a small pig. They washed both themselves and the pigs in the sea as an act of ritual cleansing. The pigs were subsequently sacrificed, and their blood was considered to act as a potent purificatory agent against demonic evil.

It is in the mysteries of Cybele and Attis that we meet the most savage form of a regenerative bath. The rite was known as the *taurobolium*. The initiate descended into a pit and was bathed in the blood of a bull, sacrificed above him. (There is mention also of a *criobolium*, which involved the slaughter of a ram.) The first documentary evidence of the rite dates from the 2nd century AD.

The rite seems sometimes to have been primarily a sacrifice for well-being of some kind; but its regenerative function is shown by certain inscriptions which use the word *renatus* (reborn) of the initiate or refer to the day of the taurobolium as his birthday. Some of the ideas that underlie this rite would seem to be obvious: the bull has ever symbolized strength and virility; and its blood is its life-substance. But in what manner the bull was associated with Attis, a 'dying-rising god', and in what sense the devotee was reborn or rejuvenated by the taurobolium is not clear.

Ritual washing for various purposes was an ancient custom among the Hebrews;

The purifying properties of water lie behind its use in both pagan and Christian rituals. The baptism of Christ in the river Jordan by John the Baptist, a painting by El Greco.

after being healed of leprosy, for instance, or after touching a corpse. Jesus is reported to have healed a blind man by sending him to wash in a pool, after anointing his eyes with clay (John, chapter 9). These examples show the belief in the power of ritual washing to remove ritual 'uncleanness' and in the curative property of water. But more significant as a forerunner of early Christian baptism was the ritual bath which had to be taken by converts to Judaism. This rite was essentially a purification from heathenism, in preparation for membership of the holy people of Yahweh, the God of Israel. An essential requirement was the total immersion of the candidate.

There is a parallelism of imagery between the burial of Christ in the tomb and the burial of the new convert under the baptismal water. In other words, in baptism the Christian is ritually assimilated to Christ in his death, dying to his former self, so that as Christ was resurrected from the dead, the Christian, thus ritually incorporated in Christ, will rise to a new immortal life.

Baptism of Babies

In the early period of the Church, most candidates for baptism were adults. Often converts put off baptism until near death, in the belief that thereby they would die purified from sin and spiritually reborn. But as time went by, the custom of baptizing infants gradually prevailed. It was natural that Christian parents should want their children to enjoy the spiritual benefits of baptism as soon as they were born into the world, but the practice was decisively affected by the doctrine of Original Sin.

According to this doctrine, a newborn child, though incapable of actual sin, was held to be subject to God's wrath because it shared in the inherited sin of mankind. A baby which died unbaptized was condemned to hell (or to Limbo, a special compartment of hell). The practice of infant baptism led to the introduction of the smaller elevated font, which replaced the baptistery of earlier churches: and also to the separation of baptism from confirmation, which was originally part of the baptismal ceremony in the Early Church and was regarded as imparting the gift of the Holy Spirit to the baptized through the laying-on of the bishop's hands.

The Reformation did not disturb the status of baptism as the essential rite of Christian initiation for Protestants as well as for Catholics. Indeed certain sects such as the Anabaptists and Baptists laid primary stress on its importance; but they insisted on a return to adult baptism by immersion, maintaining that baptism should signify the deliberate acceptance of Christ, which was impossible for an infant.

Today baptism is usually taken to symbolize acceptance of membership in the Christian community, rather than to effect a mystic rebirth, such as Paul taught. The Roman Catholic Church retains the most elaborate baptismal ritual in the West: it includes preliminary exorcisms, placing of salt in the candidate's mouth, anointing with spittle and oil, and the holding of a candle.

Purification

Ashes are the residue of fire, and just as fire is regarded in mythology and folklore as something which purifies and also regenerates, or brings new life, so the same properties are associated with ashes. Some primitive peoples regard ashes as the 'seeds' of fire, falling from it as it dies in the same way that the seeds of plants do, and so containing the life of the fire itself.

The ancient Jews sacrificed a red heifer by fire, the ashes being used to purify the unclean. The ancient Egyptians burned red-haired men, not as a purificatory rite but so that their ashes could be scattered on the fields to quicken the seed in the earth.

At the root of the custom of burning living creatures in sacred fires to fertilize the soil lies the conviction that ash is the soul of fire and so brings renewal. It was long a folk custom in Europe for the ashes of the Midsummer fires to be spread on the crops or fed to farm animals. In modern Germany a flaming Easter wheel is rolled down the hillside and its ashes are then spread on the fields.

Ashes have also played their part in the rites of rainmakers and in control of the weather. South American tribes, particularly the Muyscas of Colombia, throw ashes into the sky to condense the clouds and induce rain, or scatter ashes on water as a charm to produce fair weather. In Central Europe ashes were spread on the fields to prevent hailstones, and in France as a defence against lightning.

In New Guinea it was believed that the qualities associated with one living creature could be magically transferred to another by a ritual involving ashes. A snake was killed and its ashes smeared on the legs as a defence against snake-bite. Even today certain South American tribes mix the ashes of their loved ones with their food and drink in order to absorb the qualities of the dead.

An interesting combination of the agricultural use of ashes with the belief that the ashes of something holy contain magical power came to light in 1857 at the trial of the Cornish well-sinker Thomas Pooley. Charged with blasphemously recommending the virtues of the ashes of burned Bibles as a fertilizer and for the treatment of potato disease, he was condemned by an unsympathetic bench of magistrates to 21 months' imprisonment in Bodmin Gaol, where he shortly afterwards went mad.

In Ireland, the Isle of Man and Lancashire divination by ashes was carried out at Hallowe'en, when a curious love ritual was sometimes performed by single men. The bachelor would sprinkle ashes or seeds along some quiet lane and then wait and watch. The first girl to pass along that way after him was destined to become his wife.

An entirely different way of looking at ashes is found among medieval alchemists, who saw them as the dead body of a substance. If you burned a piece of wood, the smoke rising up was the 'soul' of the wood and the ashes left behind were its corpse.

A similar connection between ashes and death lies behind their widespread use as a badge of sorrow, bereavement and repentance. In Roman Catholic churches on Ash Wednesday, the ashes of the palms used on Palm Sunday the previous year are sprinkled on the heads of penitents.

Flagellation

Whipping has long been thought to cure boys of almost everything that needed curing, and some 20th century boarding schools have not let the tradition die.

Dr Christian Paullini, the 17th century German author of *Flagellum Salutis*, is only one of a long line who recommend flagellation to cure schoolboys of idleness, women of shrewishness, thieves of criminal behaviour.

In such cases the whip is laid on partly in punishment but mostly to rectify personality flaws. It sets out to cure by ritual purification, to drive out evil from the recipient's body and mind. We may no longer believe that illness is caused by evil spirits or demonic possession; but some of our therapeutic techniques derive directly from this attitude. In the history of flagellation, this purificatory aspect has far more importance than another main ritual use of the whip, in the ordeal or test of endurance.

Wherever a devout individual or community has perceived evil needing to be driven out, the whip has made its appearance. Many societies cleansed their community by the use of a scapegoat, on to which all the evil afflicting them was laid before it was killed – often by beating it to death. The Bible (apart from Solomon's adjuration in the Proverbs not to spare the rod) clearly pictures the Messiah in this way, in the book of Isaiah: 'he was bruised for our iniquities . . . with his stripes we are healed.' The tradition of exorcism – the driving out of evil spirits from houses or bodies – is full of tales of flagellation. And of course the ascetic and ecstatic religions found flagellation a firm ally.

Penitential Lashes

The ancient Greek cult of the Spartans had an annual purifying Feast of Flagellation; and early Christian monasteries resounded with the crack of the lash, but far more frequently. An 11th century cardinal reckoned that 1000 self-inflicted lashes were the spiritual equivalent of ten penitential psalms. The early Franciscans turned also to the whip. The object was mortification of the flesh and repression of any unchristian fleshly urges.

Out of this spirit of purification and penance came also that weird phenomenon, the Brotherhood of the Flagellants – never a real religious order, never recognized by the Church, but immensely widespread in 14th century Europe. Perugia, in central Italy, saw the beginning of mass flagellation in public in the 13th century; in the next century the practice took on new strength and spread like the plague that coincided with it. But the Flagellants did not turn to the whip because of the Black Death; they were active especially in Germany, before the plague had reached that far. Certainly, though, the plague gave them their justification for bloodthirsty penance, and brought thousands of converts after 1349, the year of the plague. The Flagellants massed in public, vast crowds of partly naked men and women, lashing themselves and each other twice daily for $33\frac{1}{2}$ days, with devices ranging from little cords to leather thongs knotted and holding metal points, for the more extensive penitential spilling of blood.

The Flagellant cult went to the New World with the conquistadores, giving rise to the movement called Los Hermanos Penitentes – still thriving, still self-flagellating with whips of cholla cactus in parts of New Mexico and southern Colorado. Their whips fly most during Holy Week, but also during the initiation of new brothers, the only time a brother is lashed by anyone but himself.

The Flagellants and their fellows used the whip to punish the sins inherent in the flesh and to scourge evil from the spirit. But this ecstatic flagellation has a positive side, too: it becomes a means of achieving a higher plane of consciousness, a more exalted state of being, through pain. The ordeal, too, aims to produce an exalted state: the initiate is not only being tested for endurance and courage, but is being directly infused with some higher power to fit him for his new role in the community or the secret society. The aspiration to a higher plane is also

offered as the reason for the orgiastic aspects, including flagellation, of the various cults of evil that have proliferated in past centuries and apparently still thrive today.

Mention of the sexual deviation known as sado-masochism stirs up powerful emotional reactions. Undoubtedly many of the people claiming today to be practising Devil worshippers or black magicians may well be using the traditions of evil as a smokescreen behind which they are performing the usual antics of the sex orgy, deviant or otherwise. They can be said to be involved with orgies for orgies' sake, disguised as satanism.

Pilgrimage

The word pilgrim itself is derived from the Latin *peregrinus*, and means simply a wanderer or stranger. Although 'pilgrimage' (*peregrinatio*), means literally no more than 'wandering about', the word has come to mean wandering with a purpose, and a pilgrim is one who temporarily abandons his or her normal pursuits in order to seek the spiritual and moral benefits believed to be obtainable in some particularly holy place. A palmer, on the other hand, was one whose whole life was spent in wandering from place to place.

Wherever there have been holy persons or holy places, there have been pilgrims to visit them. Perhaps the first problem to consider is why some places and some people are regarded as more 'holy' than others. It seems that in the religious history of mankind, the world of men and the world of the

supernaturals – gods, spirits, demons, ghosts – have been believed to exist for the most part in parallel. However, there are certain points at which the parallel worlds meet, points at which supernatural power comes, as it were, to a focus. Sometimes the original reason for such belief in the concentration of power is unclear. But certain places – for instance, mountains, caves, rivers and springs – were very early thought of as dwelling-places of the supernaturals, where power was intensified; and when early man worshipped, he did so in such places. Later, when temples were constructed, they too were thought of as the homes of the gods to which they were dedicated, consecrated by the presence of the deity within them. Holiness – supernatural power – is contagious, and anyone wholly dedicated to the service of a deity partakes of this same quality.

Right Most ailments of character or psychological make-up have been 'treated' at one time or another by flogging. A female figure with dark wings wields the lash as part of the initiation of a young woman into the ecstatic cult of Dionysus: fresco from the Villa of the Mysteries outside Pompeii. Spiritual inadequacies have received a larger measure of treatment by this rather ambiguous method. Human beings have always been willing to suffer pain for religious magical reasons.

Below left Young fakir in South India, his tongue pierced with a skewer in celebration of one of the many Hindu religious festivals.

Below Ash-daubed Indian holy man: ash, the residue of fire, is widely regarded as a substance which purifies as it regenerates.

Jørgen Bitsch

Balu Mondhe
Scala

There were also sites at which a deity was believed to have revealed himself or herself, sites connected in some way with holy history, shrines of the great departed and places at which oracles were delivered and interpreted. Any of these might serve to mediate the power of the supernaturals to ordinary people: hence they were sought out, and became places of pilgrimage.

The reasons which prompted people to become pilgrims doubtless varied greatly. On the one hand, there was the subjective desire to acquire power, merit and those other benefits (the expiation of past sins, for instance, and the healing of present diseases) which might be held to derive from exposure to the focus of holiness. On the other hand, there was the desire to worship and do reverence to the supernaturals themselves. Yet there were other motives than such purely personal ones. In some religious traditions, pilgrimage might simply be part of one's accepted religious duty; and although merit might well accrue the motive was social, rather than personal. Chaucer's pilgrims, for instance, had a collective, as well as an individual motive for making the journey in spring to the shrine of St Thomas.

In the ancient world, pilgrimages were very often connected with seasonal festivals, and especially with the New Year Festival, or its equivalent, at which atonement was made for the sins of the past year and the world was symbolically renewed for another cycle. It is not known exactly who attended such festivals in the ancient Near East – in Mesopotamia, Egypt, Israel – but the later practices of Judaism and Islam make it clear that the custom of visiting holy places,

and particularly the great temples, at certain seasons of the year has deep roots. The pilgrimage to Jerusalem for the Passover ceremonies, for example, lasted until the destruction of the Temple in 70 AD.

Possibly the longest unbroken tradition of pilgrimage to one particular place is seen in the Moslem pilgrimage to Mecca. In pre-Islamic times the tradition of visiting the Kaaba was already well established, but under Mohammed pilgrimage (*hajj*) was elevated into one of the five pillars of the faith, and it has always been the religious duty of every Moslem who is able to do so, to go on pilgrimage to Mecca at least once in his or her lifetime.

Elsewhere in the ancient world, old places of pilgrimage now exist only as archeological sites – for instance, the hall in which the Mysteries of Eleusis were once celebrated, near Athens, and the sites of the oracles at Delphi and Dodona. The function of some places of pilgrimage have been radically altered. The great pre-Christian temple at Old Uppsala in Sweden, for example, was once visited by great crowds of pilgrims at the seasonal festivals. In the 12th century the coming of Christianity led to the destruction of the temple with its images of Thor, Odin and Freyr, and the building of a church on its site; but the attraction had gone and, soon after, the capital of the Svea kingdom was moved elsewhere – an eloquent testimony to the secular significance of pilgrimage centres.

The Indian sub-continent has a vast number of sacred sites, which Hindus, Buddhists, Jains and others visit as often as circumstances permit. However, for the Hindu there is no qualitative difference

Above In the late Middle Ages long lines of Flagellants travelled across Europe, beating each other and themselves in penance for their sins and those of society.

between worship at the local shrine and the visit to a particularly important holy place. Worship, to the Hindu, is invariably a matter of individual concern, connected both with the reverence due to the gods or (more usually) the Supreme Being, and with the acquisition of individual merit. Pilgrimage raises both these concerns to a higher level, but does not really change them. To the Buddhist, although the motive of worship may in theory be unimportant (Buddhism denies the existence of a Supreme Being and classifies the gods as merely higher forms of universal life), the motive of the acquisition of merit is very much present. For Hindu and Buddhist alike, the gaining of merit leads to an improved status in the individual's next life, and thus ultimately to release from the wheel of rebirth.

Among the holiest of goals for Hindu pilgrimages are the seven great rivers, especially the Ganges; and of the cities on the rivers, probably the best-known is Benares (Varanasi), with its hundreds of temples, large and small, its ghats (places where the dead are burned), and its crowds of pilgrims at all times of the year. Every inch of the Ganges is sacred, but none more so than the holy places, Gangotri, Kedarnath and Badrinath, at the sources of the river's three main branches, the Bhagirathi, the Mandakini and the Alaknanda. The great Ganges pilgrimage begins at Hardwar, 'Hari's gate', and passes through

Sonia Halliday

Pilgrims seeking to pay devotion to our Lady of Lourdes and suppliants hoping for relief from their ailments are among the two million annual visitors to this city. St Bernadette's visions of the Virgin Mary transformed the small town of Lourdes into the greatest centre of pilgrimage in the Roman Catholic world: the spring which miraculously appeared in the barren floor of the grotto is believed to be healing water, capable of curing even the hopelessly crippled: pilgrims at Lourdes.

Rishikesh, the town of ascetics, to the three sanctuaries. The entire pilgrimage, performed in May, June and July, covers over 600 miles, and although transport is available for much of the way, there remains a good deal which has to be undertaken on foot, often in very difficult conditions. Recently a Western youth who attempted the journey barefoot had to have both feet amputated as a result of frostbite. Of course, where there are difficulties to be surmounted, this only adds to the merit acquired, as well as serving as a necessary mortification and disciplining of the body. The best-known (though now seldom practised) pilgrim austerity is that which requires the seeker after perfection to measure his length along the entire road.

Compassion for the World

The Buddha himself neither recommended nor forbade the practice of pilgrimage, but shortly after his death, his relics were distributed and placed in monuments (*stupas*), which very soon became centres of pilgrimage. Indeed, the technical term for the first stage in Buddhist ordination (into the order of monks, or *bhikkhus*) is *pabbaja*, meaning

'going forth from the world' or, in a sense, becoming a pilgrim.

Today, the main centre of Buddhist pilgrimage in India is Buddha Gaya, the place at which the Buddha gained enlightenment. Outside India there are many Buddhist shrines, the best-known among them being the Temple of the Tooth – a relic of the Buddha preserved in an inner chamber on a golden lotus flower within nine caskets of gold – in Kandy, Sri Lanka. Also in Sri Lanka is perhaps the most universal of pilgrimage centres, Adam's Peak, with its sacred footprint, believed by Buddhists to be that of the Buddha, by Hindus to be that of Shiva, by Christians to be that of St Thomas, and by Moslems to be that of Adam.

In Christianity, the practice of going on pilgrimage began in the early Church, achieved great popularity in the Middle Ages, and is by no means forgotten – particularly by Catholics – in the modern world. The first goal of Christian pilgrimage was the Holy Land, and especially Jerusalem. Among the earliest records in post-biblical times is that of 'the Bordeaux pilgrim', who went to Jerusalem in 333 AD. Despite political difficulties in gaining access to the holy places (a factor which was one of the causes of the Crusades), the practice has continued to this day, though the modern pilgrim visits all the actual or supposed sites of sacred history, and not just the Holy City.

As the focus of Christendom shifted from Jerusalem to Rome, the presence in Rome of the tombs of Peter and Paul, and the catacombs, caused a corresponding shift in pilgrimage to these more specifically Christian sites. At the same time, the development of the doctrine of purgatory, and the

belief that the individual's time in purgatory (or that of his relatives) could be lessened by acquiring merit, caused the growing practice of the granting of indulgences as a reward for faithful pilgrimage. Thus when the Papal Jubilee was celebrated in 1300, the indulgences offered on that occasion are said to have drawn more than 20,000 pilgrims to Rome. The early Christian Middle Ages also saw a vast – and frequently dishonourable – trade in sacred relics, theoretically repositories of divine power, but often in practice nothing more than, as the cynical Chaucer expressed it, 'bones and ragged bits of clout, relics they are, at least for such are known . . .'

Pilgrimage and the viewing, touching or kissing of such relics were closely connected, and the superior centres of pilgrimage gradually acquired vast stores of relics. In 1446 a German pilgrim to the shrine of Thomas Becket at Canterbury recorded that '. . . we were shown the sword with which his (Becket's) head had been struck off. Then they also showed a remarkable piece of the holy cross, and one of the nails, and the right arm of the honourable knight Saint George and a single thorn from the crown of thorns, mounted in a monstrance.' Elsewhere in England, for instance at the celebrated shrine of Glastonbury, which was almost certainly a Celtic cult centre before being Christianized, stores of relics were kept and miracles of healing were recorded as late as the 18th century, long after the Reformation.

Healing and Disillusion

Pilgrimage for the purpose of healing was common in the Middle Ages. The Venerable

Bede told of the place where Oswald, King of Northumbria, fell in battle against the Mercians: 'Many people took away earth from the place where his body fell, and put it in water, from which sick folk who drank it received great benefit. This practice became so popular that as the earth was gradually removed, a pit was left in which a man could stand . . .'

It has become a commonplace of Church history that the excesses of popular devotion to sacred places and the relics of holy persons were among the causes leading to the Reformation. In the 16th century a chorus of protest was raised by the reformers, with Martin Luther as their head. In 1510 Luther went to Rome, on Church business but entirely in the spirit of pilgrimage, intent on making the very best of whatever spiritual benefit the city could offer him. His sense of disillusion grew, largely as a result of the sheer levity of many of the sacred proceedings. He did not then doubt that merit was to be gained; what he did doubt was that it could be transferred to the dead. There is a story that he ascended Pilate's staircase on hands and knees in the approved manner, hoping thereby to extract his grandfather from purgatory. At the top he stood up, and said to himself, 'Who knows whether it is so?' On such doubt was the Reformation based.

But the doubt of the reformers led directly to the distress of the faithful. In England, the shrine of Walsingham, reputed to contain a few drops of Mary's milk, was suppressed at the Reformation. Although Protestantism has always looked with disfavour on the custom of pilgrimage and the religious views on which the practice was based, the Roman Catholic world has continued to believe in the efficacy of holy places. Many of the old shrines have disappeared beyond recall; but others have been reopened – Walsingham, for example – and new shrines have arisen. The most celebrated of these is certainly that at Lourdes, in the French Pyrenees, where in 1858 a peasant girl, Bernadette Soubirous, saw visions of the Blessed Virgin. All the classical features of the pilgrimage centre are there: manifestations of holy power, a sacred spring, and healing miracles. There are also similar centres of pilgrimage on the American continent, for instance at St Anne de Beaupré, near Quebec.

It seems that it is only the sceptical Western mind that is unable to accept the premises on which the case for pilgrimages rests. The intuitive religious mind believes implicity in the supernatural world, and in its manifestations in the world of time and space. Wherever those manifestations take place, man may profitably come to worship and pray and receive strength.

> There's no discouragement
> Shall make him once relent
> His first avowed intent
> To be a pilgrim.

To such a man or woman, the words of the great allegorizer of pilgrimage, John Bunyan, express part of the assured order of things.

Atonement

The word means literally 'at one-ment' and refers to reconciliation between man and God, who became at one with each other. Theories of atonement assume that the proper relationship between a man and his god has been broken by a 'sin' or offence, but that the relationship can be restored.

In the history of religions there are two main ways in which a man can atone for sin. One is by sacrifice, by giving up an animal or something which he owns and offering it to the offended god. The other is by giving up the sinful action itself, by repentance and determination not to sin again.

Both these ways of atoning appear side by side in the Old Testament, together with another belief, also found in early Greek religion, that the sins of the people can be literally banished by transferring them to a scapegoat, which is then driven out of the community. As part of the ritual of the Day of Atonement (described in Leviticus, chapter 16), the sins of the people were recited over the head of a goat, which was then led away into the desert, carrying the sins of the people with it.

The ancient Hebrews who invented the idea had no word for 'scapegoat'. The goat in question first makes its appearance in Leviticus, chapter 16. Its function, as part of the expiatory rites performed by the High Priest on the Day of Atonement, is to have all the sins of the children of Israel put upon its head, and to carry them away into the wilderness. The goat, so to speak, escapes with a burden of alien sin – hence its name. But it is not a name that occurs in the original Hebrew of the Book of Leviticus. It is true that the Authorized Version speaks of the high priest Aaron taking two goats and casting lots upon them, 'one lot for the Lord, and the other lot for the scapegoat'. But in the Hebrew it says, 'one lot for Yahweh (Jehovah), and the other for Azazel'. To this day, no one is absolutely sure who or what Azazel was, but when William Tyndale (c 1495–1536) made his translation of the Old Testament from the Hebrew text, he also had the Greek and Latin versions at his elbow, and he took a

hint from them to translate the mysterious Azazel as 'scapegoat'. In subsequent verses of the same chapter of Leviticus, however, Tyndale had to twist both the English and the Hebrew syntax to make sense of the word Azazel, and he wrote of letting the goat go 'for a scapegoat', when he should have written 'to Azazel'.

The point is of more than linguistic interest. Most authorities on the subject take Azazel to have been a demon that lived in the desert. He is not mentioned elsewhere in the Old Testament, but the author of the apocryphal book of Enoch evidently took Azazel to be a demon from his reading of this chapter of Leviticus, and developed an elaborate legend about him, on which Milton drew when he made Azazel Satan's standard-bearer in *Paradise Lost*. If Azazel was a demon, then the ritual described in Leviticus was intended to symbolize the purging of the land and people of Israel from guilt and the transmission of their sins, on the goat's back, to the evil spirit to whom they were believed to belong, and whose abode was in the desert, cut off from human habitation. It is also possible that the goat was chosen for this task because goats were sacrificed to Azazel in illicit pagan rituals.

The meaning of the name Azazel is disputed, some scholars connecting it with an Arabic word meaning 'to place far apart'. But some early Jewish authorities interpreted Azazel as the name of a 'strong and difficult place', and this seems to be the interpretation followed by the translators of the New English Bible (1970). They translate *azazel* as 'precipice', and write of 'the goat on which the lot of the Precipice has fallen'. But this makes the marked antithesis between Yahweh and Azazel feeble, to say the least.

In view of the less well-defined meaning

As long as the doctrine of hellfire was preached the sin eater, who took upon himself the sins of someone who had just died, could always find work; the unsaved dead were said to be doomed to the everlasting torments of hell: illustration from a 16th century Flemish manuscript showing the sinfulness of man.

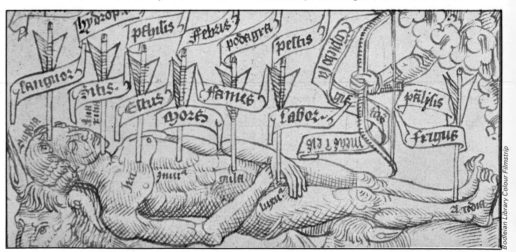

The Scapegoat by Holman Hunt: the goat to which the sins of the people were transferred and which was then banished into the desert.

given to the term in modern usage, where anyone from the late Stephen Ward to Lieutenant William Calley can be hailed as a 'scapegoat', it is necessary to dwell on one or two features of the ritual described in Leviticus. In the first place, the goat chosen to be sent to Azazel may be assumed to be entirely innocent of the sins which he is transmitting. Secondly, it is significant that the goat is chosen from among two by lot, so that an element of chance or randomness is introduced deliberately into the ritual. Thirdly, and most importantly, the scapegoat is not sacrificed to Azazel (or anyone else): its blood is not shed. Indeed, it would have been sacrilegious in the extreme to have made a sacrifice of it to an evil spirit. The scapegoat is made to stand alive before Yahweh, but it is the other goat that is sacrificed to him.

This needs to be emphasized, because Jesus Christ is sometimes spoken of as a scapegoat. It is true that the scapegoat is also a vicarious 'carrier' of the sins of others, and that he figures in a rite of atonement. In the New Testament, Jesus Christ atones for the sins of humanity which he did not himself commit, but, unlike the scapegoat, he does suffer a sacrificial death. In his epistle to the Hebrews, Saint Paul writes of the blood of Christ being incomparably more efficacious to purge the Hebrews' consciences than the blood of bulls and goats

offered in sacrifice. But as the scapegoat was never regarded as an offering to anyone, least of all to God, the notion of the scapegoat is not developed in the New Testament and later Christian doctrines of atonement and salvation through Christ.

The Hebrew institution of the scapegoat is not without parallels in other cultures, and may have been derived from earlier Semitic or even Sumerian rituals. An ancient Babylonian text suggests that one way of curing a pain in the neck in the second millennium BC was to sacrifice the neck of a beast, and there is a reference to the 'horned animal which alleviates pain'. The meaning of these texts is often obscure, and keenly disputed by scholars, but a sacred poem enjoining a sick king to fire an arrow which will shoot his sickness away into a gazelle points to the idea of an animal carrying human disease away. In a well-known chapter of *The Golden Bough*, Sir James Frazer cites examples from many places in the world of the demons or afflictions of whole communities being carried away by animals or in boats committed to the sea or a river.

The Substitute Victim

If the Hebrews did take over an ancient pagan custom, they characteristically gave it a spiritual content by making the goat take away not disease or physical affliction, but the sins and errors of the people themselves. But even this adaptation of the scapegoat idea is not confined to ancient Israel. Frazer quotes a Victorian missionary's account of the sacrifice of a 20-year-old girl in a village

in Nigeria, who was dragged alive along the ground, face downwards, from the king's house to the river, a distance of two miles, as if carrying away the 'weight of all their wickedness'. Two human victims, it seems, were sacrificed annually, after they had been purchased from the interior of the country with money raised by public subscription. 'All persons,' writes Frazer, 'who during the past year had fallen into gross sins, such as incendiarism, theft, adultery, witchcraft, and so forth, were expected to contribute 28 *ngugas*, or a little over £2.'

Frazer was more interested in points of similarity between geographically widespread cultures than in their differences, so that his examples of 'scapegoats' only approximate to the scapegoat of Hebrew ritual. It will be noted that in the Nigerian example the notion of a substitute victim is present, and the evil which it is intended to drive away is spiritual rather than physical; the ritual is also, as the Hebrew ritual became eventually, if it was not so from the beginning, an annual one. But the Nigerian custom differs in the important point that the substitute victim actually was put to death, whereas in ancient Israel it was merely banished.

Nearer to the Hebrew conception in some respects is the custom reported in the 16th century from Halberstadt in Thüringen of turning a man 'believed to be stained with heinous sins' out into the city streets throughout Lent and, in particular, refusing him admittance to any church. The man in question (a new man was chosen each year)

Left The scourging of Christ, from the *Très Riches Heures du Duc de Berry*: Jesus has frequently been thought of as a scapegoat, in the sense that by his suffering and death he atoned for the sins of others. An almost universal phenomenon in the history of religion, sacrifice is the main means by which man acknowledges his dependence on the unseen powers who control life and death.

Right The head of 'Tollund Man', with the rope with which he was strangled or hanged around his neck, discovered in a peatbog in Denmark; he was probably sacrificed to the goddess Nerthus, guardian of the fertility of the fields.

loose and not killed in sacrifice – are no less interesting than the broader meaning of the ritual which has made the scapegoat a familiar notion throughout much of the inhabited world.

The scapegoat ceremonies were given up in the 1st century AD but the Jewish Day of Atonement remains an important festival, at which the faithful fast and repent.

Christian theories of atonement are connected with the scapegoat through Isaiah 53. verses 4–6: '. . . he was wounded for our transgression, he was bruised for our iniquities . . . and with his stripes we are healed.' Christians identified the 'man of sorrows' of this passage with Jesus, and it became a central doctrine of Christianity that Jesus had reconciled man with God through his life and death, as he himself had suggested.

Different Christian thinkers have put forward different views about the mechanism of the Atonement, but that the coming of God to earth as a man made it possible for sinful man to be reconciled to God is accepted by all denominations.

Sin Eater

The function of the person known as a 'sin eater' was to act as a human scapegoat for the sins of someone who had just died. By eating bread and drinking either milk, beer or wine that had been placed on the body of the corpse, the sin eater took upon himself the sins of the departed, absorbing them into his own body. He was paid a small amount of money for saving a soul from hell in this way.

Sin eaters were first recorded by the antiquary John Aubrey in the 17th century, in his book *Remaines of Gentilisme and Judaisme*: 'In the County of Hereford was an old custome at funeralls to hire poor people who have to take upon them all the sinnes of the parting deceased . . . The manner was that when the corpse was brought out of the house and layd in the biere, a loaf of bread was brought out and delivered to the sinne-eater over the corpse as also a mazar bowl of maple full of beer (which he was to drinke up) and sixpence in money in consideration whereof he took upon him (*ipso facto*) all the sinnes of the defunct and freed him or her from walking after they were dead.' In North Wales, according to Aubrey, milk was used instead of beer.

Although later references to sin eaters are scarce, they probably survived in remote places in the British Isles until well into the 18th century.

was finally readmitted to church and absolved from his sins on the day before Good Friday. But again this human scapegoat differs from the goat in Leviticus, in being himself a sinner. Another example of a human scapegoat cited by Frazer is based on a Byzantine account, derived in turn from the Greek poet Hipponax of Ephesus (6th century BC). It was the custom in the time of Hipponax, when a city was visited by plague or famine, to choose an ugly or deformed person to take upon himself all the evils afflicting the city. He was brought to a suitable place, where dried figs, a barley loaf, and cheese were put into his hand. When he had eaten these, he was beaten seven times on his genital organs

with squills and wild fig tree branches (thought to avert evil influences, and so, in this instance, to guarantee the power of the sexual organs to ward off evil), and then sacrificed on a pyre, after which his ashes were cast into the sea.

These examples resemble the ancient Hebrew ritual only in their use of a substitute victim onto whom a whole community can project its ills. It may be that this answers to a universal human impulse, and that the Leviticus scapegoat in this respect typifies a universal element in human culture; but to the modern investigator, the unique features of the Hebrew ritual – the innocence of the victim, its selection by lot, and the fact that it was let

Sacrifice

In May 1950 a Danish archaeologist, Peter Glob, was called from his classes at Aarhus University to view a body. It had been discovered at a depth of almost seven feet in a peatbog in central Jutland. 'As dusk fell,' he later wrote, 'we saw in the fading light a man take shape before us. He was curled up, with legs drawn under him and arms bent, resting on his side as if asleep. His eyes were peacefully shut; his brows were furrowed and his mouth showed a slightly irritated quirk as if he were not overpleased by this unexpected disturbance of his rest.' Naked except for a leather belt and leather cap, the rope with which he had been strangled (or perhaps hanged) 2000 years ago was still around his neck.

'Tollund Man', as this discovery became known, may have been an executed criminal, but it is more likely that he had been sacrificed to the goddess Nerthus, the guardian of the fertility of the fields. Today he rests in a Danish museum, where the tourist can join the scholar in seeing a tangible piece of evidence of the nature of ancient religion.

Not all sacrifices were of human beings. But religion in the ancient world, and in parts of the modern world, involved so many forms of sacrifice that a full account of the history of this rite would be almost indistinguishable from the history of religion as such. It is this that modern man finds so hard to understand. To be sure, the word 'sacrifice' is still used: but in such a loose way as to obscure any original meaning it may have possessed.

It is first of all necessary to recognize that for most of history man has believed unquestioningly in the objective existence

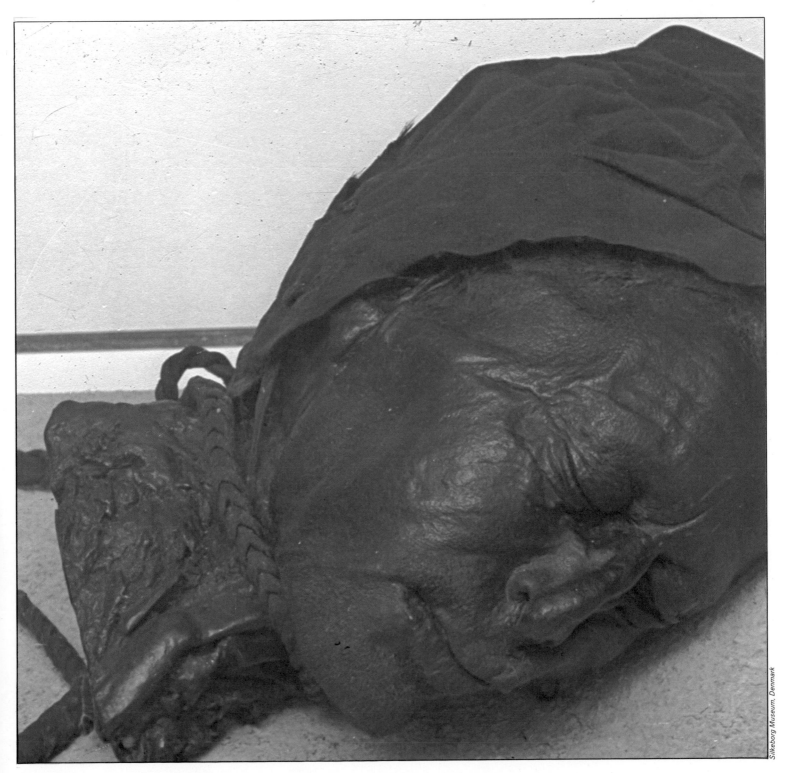

Musée de l'Homme, Paris

of a world parallel to his own, an unseen world peopled by gods, demons, ghosts, spirits, any one of which might influence his life in innumerable ways. Although for much of the time the workings of the unseen world were unpredictably mysterious, it was nevertheless believed that there were points of contact between the worlds, and that some degree of influence could be exerted at these points. In effect, the two worlds had to be kept in balance, and this involved man's acknowledgement of his proper position in the universe, and of his dependence on the unseen powers who controlled life, growth and death.

Sacrifice was the main means by which he sought to make this acknowledgement. A wellnigh universal phenomenon in the history of religion, it should always be understood as a mode of communication between man and the unseen powers, and an expression of his intentions in relation to those powers. The word comes from the Latin *sacrificium*, denoting a victim killed and consumed on the altar, that is, an object or animal which has been made *sacer* (holy) by being devoted wholly to one or other of the gods. A sacrifice is therefore something consecrated to a deity, either with a view to bringing about a certain result or reciprocal act from the deity's side, or with a view to establishing fellowship between man and the god.

A sacrifice may be offered as a gift, as an act of atonement or as an act of fellowship and communion, but it is not always possible to distinguish sharply between these aspects. In the ancient world, for instance, the giving of a gift was in itself a means of establishing fellowship between giver and recipient, of restoring a broken relationship and of influencing the recipient. A king or emperor could not be approached at all unless gifts appropriate to the standing of the person concerned were offered, and there is a close connection between sacrifice and prayer, where a deity is approached in a similar way.

Clearly, a good deal depends on the worshipper's prior image of the deity, and on the degree to which the god is thought to be accessible to human approach. In many primitive societies the High Gods of the sky are the most remote of the gods, and it is interesting that in many cases no sacrifices are made to them. They may once have created the world, but are no longer concerned in its day-to-day running, which they have delegated to lesser entities; it is to these spiritual beings that the majority of sacrifices are offered. If they are believed to be dwelling in a celestial paradise, the offering will normally be made by fire, which acts as a mediator between the two worlds; in the case of gods and goddesses of the earth the sacrifice may be buried, poured upon the ground, hidden in a cave or – to return to Tollund Man – sunk in a peatbog. Offerings to spirits of the forest may be left on a tree trunk, offerings to household gods may be made on the doorstep or hearthstone. Whatever the means, the basic purpose of sacrifice remains constant: to acknowledge

Above The blood shed by a sacrificial victim symbolized the offering of life to a deity; in some cultures it was also thought to communicate new life to the fields: Illustration from *The Book of Life of the Ancient Mexicans*: the Aztecs sacrificed human beings to the sun to ensure fertility in the coming year.

Right The book of Genesis tells how God tested the strength of Abraham's faith by commanding him to sacrifice his son Isaac: 16th century Italian painting showing an angel preventing Abraham from offering up his son.

man's dependance on the supernaturals and so ensure their continued benevolence.

The supernatural world, like the world of men, was believed to form a hierarchy, and it was therefore necessary for an individual to approach only those deities or spirits that occupied a position comparable to his own. In the ancient world, sacrifice to the greatest gods might be offered only by the king, acting on behalf of his people and usually only once a year, as with the sacrifices offered by the Chinese emperor to Shang Ti (Imperial Heaven) at the Altar of Heaven in Peking. At other times, the king's prerogatives would be delegated to members of a college of priests, who would act as mediators between men and the gods, taking care that the sacrifices were performed correctly. The individual in his home might of course offer sacrifices to lesser deities without the need for mediation, just as he might approach the lesser officials of the secular state.

The places in which sacrifices were offered varied greatly. In primitive cultures, they were natural sites of peculiar sanctity (caves, hills, groves and the like); or tombs of the powerful dead. Such sanctuaries as these could strictly speaking be anywhere, consecrated for the purpose by the repetition of the appropriate sacred texts. However, with the advent of urban civilization, the necessity for a focus of sacred presence in the midst of the city led to the construction of temples as dwelling-places of the gods; and it was here, on the temple altar or altars, that sacrifice was mainly offered. The temple was often conceived on the analogy of a royal court, with the temple staff as the god-king's servants. Sacrifice was made to the god as an adjunct of personal and communal requests, and also as a regular feature of the daily life of the divine court. Thus the god would be given regular nourishment as well as being honoured by the worshippers' gifts. Today the Hindu temple in India corresponds most closely to this once universal form of sacred symbolism.

Sacrifice in a Hindu temple takes very innocuous forms. Except in a very few cases, what is sacrificed is food, drink, flowers and coloured powders (although at some temples of Kali, blood sacrifices still occur). The sacrificial altar has disappeared, and the offering is simply placed before the image, before being, in many cases, distri-buted among the worshippers. However, it must be recognized that this is the end product of a long development. In Vedic times (beginning in perhaps 1200 BC and reaching down into the Middle Ages) the practice of blood sacrifice was common in India, and the earliest Indian holy scriptures, the *Vedas* and *Brahmanas*, form in effect a sacrificial manual of great complexity. The entire Vedic religion centred on sacrifice. It was sacrifice that regulated relations between men and gods, that maintained the order of the universe and provided the only conditions on which man's life was believed to be possible.

An ancient Hindu text states that the gods exist by gifts from below, just as men exist by gifts from above. The idea may seem excessively naive, but there is evidence from a number of ancient religions that this was indeed believed to be the case. A well-known example is found in the ancient Babylonian *Epic of Gilgamesh*, which contains a story of a great flood. The gods were utterly famished when the flood cut off their supply of sacrificial food; and when the waters finally abated and Utnapishtim emerged from his Ark and offered a sacrifice, they gathered round the smoke 'like flies'. An echo of this is found in Genesis, chapter 8: 'Then Noah built an altar to the Lord . . . and offered burnt offerings on the altar. And when the Lord smelled the pleasing odour . . .'

Reddening with Blood

The practice of cremating the dead had much in common with the practice of offering sacrifice by fire: in each case the fire (the god Agni) acted as mediator between the two worlds, and the dead were transported to the heavenly regions, where they enjoyed the same conditions as the gods, and where the same kind of offerings could be made to them. At the opening of the *Gita*, Prince Arjuna is finding reasons why he ought not to engage in battle with his relatives in an opposing army, and observes that if one destroys a family (which he is about to do), then the rules of the family collapse; and since one of the rules has to do with the offering of sacrifices to the departed ancestors, the sacrifices will no longer be offered, and the ancestors will 'fall out of blessedness, cheated of their offerings of rice and water'.

The image of famished gods and ancestors toppling out of heaven is an intriguing one, but sacrifice was seldom conceived on this elementary level, or at least, the conception was soon outgrown. More important is the image of the temple as the court of the divinity, at which gifts were offered. With very few exceptions, sacrifice was offered in accordance with larger or smaller cycles of time. Like prayer, it might follow a daily cycle, dictated to some extent by the 'needs' of the god or goddess to whom it was offered. But the greater sacrifices were annual, falling at various points on the calendar (which was usually lunar) or at the solstices.

Over and above the annual or seasonal cycle, there was in some cases a multi-annual cycle. For instance, at the pre-

Sonia Halliday

Left Goats have been sacrificial animals in many cultures; the Greeks, for instance, sacrificed 500 in thanksgiving for their victory at Marathon. Mosaic showing a goat being killed.

Right A goat is ritually killed in modern Nepal and its head is carried on a tray; during the October festival of Bassain the Nepalese army sacrifices more than 30 bullocks and many goats to Durga, the Hindu goddess of victory.

Christian temple of Old Uppsala in Sweden, the greatest sacrifices of men, horses and other animals were offered every ninth year. 'It is customary,' wrote the 11th century historian and geographer Adam of Bremen, 'to solemnise at Uppsala, at nine-year intervals, a general feast of all the provinces of Sweden . . . The sacrifice is of this nature: of every living thing that is male, they offer nine heads, with the blood of which it is customary to placate gods of this sort. The bodies they hang in the sacred grove that adjoins the temple . . . Even dogs and horses hang there with men.'

This association of blood with the sacrifice is important. Blood was once thought (not unreasonably) to be the bearer of life, and special measures were taken to consecrate to the deity the blood of a sacrificial animal or man. In the sacrifices of Viking times in the North, the main action was to take the blood and spread it on the altar and walls of the temple, and sprinkle it on the participants. One Old Norse expression meaning 'to offer sacrifice' is simply 'to redden with blood'. Similar practices are found in many other religions, including that of ancient Israel, where sprinkling blood on the altar was a preliminary to burning the sacrificial beast.

Season of Growth

Apart from its significance as an offering of life to the deity, the blood-sacrifice also served in some cultures to communicate new life to the fields at the beginning of a new season of growth. A particularly grisly example is known from the Pawnee Indians. A 15-year-old girl was taken and for six months treated royally; then she was led from hut to hut by the chiefs and warriors, at each one being given a gift. Her body was painted, after which she was killed. Finally her body was cut up and distributed among the cornfields. The spring ritual of the Aztecs contained similar elements, while at the Toxcatl Festival a young man was sacrificed to the sun god after having spent a year as a quasi-king. In the Americas, the link between sun worship and blood sacrifices is particularly noteworthy.

However, the sacrificial practices best known in the West (at least by repute) are those of the Old Testament. These are not isolated phenomena: their elements can easily be paralleled from many other cultures. But for at least as long as the Jerusalem Temple stood (that is, down to 70 AD), the sacrificial system was central to Israel's worship. Jewish sacrifices were of many kinds, carefully classified and regulated by the prescriptions and prohibitions of Leviticus. There was the burnt offering, no part of which was available for

human consumption, while in the peace offering, some parts of the animal were burned and others were consumed by priests and the worshippers.

The holiest of Jewish sacrifices were those known as sin offering and guilt offering (Leviticus 4.7), in which a broken relationship between man and God was symbolically restored. The entire action of these sacrifices was hedged about with the strictest taboos; for instance, the vessels in which any sacrificial offering had been contained had to be purified most carefully and even, in the case of earthenware vessels, broken.

This same theme – the restoration of the divine-human relationship – is also attested in one of the Jewish seasonal festivals, that of the Day of Atonement, *Yom Kippur*, which has been described as the summit of the Jewish sacrificial system. On this day, bullocks and goats were sacrificed, and their blood sprinkled within the Holy of Holies in the Temple – the only occasion in the year on which even the high priest was permitted to enter this innermost sanctuary. Subsequently the sins of the people were recited over a goat, the so-called 'scapegoat', which was then led away into the desert as an offering to a demon, Azazel. In later Jewish practice the animal was thrown over a cliff. However, practices such as these passed out of use early in the Christian era, and today even the solemn Day of Atonement is observed penitentially, rather than sacrificially.

Blood of the Lamb
In the ancient world the practice of sacrifice would often be accompanied by a banquet at which the worshippers would share table fellowship with the god concerned. Meat was eaten; wine or some other intoxicant was drunk. The Canaanites, according to the book of Judges, '. . . went out into the field, and gathered the grapes from their vineyards and trod them, and held festival, and went into the house of their god, and ate and drank . . .' (9.27). 'Consider the practice of Israel,' wrote Paul, 'are not those who eat the sacrifice partners in the altar?' (1 Corinthians 10.18). He went on to stress that to partake of any type of sacrificial banquet was to establish a bond of fellowship with the deity concerned, even though it might be a demon: 'I do not want you to be partners with demons' (10.20).

In Scandinavia, the annual sacrifices to Thor, Odin and Freyr were accompanied by a banquet at which horns were drained to Odin on behalf of the king and to Freyr for a good year and for peace. Incidentally, drunkenness – the rule rather than the exception – might well have contributed to the sense of divinity which the worshippers undoubtedly felt on these occasions. In India, precisely this type of situation is reflected in the soma sacrifice. It is not known for certain from which plant soma was extracted, although it has been suggested that it was the mushroom *Amanita muscaria*, but it is certain that it was the drink of the gods, that it was offered to the gods, and that it was at the same time shared by the worshippers.

Another type of table fellowship is seen in the Jewish celebration of the Passover, which is shared by the family in their home in remembrance of the release of the Israelites from Egypt. The Passover lamb was in later times sacrificed in the Temple, but the meal was an entirely separate concern; it is still the high point of the Jewish ritual year.

Early Christian teaching saw the Jewish sacrificial system (and particularly the sacrifices of purification and atonement) as having been summed up in the death of Jesus Christ. Jesus was the 'lamb without blemish or spot' (1 Peter 1.19) offered to take away the sin of the world. He fulfilled the role of the high priest on the Day of Atonement; 'he entered once for all into the Holy Place, taking not the blood of goats and calves but his own blood' (Hebrews 9.12). In the vision of John in the book of Revelation he was 'a Lamb standing, as though it had been slain' (5.6). In his death, therefore, the only possible offering for the sin of the world had been made, once and for all, and no further sacrifice need be made. Catholic teaching speaks of 'the Sacrifice of the Mass', and in this way incorporates much of the idea of table fellowship with the deity which accompanies sacrifice. However, there is no assertion that Christ is sacrificed afresh each time the Mass is celebrated: instead it is expressly stated that what is involved is a re-presentation, a continuation and a renewed application of Christ's death.

There have been, at least in the Indian and Western traditions, more or less elaborate protests from time to time against the view of deity which the sacrificial system implies. The Indian protest is made mainly in the interests of a metaphysical doctrine of God as pure Being, who cannot be adequately conceived in the form of an image before which sacrifices might be offered. In many areas of Hinduism, sacrifice is interpreted in a purely spiritual sense, and it is taken as meaning an attitude of faith and devotion.

The Western protest might be said to have its roots in the Old Testament, and to rest its case on the priority of the ethical over the ritual in man's relationship to God. Hosea may serve as the spokesman of those Israelite prophets who condemned sacrifice in one form or another (though it may be suspected that they were in fact condemning less the sacrificial system as such than either the Canaanite form of it or a purely mechanical view of its efficacy). Hosea wrote – or said – on behalf of God: 'I desire steadfast love and not sacrifice, the knowledge of God, rather than burnt offerings' (6.6).

Most people today would probably agree with him. The process of secularization has meant many changes in man's view of the world, not least in his conception of the supernatural, and sacrifice can have little place in a world from which the supernatural is so firmly excluded. It must remain an open question whether 'modern man' is right in this. It is certain, however, that the symbolical links with the spirit world, which sacrifice regulated and normalized, have been broken.

Sacraments

In seeking to possess himself of supernatural power or grace, man has instinctively felt the need to use forms of ritual action and manipulate material objects deemed appropriate to his purpose. There are some notable exceptions to this general tendency: for example, the mystic endeavours by mental or physical effort alone to achieve some desired spiritual state or virtue. However, since human nature is compounded of material and non-material elements, what has been called 'the sacramental principle' is both a necessary and intelligible pattern of behaviour, and its ritual operation is often closely akin to magic.

The ancient Egyptian ceremony of the 'Opening of the Mouth' provides a particularly graphic instance. The rite was carried out shortly before the embalmed body of a dead person was lowered into the sepulchral chamber of the tomb. The process of mummification had ensured the preservation of the corpse from decay; but if the deceased person was to live in his tomb, as the Egyptians fervently hoped, it was necessary to restore to his embalmed body the ability to see and breathe, and to take nourishment.

The ritual 'Opening of the Mouth' was a curious compound of symbolic and practical action. It was symbolic in so far as the action was performed on the corpse, which was completely swathed in bandages, with a mummy-mask over its head and face. In other words, in the ritual actions of touching the mouth and eyes, to restore the use of these organs, actual contact was not made with them; it was enough to touch the appropriate parts of the mummy-mask as an 'outward and visible sign'. However, the action was not just ritual miming; certain other factors were involved for the achievement of the desired result, as the Egyptians conceived it. A peculiarly shaped implement of bronze called a *mshtiw* had to be used for 'opening' the mouth and eyes. The ritual action had to be accompanied by the reading of a prescribed text which stated the intention of the act: to do for the deceased what had once been done by Horus for his dead father Osiris. Further, the rite had to be performed by a special *sem*-priest, while a lector-priest read the text. On analysis, therefore, to endow the dead person with supernatural power, the rite of the 'Opening of the Mouth' involved three elements: ritual action that required the use of a specified implement; a solemn statement of intent by an ordained minister; and the authority of a divine precedent.

In the celebrated Eleusinian Mysteries, the initiates, who had been fasting, partook of a special drink called the *kykeon*. It was made of meal mixed with water and flavoured with soft-mint. The initiates drank this potion in memory of what the goddess Demeter had done at Eleusis during her search for her daughter Persephone. In sorrow, she had fasted, but finally had assented to drink a potion concocted as the kykeon. In the Homeric Hymn to Demeter, the authenticating occasion is described: 'And Metaneira mixed the draught and gave it to the goddess as she bade. So the great queen Deo received it to observe the sacrament.'

These examples, selected from many, attest to the operation of the sacramental principle as a natural pattern of man's behaviour when in quest of supernatural power or grace. It is easy to describe the examples cited as magical transactions in a denigrating sense, but a more wisely sympathetic approach would evaluate them as significant expressions of the spiritual aspirations of mankind, of which the Christian sacraments are more sophisticated and refined examples.

Christian Sacraments
The word 'sacrament' has acquired its distinctive theological meaning from Christian usage. The Latin word *sacramentum* meant originally the pledge of security deposited in public keeping by the parties engaged in a lawsuit, or the oath taken by Roman soldiers to the emperor. In the Western Church, the term was adopted to translate the Greek *mysterion*, which had long been used as a designation for the secret rites of the Mystery religions.

Catholic Christianity, both Eastern and Western, recognizes seven sacraments, of which two are distinguished as the greater sacraments. These are baptism and the Lord's Supper, the institution and ordering of which are clearly recorded in the New Testament. The origins of the five lesser sacraments are obscure, and their recognition throughout the Church was gradual. The interpretation of the sacraments has greatly occupied Christian theologians throughout the centuries, and many of their definitions, and the practices which have stemmed from them, have provoked great controversies. Rejection of certain medieval doctrines concerning the Lord's Supper or Mass characterized the Protestant reformers. Protestants generally recognize only baptism and the Lord's Supper as sacraments.

Body and Blood
The seven sacraments of the Catholic Church are: baptism; the Lord's Supper; confirmation; holy orders; penance; matrimony; and extreme unction. The supreme sacrament is that variously described as the Lord's Supper, Holy Communion, Eucharist or Mass. The institution of the rite is first recorded by St Paul, c 55 AD (1 Corinthians, chapter 11) and is described, with some slight variations, in the gospels of Matthew, Mark and Luke.

The words of institution which were used by Christ gave the rite a twofold significance. The consumption by the faithful of bread and wine, specially consecrated as the body and blood of Christ, signified an act of communion with Christ effected by the taking into the body of the consecrated elements. The symbolism of the broken body and outpoured blood implied sacrifice, thus making the rite commemorative or representative of the crucifixion of Christ, interpreted theologically as the atoning sacrifice offered for the sins of mankind. These implications inspired the development of two of the most notable doctrines of medieval Christianity: transubstantiation and the sacrifice of the Mass.

According to the doctrine of transubstantiation, the substance or essence of the bread and wine are transformed by the words of consecration into the body and blood of Christ, although they still retain their outward appearance of bread and wine. This doctrine led to the idea that, at Mass, Christ is present on the altar, and could be carried about in processions of the sacred host (the consecrated bread). The doctrine of the sacrifice of the Mass teaches that, at each celebration, Christ's sacrifice is represented to God the Father, often with some special intention. Thus at Requiem Masses, the sacrifice is for specified souls.

Left Central to the action of the Christian Mass is the taking of the consecrated bread and wine; Christians disagree about whether this ceremony is symbolic or whether it is a literal 'eating of the god', the consumption of Christ's body and blood. Certain aspects of this ceremony may be compared with cannibal practices.

Below Cannibalism is often based on the belief that by eating a person you acquire his characteristics.

Mary Evans Picture Library

Dance, Drama and Games

Dance

While western man generally regards the dance as a pastime, many other people, especially in non-literate societies, still dance as a form of prayer or magic, directed to a variety of practical ends. Ritual dances of today serve many functions, particularly as celebrations of life's crises, for healing or as efforts to promote the fertility of crops.

Puberty rites survive among aborigines in various parts of the world. The *waiang-arree*, for example, is the circumcision rite of the tribes of Broome on the west coast of Australia. After initiations and a climactic group dance by men and boys in a double circle, the novices become fully fledged members of tribal society. They have learned the secrets, they have symbolically died and have awakened to a new status.

Women may hold their own rites for pubescent girls. Choroti and Lengua women of South America danced for a month, circling the girl with slow steps, and striking the ground with bamboo staffs topped by deerhoof rattles. In this rite for demon exorcism they had the aid of four singing medicine-men. In the Maipure tribe of Venezuela the older women chase away demons, who are really masked men miming wild beasts. An Apache girl of New Mexico joins in a circle dance with attendants. For four days four men, the masked *gahe*, impersonate horned mountain spirits with pointed swords and angular gestures. During the ceremony the girl practises her future tasks as a woman. Such instruction is an important function of these rites.

Therapeutic dances may also take the form of circling or demon impersonations. They may show startling, individualistic whirls or spasms, depending on the purpose and location. They achieve therapy by inducing ecstasy, by curing a disease, or both. Ecstatic dances bring worshippers into communion with supernatural beings, by means of regulated movements, hypnotic musical accompaniment and sometimes with the aid

Although dancing, in the West, is generally regarded as a social pastime, or entertainment, dances in Africa still retain their ritual character: Nigerian stilt dance, a test of skill.

of narcotics. The most spectacular mystic cult is that of the Turkish dervishes. Rufai or howling dervishes stamp and spring in a double circle, swaying and jerking their bodies. Mevlevi dervishes whirl individually, faster and faster – the upraised right hand receives supernatural power and carries it to earth through the lowered left hand.

Balinese men dance themselves into a near-suicidal trance, as they direct their kris daggers against their own breasts. The frenzy of the Asiatics brings to mind medieval dance manias – the St Vitus tremors which are now extinct, and the self-flagellant ecstasy of Penitentes, who still celebrate their Eastern rites in New Mexico and the Philippines, to atone for their sins.

Asiatic shamans whirl themselves into a trance not only for mystic experience, but also for the cure of illness. Siberian shamans of the Tungus and Yakut tribes commune with the spirits of ancestors or animals and they effect cures by means of a revelation. Noisy exorcisms are the aims of the masked Devil Dancers of Sri Lanka and the Nalke and Paraiyan castes of India. These inspired men (rarely women) have their counterparts in the New World, especially among the Eskimo and the tribes in the jungles of the Amazon. They restore sick patients by bringing their souls back from the spirit land.

The New World received other ecstatic cults from Africa, under various names. Negro slaves brought the *vodun* cult (from which the word Voodoo is derived) to Haiti from Dahomey. The Bantu perpetuated their Macumba in Brazil, making many adaptations to the new environment. For instance, they know their ancestral gods by the names of Catholic saints as well as by the tribal names but they have preserved the essence, the traditional movements, songs and drums, and retain the strict ritual organization, with male and female priests. The worshippers impersonate deities in traditional movements, such as undulations for the snake god. As the deity 'rides' a worshipper, he or she may lose consciousness or become violent. Priests, who remain conscious, must often restrain ecstatic individuals, and help them regain consciousness. Though these rituals appeared malevolent to missionaries, they actually benefited the participants by relieving psychic tensions and by effecting better rapport with fellow human beings.

Masks with Staring Eyes

Missionaries saw such ecstasy arising within the groups of Christian converts. The Shouters and the Holy Rollers are among the sects which seek communion with Jesus in a semi-trance. Any member of a congregation can start a gospel song. A pianist and steel guitarist pick out counter rhythms; then the entire assembly syncopates the melody with hand-clapping, tambourine or triangle. As the worshippers rise from their chairs, some flex their knees rhythmically; some shuffle their feet; some skip in the aisles with spasmodic foot twists. They jerk their torsos or sway with upraised arms, shouting 'Halleluia', 'Thank you, Jesus!'.

In the New World, medicine dances of native origin cure mental and physical ailments. The Iroquois of New York State and Canada hold many medicine dances with traditional songs. At midwinter the Society of Maskers represents disease spirits and exorcises spirits which have afflicted members of the traditional native religion. In wry, wooden masks with staring eyes and long hair, they enter the sanctuary, the specially sacred area of their meeting place, crawling, whinnying and knocking turtle-shell rattles on floor and door. They hop about grotesquely, causing mingled awe and mirth. From a fireplace they collect ashes and rub them on the hair and arms of patients who are suffering from toothache or some other ailment. Finally everyone joins in a circle dance and a subsequent feast of corn mush. The Iroquois hold equally jolly medicine dances to propitiate the spirit of an animal that has taken offence at some ritual misdemeanour and has afflicted a man or woman. If a shaman decides that a bear spirit has caused cramps, for instance, he recommends a ritual for the bear. After a prayer and a tobacco offering, ritual conductors lead a circle dance, imitating bears with waddling and growling. Then the spectators join in a mimetic counter-clockwise circuit. They stamp, kick, eat nuts and berries, the bear's favourite food, and end by greatly cheering the patient.

Other tribes, like the Navaho of Arizona, hold long curative ceremonies, with singing and sometimes with masked spirit impersonations. They have special success with emotional ailments, by virtue of the musical and dance rhythms. They do not try to cure

Camera Press London

ailments brought by the white man from Europe.

To encourage a plentiful supply of food dances are performed to honour animal spirits in hunting rites, and plant spirits in agricultural rites. They vary greatly in accordance with the environment, fauna and flora. Animal dances, which are usually imitative, please animal spirits before a hunting expedition and appease them after a successful kill. Early man and some groups of modern men have held beasts in awe, not only because of their food value but also because of their agility and power. These animists endow all creatures with souls. Their animal mimicry is often very realistic. Boys of the Australian Kemmirai tribe imitate kangaroos by jumping, holding up their hands before their chests, or scratching themselves. African mimes can be great comics, such as the monkey men near Odienne of the Ivory Coast of West Africa. Tewa Indian men of New Mexico act like deer in some animal ceremonies; they gallop lightly or stand and tremble, nervously turning their antlered heads from side to side. In another version, however, they have stylized the mime; they stand erect as they sing and tread the ground.

Many animal dances survive as entertainments. Japanese folk festivals include realistic masked deer, bears, dragons, herons, cocks, and a comic lion imported from China. Turkish festivals enliven begging processions with camels and foxes in skins. England's prehistoric dramas survive

in the Mummers, with real skins or shaggy imitations made of newspaper. The stylized reindeer of Abbots Bromley are six men who hold antlers in front of their heads as they face each other in two files, cross over and interweave sedately.

Agricultural dancers of today rarely impersonate plant deities. The Aztecs appointed elaborately garbed priests or priestesses for the impersonation of deities like Cinteotl, god of maize, in their seasonal ceremonial dances. The ancient Egyptians and Greeks also visualized their agricultural deities, like Dionysus, god of wine and seasonal rejuvenation. Iroquois women, however, merely symbolize the spirits of corn, beans and squash, without imitative attributes. Tewa women represent corn in great communal dances for the harvest, huge circuits and intricate lines danced by hundreds of men, women and children.

As in the case of animal mimicry, some agricultural dances are losing their religious significance but retain their ancient patterns. Balkan peasants still celebrate the harvest with circle dances by men and women – *kolos* of Serbia, *horas* of Rumania, Greece and Israel, descendants of the ancient Greek *choros*, yet even more complex in steps and rhythms. The Tarascan Indians of Mexico still perform a sowing dance for women.

Folk dances and singing games preserve the forms of other occupational dances besides the hunt and agriculture. The Spanish *Filada* mimes spinning; the German *Webertanz* represents weaving; the Danish Shoe-

maker's and Tinker's Dance, the English Sailor's Hornpipe and Cobbler's Jig indicate these occupations.

Dancing Class Distinctions

The various classifications of people within a society, by birthright, occupation, age and sex, affect dance participation. In Western society such classifications are not rigid, but in many parts of the world social status determines a person's rights as a dancer.

Social organization, which may involve ritual organization, has evolved an infinity of patterns and restrictions. India's caste system is probably the world's most rigid division of people into gradations of prestige and occupations. The low caste, the Paraiyans, clatter in masked, shamanistic trance movement, the purpose of which is curative. Peasants of Maharashtra in south-west India perform calendric festive dances, such as the *kolattam* stick dances. The Devadassis (female temple dancers) excel in the fine art of Hindu *Bharata Natyam*. Hilltribes like the Todas cling to ancient round dances.

Past civilizations have similarly, though less rigidly, divided people into social and choreographic classes. Europe's medieval feudal system separated people by location and simultaneously by occupation. Aristocrats in their castles held lavish festivals with comic dances by professional clowns and paired dances by the elegant men and women, including *caroles* and later on *pavanes* and *gaillardes*. Burghers in the cities tried to emulate the aristocrats, but they also took over dances from the peasants

Left Basuto girls, their faces symbolically concealed behind masks made from beads, perform an initiation dance.

Right Caroles, or ring and chain dances, spring from ritual practices thousands of years old. Two variations are the Sardana of Spain (*above*) and the Israeli Hora (*below*).

like the rough *weller*, which they eventually developed into the waltz. The peasants or serfs were the custodians of ancient, pagan ritual dances. Partly as tradition, partly as release from an arduous life, they continued to impersonate the awesome animal maskers at Twelfth Night and Carnival. In many parts of Europe, the descendants of these peasants perform folk dances for harvests, for weddings and for tourist shows.

In Mexico the Aztecs developed a similar class system between the 12th century and the 15th. They expressed their social-ritual divisions during huge seasonal ceremonies. Priests and war captives, who were also sacrificial victims, impersonated deities. Warriors held ritual combats, not unlike the sword dances of northern Europe. Nobles held special dignified dances, in double file. Women had special roles, as priestesses. In some serpentine dances harlots were the partners of warriors; in other serpentines respectable virgins of the merchant class joined youths of their class. Serfs never participated; they watched the ceremonies, or were drafted as sacrificial victims.

Telling the Men from the Boys

The Aztec caste system was exceptional in the New World. Most native tribes had a comparatively democratic organization, based on clans, and some still do. Iroquois society is divided into hereditary clans, which are traced through the women. All social and ritual activities hinge on the interaction of two groups of clans, termed moieties by anthropologists. Members of each moiety have their assigned places in the sanctuary and in the dance line. They must sit at opposite sides of the sanctuary. Generally they participate in the same ceremonies. In New Mexico, however, the members of the two moieties often have separate ceremonies. The summer moiety manages the summer dances for crops, while the winter moiety is in charge of winter ceremonies for animals.

Age grades nowadays have little effect on dance arrangements, except that in Europe and America children keep up singing games. In some aboriginal esoteric rites children are not admitted. In puberty rites they are the leading performers. In the now obsolete war societies of the Indians of the American Great Plains the boys were members of certain societies according to their particular age grade. Today in most American Indian and other folk dances, children participate, usually at the end of a dance line, copying their elders. While aboriginal dances involve elders as vigorous as their grandchildren, Western man tends to assume that energy is a prerogative of youth. The idea that modern dancing is for the youngsters has a long history. In the Middle Ages it was customary for the older couples to march slowly through the *branle double*, for younger couples to engage in the *branle gai*, and for youngsters to leap through the lively steps of the *branle de Bourgogne*.

Another form of segregation, according to sex, has deep-seated biological and sociological motivation. Men dance for war and the hunt, but women for peace and horticulture. The sexes may dance alone in their special rites, or they may occupy separate parts of a dance line, perhaps with different steps. Rarely are women the partners of men. That is a recent development in the social and stage dances of Europe and America.

The Geometry of Dance
The dance functions, organizations and inter-personal relationships find expression in visible and audible patterns. The ingredients of the visible pattern are posture, arm gestures, footwork and geometric formations. They are usually synchronized with sound effects. Some rituals call for imitative body postures or special gestures. Other rites, as for harvests and most sociable dances, emphasize steps that carry the dancers over the ground in simple or elaborate formations. Local factors also determine the kind of ingredient. That is, different peoples emphasize certain ingredients in special ways called style. Many African tribes and their New World descendants move the whole body expressively, even acrobatically. India's art dancers emphasize arm gestures. European peoples like footwork – small, intricate steps in the Balkans, high leaps and kicks in the Basque Provinces. In southern Spain the men and women of Andalusia excel in sinuous torso and arm movements as well as in intricate footwork. Peasants of northern Spain prefer circle dances or interweaving 'longways'; this term is used for dances performed by two rows of dancers standing opposite each other in parallel lines. Ireland's folk dancers are masters of every kind of geometric floor pattern.

Postures have certain universal connotations. Dirges and other sad dances produce flexed bodies, while in gay moods the torso is thrown out and the head raised. Heavy animals like bears or buffalo suggest a bowed position in mime; while birds suggest light, upward imitation of flight. At the same time, every tribe and national group shows local posture tendencies. West African Negroes and Spanish flamenco dancers exaggeratedly extend their backs; English Morris dancers tilt backwards; Basques hold themselves erect; Serbians and Indians of North America tilt forwards or even flex their bodies. Within these regional postures, age grades cause variations. American Indian war dancers remain fairly erect, if the men are old; they flex and extend to extremes if they are young.

Speaking with Their Hands
Sex also has an effect on traditional postures. In many parts of the world, from America to Russia, women are supposed to dance with a meek posture, head bowed feet close together, while men may expand and stretch. In Chinese theatre, male characters often assume a straddling posture, but female characters hold legs and arms closed in. Within these conventions there are also individual variations. Even in stylized group dances some individuals move joyously and others meekly. In mime some experts have more extreme interpretations of flexion and extension than others. Also – a more elusive constituent – some dancers use more force than others, in their more emphatic exhibition.

Gestures of the arms and hands similarly express universal moods and thoughts, and also regional and individual variations. Dance gestures, which ultimately derive from daily gestures, are always stylized; they may be simple and intelligible or elaborate and obscure. The gestures of European folk dancers are simple compared to the code of India. Everywhere gestures can be imitative or symbolic, involving the whole arm or just the fingers, executed with or without props. They can be realistic, expressive of emotions, or decorative. In ancient and modern India *nritya* signifies narrative, stylized gestures, while *nritta* is decorative. Both types contrast with the forthright, realistic gestures of European dances such as the Swedish flax-reaping. For an understanding of nritya and of Katha-Kali folk dramas, the spectator must know the sacred myths, the tales of Krishna, Shiva and legendary heroes. He must also know the meaning of the hundreds of finger positions and arm positions. The gesture code has been simplified in the ritual dances of Manipur in north-east India, the Indonesian enactments of the *Ramayana* and *Mahabharata*, in the narrative gesture dances of Samoa and the Hawaiian *hula*.

The only American Indians with a gesture code are the tribes of British Columbia, though the Aztecs and Maya apparently had ritual codes. Their manuscripts show gestures similar to those of Balinese priests lowering their hands to the earth or raising them to the sky. These codes of Asia and native America have had little or no effect on art dances of Europe and America. Ballet dancers persevere in a set of conventionalized positions for love and sorrow; followers of the American pioneer, Isadora Duncan, invent their own gestures; followers of the German pioneer, Mary Wigman, show the influence of Indonesia's decorative hand positions with overstretched fingers. In general, dancers of the Western world neglect gesture in favour of footwork.

Focus on the Feet
Footwork or steps may be the basis of a dance, a rhythmic background to gestures, or a means of progression. The leaps of Basque men, the intricate crossing of the feet of the Scottish dancer, the brushes and flaps of an American tap dancer take the full attention of performer and audience, perhaps formerly as ritual, certainly now as exhibition. The high leaps of the Basques and the similar leaps of the men of the Ukraine and Georgia may hark back to ancient vegetation rites to promote the leaping of plants into life. The jumps and turns of Balkan folk dancers and of England's Morris men may also have

ancient roots in supplications to the earth and the seeds.

On the other hand, the footbeats of India and southern Spain appear as rhythmic backgrounds to the filigrees of arms and hands. In contrast with such virtuoso uses of feet and legs, the simpler steps of most folk dances serve as a means of progression. In their forward, backward or sideways movements European groups and couples may use the polka or waltz steps. More frequently they run through their formations as do people in other parts of the world.

Closed or open circuits are the most commonly found ground patterns of dance. In closed circuits the participants may move in the direction of progression or they may face the centre and then step sideways. They can move clockwise, as commonly in hunting cultures and in north-west Europe, or counter-clockwise, as in agricultural rites of south-east Europe and Africa. Some peoples regard the latter directions as sinister and evil, as the Algonquins of America's Great Lakes and the medieval English, who considered 'widdershins', meaning against the sun, as the witches' direction. The closed circle, single or double (in couples) has its limitations. The open circle is really a follow-my-leader line and offers many possibilities of serpentining, winding into a spiral, and so on. It is known among the Bambuti Pygmies of Africa, the French Provençale *farandole* dancers, and agricultural American Indians.

Straight lines are less common than circling patterns. They take many forms. Simplest are the multiple stationary lines of the Maori in New Zealand, and of Africans such as the Watusi, who lay more stress on gestures and leaps than on formations. Two parallel lines offer more artistic possibilities, and have greater scope for dramatic expression. The facing lines may be two groups of warriors, or two lines of men and women in a mime of courtship, repulsion and magnetism. The former type has shown most elaborate developments in the sword dances of Europe. The latter type persists in various parts of Africa, in simple patterns; it has evolved into the intricacies of the 'longways sets' of Scottish and New England country dancing and also into the patterns of Pueblo Indian harvest dancers. In many of these longways the approach-and-recede pattern is combined with the serpentine motif of the open circle, as in the Virginia Reel. In this and many other longways the arch pattern introduces an ancient tree

Brian Shuel

The Syndics of the Fitzwilliam Museum, Cambridge

symbolism into geometric formations: successively, partners hold up their joined hands and other couples run through the arch. American Indians have adopted this ornamental pattern, Yucatan Indians with the aid of actual flower arches, and Great Lakes Indians by holding hands.

Group formations may combine with couple patterns in European folk dances, from Israel to Finland. In Moravian dances the couples circle counter-clockwise. At the same time they change from parallel progression with joined hands to separation, reunion, pivoting, and so forth. In the French quadrilles and American square dances all circle and then the four couples successively cross over, break up into small circles, finally spinning by twos in the swing. In these folk dances couples and individuals conform to regulations, unlike the undisciplined present-day dancing.

Maze, Snake and Goddess

Among later Greek writers there is a persistent tradition of a maze or labyrinth dance in Crete, in which the dancers pursued a winding course suggestive of the devious passages of a maze. The fact that the palace at Knossos . . . is complex in plan and suggests the Labyrinth of legend, perhaps lends some support to this tradition. Dances of the maze type are common to many early peoples in various parts of the world, whether they have Labyrinthine buildings or not. Some historians trace them all to a very primitive dance form which is really an imitation of the crawling of a serpent. The importance of the snake in Minoan religion is well attested, and it is possible that in primitive times a python or other large snake . . . was kept as an embodiment of the goddess. Some students think that a snake-line dance was performed in the gloom of the many caves in the mountains near Knossos, and that it was climaxed by the exhibition of a living python. Such a performance would have been weird and spectacular in the highest degree.

Certain figurines indicate also that there were in Crete, snake-handling rituals, in which woman votaries carried small living snakes in their hands. Earlier, such figurines were interpreted as 'snake goddesses', but recent studies have shown that they portray worshippers, dancers, or priestesses. Snake-handling rituals in the United States and in other parts of the world are usually accompanied with shouts and hymns, and with a shuffling sort of dance.

Lilian B. Lawler *The Dance in Ancient Greece*

81

Left and below right The devil dances of Liberia, West Africa, are performed on occasions such as the death of a king or at harvest time. The dancers made anonymous by their costumes and usually wearing terror-inspiring masks, represent malignant supernatural powers or devils: by imitating these evil spirits they hope to propitiate them.

Right War dances, in preparation for battle or to celebrate a victory, also attract attention to the masculinity of the participants: Chuka dancers in Kenya.

Patterns in Time and Space

The various ingredients of the dance are combined into structures by patterns in tempo or variations of steps. Quadrille types open with the circling, continue with a 'body' of distinctive formations, and close with a promenade and swing. The original French quadrilles were suites, with precise, named sections, like the Morris dances with their five successive dances. Many dances have simpler forms. Some, like the Palestinian *hora*, continue with the same step and formation of an open circle, but they build up excitement by a crescendo in speed and intensity. Others use the simple device of contraction, like the German *Siebenschritt*, with its ever shorter and shorter series of steps. A common device is the two-part set of slow and fast dance, like the Renaissance *Pavana* and *Gaillarda*, the later Minuet and Rondeau, the present Hungarian *Lassu* and *Gyors*, the Norwegian *Gangar* and *Springar*, and the Tewa Harvest slow and fast dance. Each part has distinctive steps, first processional, then lively and leaping.

Dances often combine with other activities into traditional dramas, with preparations, intensifying action, and aftermath. African possession cults and the corresponding Holiness Church services start with prayer and solemn music; work up to a climax of frenzied solo and circle dancing, with interludes for speeches; and they calm down into a benediction and song, with in Africa a concluding feast. This is the structure of the Greek Dionysian rites and the resultant Greek dramas and medieval Passion Plays. While these dramas last only a few hours, some rituals occupy many days, like the 27-day Midwinter rites of British Columbia tribes.

Dance Music

Over thousands of years dances have developed an infinite variety of muscial accompaniments, costumes and settings. Musical accompaniment may involve separate musicians, single or grouped. Drums of many sizes and shapes are almost ubiquitous; they are most advanced in Africa. Stringed instruments have spread from the Near East to most of Asia and Europe, and thence to the Americas. Gongs characterize Southeast Asia. Flutes and other wind instruments are sporadic, varying from the tiny flute of the one-man flute-and-tabor music in England, Spain and Mexico, to the enormous horns of Tibet and native Chile. Europe has evolved the most complex instruments and ensembles of strings, accordions, pianos and other instruments. The most elaborate ensembles, the orchestras of the modern world, have the least significance, while the drum-and-voice combinations are closest to the original magical intentions.

These separate accompaniments generally conform to the mood, tempo and metre of the dances, and they have the same structure. They may thus be in triple or double time; or in irregular metres. They may synchronize with the footwork of the dancers and with each other, or they may be in syncopation or antiphony. The relation-ship is closest when the dancers produce their own accompaniment, as the sole musicians, or as enrichments of the background music. Dancers may manipulate their instruments, as they sing or chant, or move them automatically as part of their clothing, or create rhythmic sounds with parts of the body.

Sometimes drummers dance, kneel, leap, as they beat the rhythms. Small drums are used by tribesmen of New Guinea; the Santals and Oraons of Bihar in India have more cumbersome ones slung around their shoulders; gypsy men of Turkey and Macedonia perform remarkable feats with huge, double-headed instruments. The tambourine players in the Italian *tarantella* have a relatively lightweight instrument with a simple playing technique. Almost as impressive as the gypsy drumming is the self-accompaniment of Mexico's Concheros, who strum rhythmic chords on a lute-like instrument, made of an armadillo shell, as they stamp out their dance steps. In the New World such music may be a substitute for ancient native rattles. Iroquois men shake horn or turtle-shell rattles. Many tribes shake tortoise rattles for rain. The Siouans of North America and the Yaqui of Mexico use deer-hoofs, on sticks or on their belts. Yaqui clowns, who play an important role in the dance, strike a rattle with brass discs on the palm of the left hand. At the same time they wear bells dangling from their belts, and rustle anklets of butterfly cocoons filled with gravel. Many dancers wear such jinglers on their belts, hems or ankles.

More skill is involved in the manipulation of castanets, held in the hands, with different timbre for the right and left hands. The castanets of Spain are descendants of ancient finger-cymbals; Andalusian women often have the same poses as the cymbal players of Egypt and Greece. At the same time they and their partners stamp out intricate sounds with their hard-heeled shoes. Flamenco dancers also stamp *zapateados* but they clap their hands or snap their fingers. They belong to a widespread cult of stamping either with or without shoes and of handclapping in counter-rhythms.

Dressing for the Dance

Costumes sometimes add such sound effects to the visual design. Morris men jingle the bell pads on their shins as they leap and simultaneously wave kerchiefs or strike sticks. Nautch dancers of India jingle ankle bells and stamp while they pirouette and whirl voluminous skirts. But many props are soundless, like the fans of Japanese geishas or the long sleeve extensions of

Spear dance by the Wogogo tribesmen of East Africa: one of the many versions of the war dance, performed throughout the world with sword or shield, spear, sticks or bow and arrow.

Chinese theatre dancers. The manipulations of the fans are symbolic and represent falling leaves, waterfalls, and many other things. Some props are realistic or descriptive, or simply decorative. Tewa men manipulate feathered wings to simulate eagles. An American stage dancer, Loie Fuller, whirled hundreds of yards of cloth as flames under red lights. Isadora Duncan's disciples wafted silk scarfs merely for an effect of lightness.

Masks similarly serve many purposes, most importantly symbolic or imitative purposes. The Iroquois False-Face masks and the Tewa eagle half-masks with beaks represent supernatural beings without impeding dance movements. But many ritual masks are so huge as to preclude any dance movement except for a walk, such as the huge disc worn by impersonators of the Inca sun god and the towering demon masks of Melanesian and West African dancers. Some masks require special manipulation. Thunderbirds in British Columbian dances move their beaks on hinges. Other masks heighten character acting, like the demons, heroes and court ladies of Japanese theatre, and the comic Old Men of the Tarascan people of Mexico.

Special garments are prescribed for the effectiveness of the masks. The dancers may be completely covered in bulky grasses or in stiff and decorative kimonos. At the other extreme, they may be nude but for painted stripes. Without masks, costumes rely on other devices for their effect. Tewa Indians decorate their tunics or kilts with magical designs, zigzags for lightning, terraces for clouds and rain. Folk dancers of many lands emphasize their femininity and masculinity by costume patterns and rich ornaments. Women wear layers of full skirts which they whirl as they turn and sometimes flip with their hands. Men exaggerate their strong chests with bouffant sleeves.

Settings enhance the meaning and effectiveness of dance movements and props. Maypole dancers belong on a village green. Tewa dancers belong in their sunny semi-desert, against a horizon of snow-capped mountains, their turquoise, red, black and white costumes brilliant against the beige adobe of the homes around the dance plaza. British Columbian maskers appear more weird than ever in the dimly lit dance house, by a flickering fire. But Melanesian and Polynesian dances are set against the background of jungle or sea, the sun, and the fragrance of exotic flowers.

Environments have often changed for dances, as people have migrated to new lands, have conquered or visited other peoples. Such migrations have resulted in the diffusion of dance forms, with adaptations to their new homes, and in mixtures. Other changes such as secularization and professionalization have taken place locally and also through migrations.

Recent dance importations to North America followed the immigrations of the 19th century. Some of the immigrants have tried to re-create their seasonal festivals in the new environment. In settlements like Heightstown, New Jersey, Slovaks and Moravians attempted processionals through the streets of the village, imitating their native harvest festivals. In big cities, like New York and Detroit, they have tried to stage fragments of their dance rituals or have invented plays representing their custom.

Mixtures generally result in the course of transfers. Some of the mixtures are among the world's most picturesque dances, such as a dance representing the battles of Moors and Christians, with a Spanish libretto and Aztec movement styles. America's most accessible mixtures are the square dances, which started as diversions of British immigrants, then added Scottish motifs, later on, Danish and Norwegian motifs in the Middlewest, and, in the Southwest, figures from Spanish *cuadrillas*. Such mixture has affected art dance, too, but in a more self-conscious manner. Americans such as Fred Astaire and Paul Draper have combined European ballet with American tap dancing.

Dance in the Modern World
Professionalization has had an increasing effect on the forms and settings of dances. Certain gifted individuals in every culture

84

become so expert that they elaborate the traditional forms, or create new routines. In ancient times, as in Pharaonic funerals, and still today, as in India's Katha-Kali dramas, experts who became professional by virtue of their excellence were as dedicated to the gods as to their art. African virtuosi, like the Watusi men, do not expect remuneration. Today in the Western world, however, the supreme performers serve both art and mammon.

Secularization has resulted from professionalization, but the process is not identical. Some professionals, like Japanese Shinto priests, still serve religion. Most secular dancers, as in the ballroom, are amateurs. The process of secularization has certainly been going on for untold centuries. In many parts of the world rituals survive side by side with pleasure dances, as among the Iroquois and the Basques. For centuries special 'social' dances have been created, like the minuet, polka and waltz; these dances emphasize communications between the sexes instead of with deities.

The shift from faith to fun has followed in the wake of Euro-American industrialization and urbanization. Yet it has not destroyed all native ritual, and even in urban society, serious artists are seeking a return to faith, or to a deep, almost ritualistic dedication. The devotees, be they performers, producers, or scholars, believe that the dance plays a role in modern society, even though it is no longer integrated with beliefs and activities.

Ritual dances are taking on new forms, suited to modern Christianity. While ancient dance rituals persist in Africa's Coptic churches and in Spain's cathedrals; while stage performers enact Stravinsky's *Rite of Spring* as a spectacle, a few devotees have tried to reinstate dancing in Christian churches, particularly in the United States where a number of Sacred Dance Guilds have interpreted biblical themes in dignified movements.

Therapeutic dances survive here and there within urban culture. Inside the industrial pattern they may help the mentally ill, the problem child, and the worker on an assembly line. Many experts believe that this ancient healing function of dance has considerable potentialities for exploitation in the future.

Dance of Death
In dances of death, people reflect their attitude towards this final, catastrophic crisis in human life. Some people have regarded death with horror and they have feared the ghosts of the dead. Some express their grief in mournful ceremonies. Others try to cheer each other and the departed spirit by dance and song. Others again consider death a transfiguration, a door to another, better life. Similarly, the celebrations take many forms; impersonations of the image of death, imageless homage to the deceased, or joyous folk dancing.

Death was often personified as a grotesque skeleton, as in the medieval European Dance of Death. This is best known through frescoes and woodcuts, but it had a foundation in actual miming

dances. Death in the form of a skeleton capered in turn with sinners of all classes and ages, cardinal, labourer, child. This dance was an expression of the medieval horror of death, despite the Church's promises of a better afterlife. Clown-skeletons still cavort in ecclesiastical celebrations descended from the Middle Ages. In Catalonia, Spain, skeleton figures dance during religious holidays, notably Carnival and Holy Week, sometimes at Corpus Christi. In the *danza macabra* or *bal de la mort* of the Ampurdan area of Spain, a quadrille of skeletons carries a scythe, clock and banner. In Mexican *carnavales* Death is a horrid clown, armed with a pitchfork, descended from the Spanish impersonations.

The burial wake is another common manifestation. A motif of cheer and consolation pervades Spanish wakes. The mourners dance a lively *jota* or *canario*. Catholicism has introduced the word 'angelitos' (little angels) for the spirits of recently deceased children. Mourners celebrate wakes with a *baraban* or *lucia* in Sicily and Tuscany, and with a jig in Ireland. Negro wakes in South Carolina work up to a frenzied pitch of dance and song. Food and liquor contribute to the festivity of these wakes.

Banishing the Dead
Another form which the celebration may take is the release or exorcism of the spirits, motivated by fear of their evil potentialities as well as by affection. American Indians of many tribes perform a series of funerary and anniversary rites. The California Luiseno banished the spirit from his familiar haunts with the *tuvish* and *chuchamish* (wake), and in memorials for all the dead of the past year or several years. They imitated the character of the dead persons in the *yunish matackish*. They burned images in the *tauchanish*. Similarly, until recently, the Yuma tribe in the Mohave desert burned rush images in a circular dance and a cremation ritual termed *keruk*. The Tarahumara Indians of Chihuahua, Mexico, perform a *rutuburi* circle dance and a special death dance around their belongings, during a three-week fiesta. After a year they perform other dances – the *yumari* and *pascol*. The Yaqui tribe of Sonora, Mexico holds a fiesta and dance at the wake of a child, similar to a Catalan wake. They hold a special *matachina* dance or a *chapayekas* dance for members of these ceremonial societies. Another ritual finally releases the spirit.

Though ghosts are not feared quite as much among the Iroquois of New York State and Canada, these people do believe in them and make efforts to allay them. In case of a violent death, they dispatch a priest for prayers at the site of the murder. After four nights they sing for the release of the spirit and to aid its trip to the other world. After ten days they reinforce this supplication through song and dance. In the winter women chant and circle in the *ohgiwe* for their ancestors, with drum accompaniment. The assembly concludes with a feast and gay round dances.

Chinese and Japanese Buddhists cele-

Couple dances, with women partnering men, are rare in many parts of the world: men traditionally dance for victory in war, women for peace. 18th century Turkish miniature from the Topkapi Library, Istanbul.

brate the Feast of Lanterns as memorials to their ancestors. Japanese villagers, especially in Asage, circle counter-clockwise in the *Bon Odori*, during mid-July or in August, in connection with harvest celebrations. Men and women sing as they gesture or clap their hands; sometimes they also have a musical accompaniment.

In some instances there may be a fusion of the concept of death and resurrection. Boys' puberty rites may enact the symbolic death of the initiates and their rebirth to a new status. Funeral rites of antiquity often included the hope of resurrection. The high kicks of Egyptian female mourners symbolized new life. The Egyptian Osiris rituals and the Greek spring festival for Dionysus mimed the death and final resurrection of the deity. Babylonians and Romans had similar customs. In the Middle Ages funeral dances symbolized resurrection by a kiss between male and female performers, with the anticipation of new life. The Hungarian *Gyas Tanc* perpetuates this concept.

Relics in modern children's games of many countries form yet another manifestation. English and American children preserve the actions and song words of ancient funeral rites, as in *Old Roger is Dead, Jenny Jones* and *Green Gravel*. In their Hallowe'en masks and pranks small children perpetuate All Soul's ceremonies for the return of the spirits and propitiatory food offerings.

Impersonations of death are also found in modern art dances. Two German choreographers visualized death as an ugly thing. In *Totenmahl* or *Feast for the Dead* (1929), Mary Wigman masked her group in white, cadaverous faces, as homage to the dead of the First World War. In his *Green Table* (1933), Kurt Jooss envisaged the figure of death in wartime as a skeleton resembling the great reaper of the Middle Ages. A few years later, in 1937, the American, José Limon, created his *Danza de la Muerte* and Andrée Howard produced *Death and the Maiden* to Schubert's music for the English Ballet Rambert. These modern spectacles echo the anxieties of folk laments.

Dancing Mania

There appeared on the streets of Aachen (Aix-la-Chapelle) in Germany, in July 1374, a body of men and women, belonging almost entirely to the poorer classes, who began to exhibit the signs of an alarming disorder. Its symptoms were convulsive running, leaping and dancing, frequently accompanied by elaborate hallucinations, and those so affected seemed powerless to stop themselves; indeed, attacks could be

The *Dance of Death*, an allegorical representation of Death leading all men and women inevitably to the grave was a popular theme in late medieval art: these illustrations from Holbein's series of woodcuts on the subject show Death as a grotesque skeleton who appears to various people and is finally himself engulfed by men and women who have already died.

terminated only by forcible binding, or by the onset of utter physical exhaustion. No one seemed to know how the outbreak started, though we hear of the 'dancers' as having come 'out of Germany' and that they were popularly known as 'St John's Dancers'.

It is this name which provides a clue to the possible origins of the phenomenon. Already in the early Church, the Feast of St John the Baptist had been placed at Midsummer – incidentally, the only example in the Church Calendar of a saint celebrated on the day of his birth, rather than of his death; according to St Luke he was born six months before Jesus. It is common knowledge that in pre-Christian Europe, and elsewhere, Midsummer was a time of celebration, in which dancing, processions and the lighting of fires played their part. These elements were, it seems, transferred bodily to the Festival of St John the Baptist – a measure of which the Saint is unlikely to have approved. It is not known for certain but it appears at least likely that the dancing mania began with the celebration of a semi-Christian Midsummer in 1374. Memories of the Black Death were still strong; there was a widespread sense of fear and insecurity; and the result was a form of mass hysteria which spread with startling rapidity. Within a very short time dancing mania was reported from the streets and churches of Liège in Belgium, from Utrecht in Holland and many other towns and cities.

Predictably the phenomenon was officially attributed to evil spirits, and recourse was made to chapels of St John for the purposes of exorcism; this strengthened the connection with the saint under whose auspices the dancing had begun, though occasionally the issue became confused by the introduction of St John the Apostle in his place. The common people, too, were convinced that demons were at work but accounted for this by the theory that the persons affected had been invalidly baptized by priests living in concubinage, which added an unpleasant moral and theological dimension to the problem.

Although each separate outbreak came to an end in a few weeks, sporadic instances of the dancing mania continued for the remainder of the 14th century. The next serious wave occurred at Strasbourg in 1418. By this time the original link with St John the Baptist had been forgotten, and those afflicted were taken instead to the chapels of St Vitus (an obscure 4th century Christian saint who had long been thought – although for no clearly apparent reason – to protect sufferers from convulsive diseases) to be cured.

Again, the saint's day was closely connected with the celebration of Midsummer. The name 'St Vitus's Dance', *Veitstanz*, was applied to this new outbreak, the symptoms of which were identical with previous epidemics; this name has survived to this day as a popular name for convulsive chorea.

Dance of the Spider

These outbreaks of dancing mania in 1374 and 1418 are the best-known, but there is ample evidence to show that the disease itself had appeared earlier; there are records of similar visitations in 1237 at Erfurt in Germany and in 1278 at Utrecht, for example. It continued, though on a smaller scale, well on into the 17th century. In Italy, for instance, an almost identical disease, known as Tarantism, was popularly believed to be caused by the bite of the tarantula spider.

Dancing mania was basically a contagious form of hysteria, brought on in a situation of peculiar stress. It was largely psychological in origin, though it was not without its physical causes, such as undernourishment. As an expression of European life in the Middle Ages, its imagery was that of Christianity, though distorted.

In Scotland, three men and four women were burned at the stake at Paisley on 10 June 1697 for the crime of witchcraft, and it seems from the evidence that they were sufferers from some form of chorea. Many of the symptoms exhibited by the Convulsionaries of 18th century France, and in connection with Methodist and other Christian revival movements in Britain and America in the 18th and 19th centuries, were substantially those of the dancing mania, though not known by that name. Other parallel manifestations, ranging from the medieval Flagellants to the more recent Holy Rollers, might also be cited.

Drama

Man is a natural mimic and among the earliest evidences of magical imitation are the representations of animals in the cave art of the Old Stone Age. Our ancestors may have made these drawings to amuse themselves but many anthropologists have concluded that their work had a purpose and was a form of magic for good hunting and bountiful animal life. The idea of imitating in order to acquire was continued in the New Stone Age when man had discovered how to grow crops and vary his food supply. The first farmers believed that they could give a hint to the powers of Nature; accordingly when rain was needed they poured water out of a pail, mimicking a downpour in the hope of getting one. One of the origins of drama, therefore, can be said to lie in imitative magic.

Another procedure intended to encourage Nature by imitation was to leap in the air beside the growing grain, with the expectation that it would spring up in fullness and plenty. Here was a game of 'let's pretend', the game which children have never stopped playing. Adults also have continued to delight in pretending to be someone else and have never ceased to enjoy impersonation. In a modern society, we watch 'let's pretend' performances increasingly, because the means of presenting them are so many and so convenient, in cinema and television studios as well as in theatres. There has been continuity of mimicry down the centuries since the relish of pretending is inexhaustible.

Born of Fertility Rites

What has changed has been the purpose of imitation. The mimicry which began as magic has expanded into a huge and money-making entertainment industry. The earliest plays were the progeny of fertility rituals. Life and more life were its objectives. It is worth remembering that recreation did not originally mean 'fun and games'; it meant being re-made and born again.

It is a commonplace that conflict is the essence of drama. The first drama, which developed from routines of song and dance, presented a battle of life and death. If a tribal hero or god was shown to be slain he had also to be resurrected. He was not only a human hero. He might symbolize the death of winter and the resurgence of spring and summer; he might be the corn spirit which was hoped to be indestructible. But there were doubts and fears of pestilence attacking man and soil. So Nature had to be helped and encouraged and man, fearful of extinction, had to be comforted. (Com-

The Katha Kali dance dramas of India are enactments of sacred myths, tales of Krishna, Shiva and legendary heroes and demons. Before a performance actors meditate on the gods whose parts they will play: the central figure in this scene is the monkey god Hanuman.

plays were first written they were part of an annual religious festival, a competitive occasion with prizes awarded, and a ritualistic and traditional one, in so far as the priests of Dionysus were the judges and performances were limited to a holy week. Significantly, the principal time of continual play-going, with a day-long succession of performances, was in the spring.

The drama was still concerned with the gods of traditional mythology although it is probable that these had dwindled to little more than a literary convention by this time. The real faith of the citizens who went to the plays and were not sceptics was in the mysteries of Eleusis about which there had to be silence. The word mystery came from a Greek word for sealing the lips; it described rituals which must remain secret.

'Goat-Song' and 'Revel-Song'

In primitive religions animals, especially the bull and the goat, play a prominent part as the embodiments of physical and sexual energy. Those who now talk of tragedy are rarely conscious that this term meant 'goat-song' to the Greeks, who believed that the origin of tragedy was a tumultuous chant and dance routine in which, as the word implies, the celebrants were seen as half-bestial. When the great dramatic festival was being held in Athens the tragedies in groups of three were followed by the light relief of a satyric play. The satyrs were the semi-human, semi-divine spirits of untamed country, sometimes partly goatish, sometimes partly horse-like. A typical figure was the hairy Silenus, who was shown in pictures seated on a wine-skin.

The Greek word comedy meant a revel-song. Tragedy developed when one individual, who came to be known as Thespis (hence the name Thespians for actors) stood out from the choric goat-song. He spoke what we call a part, and then was followed by others who thus created the rudiments of a play. Comedy began as a riotous celebration of human fertility and was turned into an art when texts were written. But when the genius of Aristophanes (c 450– c 388 BC), the Athenian master of comic wit, was at its height, the original antics were not forgotten. The players wore the phallus. Perhaps that was a piece of routine which was taken for granted, like the hump-back of Mr Punch. But there remained on public view this reminder of the old caperings. *Caper* is Latin for a goat and so that animal survives today in one of our words for a frolic.

The coming of Christianity to Europe diminished dramatic performances but could not kill the impulse for a ritual release from normal canons of behaviour or the fascination of 'let's pretend'. The coming of the New Year was a natural occasion for rejoicing because the shortest

fort, like recreation, is a word which has been softened; it first meant strengthening, as in the Christian description of the Holy Ghost as the Comforter.) Thus performances were arranged to show the defeat of winter and death, and the triumph of life.

The first play of which anything is known was enacted at Abydos in ancient Egypt nearly 4000 years ago during the reign of Sesostris III (1887–1849 BC). In it the deity of life, Osiris, was defeated and killed by Seth, the demon of death. Osiris came back to life. He was impersonated in his resurrection with ears of corn springing from his body. When he rose from the dead here were the tokens, for all to see, of unbeaten vitality and fruitfulness.

The Greek historian Herodotus identified the life-giving Osiris with the god-hero of his own people, Dionysus. Dionysus was long associated with the acted drama, which the later Greek poets, especially in Athens, transformed from crude ritual songs and dances in honour of this god into written plays of high artistry and sophistication. They composed tragedies of literary splendour and comedies which mingled buffoonery with wit and topical satire, but the singing and dancing of the chorus remained. In the comedies there were still the relics of the old lusty revelling and the wearing of the phallic symbol of fertility. The texts have survived as classics to be studied and sometimes revived. When the day had passed. The Romans had their midwinter Saturnalia, with its topsyturvy festivities, and so strong was the impulse to celebrate the death of the Old Year and the coming of another season of ploughing, sowing, and eventually reaping, that the Christian Church had to accept a season of wild and even anarchic rejoicing. While the new religion celebrated its Christmas, the feast had to include some of the old pagan rites and liberties. At the Feast of Fools, first heard of in France in the 12th century AD, an Abbot or Lord of Misrule was appointed to preside over the astonishing proceedings, which were not confined to France and had some English replicas. The Saturnalian spirit could not be suppressed.

The Bessy and the Fool

The junior clergy behaved as though they were seniors. There was drinking and turbulence; there was even sacrilege with a mock Mass and priests playing dice on the altar. There was interchange of garments; men were disguised as women and women as men. There was a curious survival of the goat-song and its mummery since some revellers put on animal skins and paraded with frisking and antics through the streets. The force of tradition in this game of 'let's pretend' is shown even today in the English midwinter pantomime. In it the part of the principal boy was, and often still is, played by a girl, and a horse or cow is represented by two men concealed under an animal's hide. Ritual is continually found to have an extraordinary power of survival in the theatre as elsewhere.

The farmers all over Europe celebrated Plough Monday, the Monday after Twelfth Day early in January, with mummery. It was the day on which, if the weather was favourable, the turning of the soil began. The young men who drove a ceremonial plough painted their faces and had grotesque attendants: the Bessy, a man dressed as a woman, and the Fool, who wore an animal skin, a hairy cap and an animal's tail. An important feature of the Plough Monday rites was the driving out with brooms of supposed ghosts. There is an afterthought of that old magical practice in Shakespeare's *A Midsummer Night's Dream* in which the elfin Puck, endowed with magical powers, ends the play as a sweeper with a broom in his hand. The dramatist

Above In the modern world the dance has become increasingly secularized, as in ballroom dancing, but folk dancing even as a stage or tourist attraction retains many of the characteristics and much of the appeal of its ritual past, when it was a vital part of the community's life: Russian dancers in traditional costume.

Centre The symbolism of a dance is heightened, and it comes closest to its original ritual function, when music or rhythm is provided by only one type of instrument: children at Kabul, Afghanistan, dance to the sound of tambourines.

Below According to Hindu belief the god Shiva set the world in motion with a dance, and dancing is an intrinsic and highly formalized part of life in India: Orissa dancers in Delhi.

Peter Larsen

Camera Press London

Camera Press London

Mansell Collection

Photographie Bulloz

was likely to have seen the mummeries of January and June in his native Warwickshire.

Civic Charades
He could also have seen similar performances on May Day when, in the fullness of blossomy spring, there was good reason to implement the fertility ceremonial of the New Year. There was clowning, singing and dancing round the hoisted and decorated Maypole which began either as a tree-symbol of shooting upwards, or a permitted survival of the ancient comedian's phallus. The animal-cult came into the May Day caperings with the riding of the hobby horse.

Out of such seasonal masquerades and miming eventually came the planned and scripted performances of the earliest theatre, such as the pageants and mystery plays of the Middle Ages, in which paganism was replaced by Christian legends and devotion. These were amateur performances and free-for-all spectacles. The members of the craft guilds enacted biblical stories on wagons drawn through the towns, or in or outside churches. They were devised with simple texts and with no inhibitions about introducing comedy into sacred subjects. The title of the mystery plays was taken from the Latin *ministerium* meaning 'a service', and has no connection with the 'sealed lips' mysteries of the classical world. In these civic charades of the English cathedral cities the connection with magic was severed. They were works of faith, not of superstition. The Reformation struck a fatal blow at them, as at all forms of community drama. To the Puritans any kind of 'let's pretend' was an abomination. In their opinion, to impersonate another was to act a lie, and therefore sinful. The theatre was described as Satan's workshop, in which vice and vanity were mingled.

As the professional theatre developed during the 16th century the Puritans did their utmost to kill it but failed because the

The Athenian poets transformed acted dramas from fertility rituals into highly sophisticated written plays which were originally performed as part of an annual festival that was held in honour of the god Dionysus; the masks traditionally worn by the actors in classical dramas gave them a superhuman appearance that was in keeping with their roles as participants in a sacred ritual.

Above A Greek actor in his dressing room with the masks of a young man, a maiden and an angry father: Roman terracotta panel, copy of a Greek relief, now in the Lateran Museum, Rome.

Right A Roman statuette possibly of an elderly female character, made from ivory and dated about 2nd century AD: from the Musée du Petit Palais.

Queen and the noblemen, as well as many of the common people, enjoyed it. To this the great dramatists of the period owed their careers and English literature some of its finest poetry. The plays and players contributed a magic of their own, that of word-music and the spell of language used at its highest power. There was the magic, too, of the actor's personality and skill in presenting a wide range of characters in tragedy and comedy. The Clowns and Fools in the plays carried on the practice of the old Dionysian revels; they were bawdy celebrants of sex. The Puritans raged and the public were delighted.

The Folk Plays of Europe
None the less the old spirit of pagan mummery was not crushed. It lived on in the rustic folk plays which were performed, chiefly in midwinter, by the country people and were still to be seen in the 19th century. These maintained the primitive belief that a performance must contain a death and a resurrection. They were thus in direct descent from the drama of the Greeks and even of ancient Egypt. The battle of Seth and Osiris was long continued in the farmhouses of many European countries and

there are a number of the simple texts preserved. The characters were given various names in various places but the essential part of the story was much the same. There had to be a contest, a killing, and a life-giving cure.

Sir Edmund Chambers made a careful and most interesting survey of scripts collected from near and far. There were many variations of detail, but the normal performance had permanent characters and episodes. The mummers, sometimes called guisers, arrived and demanded entry at a house where there was a Christmas party with dancing and singing; this sometimes took place at Easter as well. Their leader, known as the Presenter, asked for the room

Above Passion Plays, the enactment of Christ's sufferings and his death on the cross, developed in Europe in the Middle Ages: scene from the famous Passion Play at Oberammergau, a village in Bavaria. In 1633 the inhabitants vowed that they would perform this drama every ten years, in gratitude for deliverance from the plague, and this tradition has attracted many tourists to the mountain village.

to be cleared and then explained in rhyme that the hero was St George who 'fought the fiery dragon, drove him to the slaughter, and by these means had won the King of Egypt's daughter.' To him entered Slasher, the Turkish knight, challenging St George to combat. They bandied words: 'One shall die and the other shall live.' From words they proceeded to sword-play. Usually the Turk was killed, sometimes St George. In either case the Presenter cried for a doctor and the doctor arrived with his magic bottle containing a herbal medicine. 'The stuff therein is elecampane. It will bring the dead to life again.' The dose had its miraculous effect. Then the clowns came in with songs and capers. Typical drolls were called Big Head, Beelzebub, Little Johnny Jack and Devil Doubt, who carried a broom.

If you don't give me money, I'll sweep you out.
Money I want and money I crave.
If you don't give me money, I'll sweep you to the grave.

The players were labourers with very low wages and were grateful for the smallest tip

and a drink of any size. A typical guising was described by Thomas Hardy, doubtless from youthful memories of Dorset, in his novel *The Return of the Native*. The Presenter in that case was disguised as Father Christmas.

Research has shown that all the elements of primitive mummery and fertility rites were brought in. The performers in some places blacked or coloured their faces. Being poor, they had to improvise their costumes and weapons and there was much use of coloured ribbons. There was the ritual broom. There was occasional use of animal skins for the players of comic parts. There was even mention of Egypt since St George had strangely gone to the land of Osiris for his bride. The main event was always the fight between the hero and the villain with its killing and reviving by the wonder-working doctor.

The folk play has been traced from the north of Scotland through Yorkshire to the south of England and across Europe to Bulgaria. There were differences in names and local allusions but all emerged from the universal feeling that midwinter demanded a recognition of light, warmth and growth to come.

Inevitably when the drama went to town and the playwright became a poet instead of a rustic rhymer the celebration of agricultural needs was forgotten. Play-making had begun as a mimetic form of prayer and became an art and a secular entertainment.

But the pantomime survives with some of the old ingredients. Its plot is a myth, and its staging asks for magical effects. It draws on the archaic tradition while it reappears with songs and jokes of the present.

Folk Plays

Two seasonal peaks, the summer and winter festivals, stand out prominently in the British calendar of folk customs. The summer customs stretch from Easter to harvest time, while winter covers customs from Michaelmas to Ash Wednesday.

Central to the summer group are the May Games and the Tree of Life, a term used to include both Maypole and Cross. The main feature of the winter group is the life-cycle, a dramatic portrayal of the death and resurrection of Nature as experienced at the turn of the year in Europe. This folk-play survives as fragments of a festival which must reach right back into Neolithic times. In the British Isles, it is known under a variety of names, the most common being the Christmas Mummers; these are play actors, local village folk, who disguise themselves by wearing masks or by blacking their faces with soot. They are known as guisers or guizards in the North of England, Geesers or Geese dancers in Cornwall. In some localities, the players appear at Easter and are called Pace-Eggers, or at Hallowe'en or All Souls Eve, when they are known as Soul Cakers. In the Isle of Man the actors are the White Boys and in Scot-

The Christmas mummers' play is a dramatic portrayal of the death and resurrection of Nature as experienced at the turn of each year: the sacrificial victim is restored to life in this scene from the Bampton Mummers.

land the Galatians. Many of the plays revolve round St George and his hand-to-hand combat with such adversaries as the Turkish Knight, the Black Prince of Paradise and Bold Slasher.

Another set of folkplays portrays the life-cycle from another angle and with a different set of characters. Since these plays are acted on Plough Monday and include a courting or marriage scene, they are called Plough Plays or Wooing Plays. They have also been found as an integral part of the elaborate sword dances in the North of England. Irrespective of type all these plays depict the life-cycle and symbolize the continuing vitality and fertility of Nature.

Although Christmas mumming as a widespread village custom has largely died out in Britain, it survives overseas in the West Indies, Newfoundland and in those parts of North America where the English traditions have been carried on by settlers. Often the mumming is little beyond the disguising of faces and dressing up in garments of the opposite sex, wearing masks, or blackening the face with soot and visiting neighbours' homes to dance and sing. If a masquerader should by mischance be recognized, this is everywhere regarded as bad luck.

Central to the plot is the death by combat, or ritual murder, of a hero at the hands of antagonists. This sacrificial death is lamented and is followed by a cure or resurrection, and the mystery of life is celebrated in song and dance. The following outline of a Christmas mummers' play performed and recorded at Symondsbury in West Dorset recently, is more elaborate than most versions and contains features not often found associated in any single version.

There are four separate scenes: the exploits of St George, Tommy the Pony (a three-legged hobby-horse), a rough wooing and the 'singing of the travels'. The actors, all men, are disguised, St George and the 'Champions' wearing tall hats with paper streamers or ribbons hanging over the faces, except for Jan, the husbandman, dressed in a smock and Bet, his wife, in long-skirted dress and bonnet. Jan carries a club made out of a young crab-apple tree. Jan enters further disguised as Father Christmas to act as 'Presenter' and to prepare the way. He then introduces the next character whom he calls 'Room'; this is an accretion for normally the Presenter himself will say 'make room'. Introducing himself, Room goes on to tell of how St George in his travels met and married the King of Egypt's daughter. He then calls in the King of Egypt, who in turn summons St George. The latter boasts of his deeds and during his vaunting, one of his friends, St Patrick, enters. He offers to help St George to fight his battles and kills the first of the antagonists, Captain Bluster, who then retires back-stage to kneel on one knee leaning on his sword. The next antagonist reels in somewhat drunk, is slain by St George and joins Captain Bluster. The third adversary enters, is slain by St George and joins the other two victims while St George, wiping his blade, calls on Colonel Spring. St George at once repeats his success, but Colonel Spring, after kneeling 'dead' beside the other three, suddenly rises to fight again before he is finally killed. The two victorious champions St George and St Patrick then express deep sorrow, lamenting for the dead men's wives and children. After discussing the merits of various doctors they call on a doctor who appears dressed in silk hat and morning coat. He talks of his travels and his skill, bargaining for a large fee before he gives his services. St George hands him a bag of money. Boasting and showing off he produces his bottle of medicine, elecampane, which cures 'all sorts' and after giving a drop to each of the four kneeling victims in turn, restores and dismisses them.

Fortune Telling Horse

In the second scene Bet enters leading in Tommy the Pony; the mummer, completely covered with a cloth, leans forward on a pole which protrudes from the cloth and is surmounted by a wooden horse's head. Bet mounts the back of Tommy and is riding him cleverly when Jan enters; she challenges him to ride Tommy. Jan accepts but is at once thrown by the hobby-horse. In a fury, Jan picks up his club and fells Tommy to the ground. Bet laments the death of her pony and persuades Jan to help her to revive it. They 'lay on hands', first blowing on them to warm them and swinging their

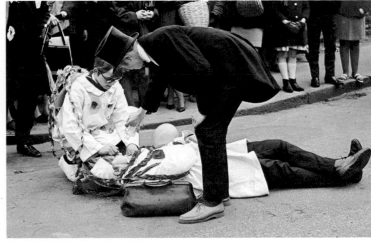

arms to make the blood flow. They try to lift Tommy up but he falls down again. Defeated they call on the Champions who march in and set the horse back on his three legs. Bet now announces that her pony tells fortunes and asks Tommy to smell out certain evil-doers; the hobby horse picks out several innocent victims, to the delight of the spectators.

The third scene opens with Jan and Bet quarrelling. Jan knocks down Bet who lies as if dead. After much rude fooling, she is revived by the Doctor, and in the next scene Jan and Bet and the Pony form a family group. The other mummers march round the group once clockwise and once anti-clockwise singing a version of the folk song *The Serving Man and the Husbandman*. At the end of each round the singers stand facing centre while Jan in reply speaks his verse rejecting the life of luxury and ease enjoyed by the serving man. At once the ring of mummers repeat their round dance, singing the verses for Jan to speak his unqualified rejection, each time seconded warmly by Bet. The Doctor makes a final speech inviting the mistress of the house to tie a piece of ribbon upon the Christmas holly bough, when on behalf of the mummers he wishes her and everyone there a happy Christmas.

The fundamental features of this type of play are the 'making of room' which may include a sweeper or whiffler to clear the space for the mystery drama; the 'calling on' or introduction by the Presenter of the combatants and other actors in turn; the dispute leading to death; the lament; the call for the Doctor; the cure and the quete or collection of the reward, important because by contributing to the collection the spectators become participators and so able to share in any benefits from the magic luck.

The other type of folkplay, the Plough Plays, belong, broadly speaking, to the Christmas season; they were performed usually in January, on the first Monday after Epiphany. The performers call themselves Plough Jacks, Plough Scots, Boggons or even Morris Dancers. Their leader is not St George but a 'Fool' accompanied by a man in woman's clothes called Bessy or Betty. There is some sort of conflict with a death and revival but there is also a wooing in which the Fool vies with his eldest son for the hand of the 'Fair Lady'. There is con-

fusion and overlapping of incidents in the two types of play. St George may appear in the Plough Play and challenge and kill the Fool who is then revived by the Doctor. The Fool then courts and marries the 'Lady'. The Fool's wooing may be found without either the combat or the cure. Some of the dialogue has obviously been borrowed from printed sources which would suggest some contact between strolling professional actors and local folk mummers.

There are many European variants of the Masquerade, some leaning toward the popular carnival festivals, some preserving an intensely individual tradition as in the Basque festivals of the *Mascarades* and the *Pastourelles*. One primitive surviving custom is the '*Poklade*' the pre-Lenten 'Play' of the Adriatic coast of Yugoslavia performed on the two days before Ash Wednesday. In this custom there are three chief actors, a Fool, a Priest and a Baba or Witch. They are served by a retinue of a score of dancers in two contingents, ten men dressed as girls and ten girls dressed as men who dance alone and together. The three characters carry bags of soot and ashes which they throw over themselves and at the spectators when they are not fooling about.

In the case of the Rumanian version of the folkplay the action takes place within the hilt and point circle of sword dancers who never cease to 'step' while the play lasts. Here the hand-to-hand combat is between a Turk and a Russian. The latter is slain and an 'Orthodox Priest' attempts but fails to revive him. One more parallel may be mentioned from the village of Haghios Gheorgios in Thrace, where a festival is kept two days before Ash Wednesday. The leading actors are two 'gypsies', who must be married men, wearing head-dresses of animal skin brought down over the faces to form masks. Their shoulders are so heavily padded as to make them humpbacked. Their hands are blackened and they wear sheep-bells round their waists. One carries a cross-bow made to shoot ashes from a horn and the other a phallus. With them are two unmarried boys dressed as their wives. An old woman, the Babo, carries a basket with a doll to represent a bastard baby. More gypsies with blackened hands carrying rods, whips and swords and a bagpiper complete the troop.

Left Scene from the Midgley Pace-Egg play performed on Good Friday: central to the plot of the folkplay is the death by combat, or ritual murder, of a hero at the hands of antagonists.

Above His death is lamented and the doctor is called upon to effect a cure or resurrection: scene from the Brighouse Pace-Egg play performed on Easter Saturday.

In the play proper, the first scene shows a gypsy man and wife sitting down forging a ploughshare. Then Babo cries that her bastard is too big for the basket and he becomes the Phallus-bearer and marries one of the Brides. The second scene shows the Cross-bow bearer stalking the Phallus-bearer whom he shoots. There is a lamentation and suddenly the victim comes to life. The forging of the plough is continued and a complete plough is then brought on drawn by the 'girls' while the blackfaced gypsies drive it. Later the two masked humpbacked gypsies are beaten with rods.

Actors of Prehistory

Further comparison of these Balkan folkplays emphasizes their close resemblance to some of the British examples. Were it not for the European analogues it might well have been assumed that the St George Mummers Play and the Plough Play were mere rustic echoes of the strolling theatrical companies familiar to country folk since Tudor days. Theatrical plays have been written round the legend of St George since the 16th century but it seems certain that the folkplays in origin long antedate any such dramatic invention and that it has been an integral part of country life familiar as an old tradition to Shakespeare and to playwrights long before his time.

The portrayal of the life-cycle with birth, death and resurrection is pre-Christian and probably pre-civilization. The principal actors can be traced back through recorded history to prehistory.

Thus the folkplay in its various forms may be regarded as a starting point for investigation into mythology, drama and religion as well as more homely institutions such as Punch and Judy, the Pantomime and the Harlequinade. Indeed one can take any of the folkplay characters and embark on a voyage of surprising discovery.

Masks: Hidden Identity

In primitive societies of today, masks are used mainly for ritual purposes. The assumed appearance is held to affect the wearer's inner nature and to assimilate it to that of the being represented by the mask. Thus a masked person is not simply a man or woman whose real identity is hidden, but he is an enigmatic entity standing outside the sphere of ordinary conduct and enjoying a freedom of movement and expression denied to ordinary men. As he has submerged his own identity by the wearing of a mask, other beings, such as an ancestor, a spirit or a totem-animal, are enabled to manifest themselves in his body and voice.

The material shapes of masks are of infinite variety. A moulded or carved surface representing the anterior half of the head and usually worn over the face of a person may be made of wood, metal, cloth, leather, clay or, in rare cases, even stone. A special type of mask, occurring in Melanesia, consists of part of a human skull combined with other materials to form a complete covering for the wearer's head and face. The transforming effect of a mask may also be achieved by applying thick layers of paste or paint to the face of a person, to which feathers and similar materials are then attached. Such mask-like disguises, usually combined with the painting of the entire

body, occurred among Australian aboriginals and among the Fuegians of South America. In a highly-developed artistic form the practice of building up a mask on a human face, is used by the Katha-Kali dancers of south-west India.

The mask in the narrow sense, which covers the face of the wearer, usually forms only part of the disguise. Elaborate costumes, often of fantastic type, complete the attire disguising a person's normal appearance. Where masks represent supernatural beings, such as gods or ancestor spirits, the illusion of superhuman height is achieved by a structure supporting an artificial head and face, which surmounts the real head of the dancer or actor. A similar effect is achieved by fitting the wearer with stilts, which are often covered by long flowing garments. The great dance masks of Melanesia are enormous structures made of bark cloth stretched over bamboo and cane frames, which are carried by one or more dancers. Such masks are intended to impress and fill with awe the uninitiated who are made to believe that divinities and ancestor spirits manifest themselves in these gigantic structures. To achieve this deception it is essential that the human wearers of the masks are completely hidden and unrecognizable.

Repository of Sacred Power

According to their function masks can be divided into two categories, the religious and the profane; the former category, comprising a large number of sub-types, predominates in pre-literate societies as well as in several historic civilizations. Among the most striking and spectacular masks are those worn by dancers in the ritual performances of various West African tribes. The Dogon of the western Sudan commemorate the death of their first tribal ancestor by ceremonies which involve the use of a series of masks of different degrees of sanctity and of varying appearance. The vertical wooden rectangle of these helmet-type masks, sur-

Some masks are surrounded by taboos and, though made by human beings, are believed to have their own individual existence, independent of the craftsmen who shaped them and the dancers who wear them: sometimes it is said that these masks are not 'made' but 'discovered'. Wearing a mask, frequently with an elaborate costume as well, is a way of concealing and submerging your own personality and identifying yourself with a spirit or other supernatural character in dance or drama.

Opposite above left A Nigerian dancer wearing a mask which bestows anonymity.

Opposite above right A masked figure arrives at a May Day celebration in Somerset, calling himself 'Gulliver'.

Opposite below Tibetan mask of a fierce protective spirit.

Below Devil mask from the Tyrol.

Tirolen Volkskunstmuseum Innsbruck

Camera Press London

Homer Sykes

William MacQuitty

mounted by upright carved animal ears, represents the main form and by its crude shape and the painting in white, black and red creates a dramatic effect; such masks are used in connection with initiation rites, burial and other ceremonies.

The task of carving these masks, which attract great magical powers, was considered highly dangerous and the woodcarvers protected themselves by observing many taboos and performing a series of propitiatory rites. They first offered a sacrifice to the greatest of all Dogon masks, which represents the deified original tribal ancestor. The making of the masks was a common enterprise of all the dancers, who assembled for the purpose outside the village. Only the fully initiated members of a secret society could with impunity approach the mask and vessel of the divine ancestor. Every 60 years they arranged for a solemn rite in the course of which the supreme ancestral mask was renewed. It is from this central mask, representing the tribal ancestor, that all the other masks derive the power to retain in themselves the imperishable life-force of the animal or departed person whom they symbolize. The transmission of this force is produced by sacred rites laid down by tradition.

Among other West African tribes, such as the Kono of Guinea, the carving of masks is equally surrounded by elaborate ceremonial. The grand master of the tribal initiation rites is the supreme guardian of all the masks. His function is hereditary, and he controls the wearers of the individual masks. Each of these receives special instructions as to how to minister to the needs of the mask of which he is in charge. He is thought of as the host of the mask and the spiritual essence dwelling in its shape.

Although the masks are fashioned by human hand, they are believed to have an individual existence, independent of the craftsmen who gave them their material shape and the dancers through whom they ultimately come to life. The myths speak always of the discovery of masks, and they are believed to have existed long before they came into the possession of men. In the mask resides the subtle spirit-substance which invests them with their latent power.

Personifying the Supernatural

In Melanesia, another area where ritual masks have been widely used, the masks were mainly associated with the cult of ancestors. In the islands of New Ireland, New Britain, the Solomons and most of the New Hebrides, this cult has largely succumbed to contact with European civilization, but in some parts of New Guinea it has retained its importance. In all these regions the masks, carved of wood or constructed of bark cloth, and sometimes more than 15 feet tall, were produced and guarded by the members of secret societies or men's organizations. Among the Papuans of south-west New Guinea masks are employed in the ritual of death. This ritual aims at expelling from the village the spirits of the dead who might endanger the living, in particular the spirits of those who fall victims to head-hunters. These spirits are personified in masked dancers, who should be kinsmen of the deceased. The manufacture of the masks very frequently extends over four to five months, and is surrounded by great mystery.

When the masks are completed they are stored in the ceremonial men's house until the day of the final rites. At that time the kinsmen of the recently deceased take the newly-made masks to the forest, and attach fresh green leaves to them and to their own bodies. Thus attired they emerge from the forest at dusk, and then dance for the whole night, imitating the movements of the cassowary, the bird associated with the sun. In the moment of sunrise, when the sun is believed to emerge from the land of the dead, the remaining men of the village attack the dancers and defeat them in a sham fight. Their victory symbolizes the successful struggle of the living over the dead. The dancers seek refuge in the house of ceremonies, and discard their masks. These are henceforth devoid of sanctity and ritual value.

In the Sepik region of New Guinea, masks carved with stone tools combined human with bird or animal elements. Their elongation and ambiguous animal forms give them an especially demonic and terrifying character. Some of these masks served in public harvest and initiation rites, others depicted the semi-supernatural founders of clans in ceremonies of a more secret nature. The uninitiated – women, children and strangers – were rigidly excluded from participating in these rites.

Masks representing supernatural beings, half-human and half-animal, occur also in other parts of the world, notably among the Indians of the north-west coast of America. Like many primitive peoples, these Indians believe that animals as well as humans are animated by souls and that the barrier between them is slight. Their sculptured masks depict strange creatures with human faces and animal horns, or beings combining the elements of men and birds. In the ceremonies of these Indians masks with moving parts played an important role. The carved and painted flaps of such masks were hinged; when closed they represented ravens and concealed the image of a human face. At an appropriate moment in the recounting of a legend the performer pulled open the flaps to reveal a transformation from animal to man.

The Eskimo carve wooden masks in the likeness of fish and various sea animals. These masks are not intended to represent the animals themselves, but to symbolize the numerous spirits associated with animals. Of a different order are the masks of shamans – priests and spirit-media – who establish contact between man and the world of supernatural beings. The shamans of the Eskimo have masks representing their guardian spirits, and they believe that by wearing these masks they establish a mystic link with the spirit concerned and induce a state of trance and possession. Other Eskimo masks depict a face which is half-human and half-animal, and they are used in rites and dances designed to propitiate the spirits of certain animals in order to prevent them from shunning man and depriving him of the animals that are necessary for his subsistence.

Different in function and shape are the death-masks used to cover the face of the dead before or after burial. Such masks made of gold, silver, bronze, terracotta or stone occurred in many ancient civilizations including those of Mesopotamia, Egypt, Greece, Italy, the Crimea, the Danube valley and parts of ancient France and Britain. Death-masks of precious metal covered the faces of the embalmed pharaohs, and from Egypt the custom spread to Syria and Mycene. The ancient Etruscans also buried their dead with masks of thin bronze. In Southeast Asia gold masks were regularly placed on the faces of dead kings of Cambodia and Siam, and the Shans of Burma used a metal mask to cover the face of a dead chief. In ancient Mexico masks, some made of jade and other semi-precious stones, were placed on the faces of prominent dead when the corpse was laid out in a grave chamber. They are without openings for mouth and eyes and represent faces of a great calm and beauty.

The Face of a God

In advanced civilizations masks have been mainly used in dramatic performances, both ritual and theatrical. One of the most notable examples of striking and elaborate masks are those worn by lama-dancers in Tibetan temple festivals. These masks, mainly of superhuman size, represent divinities, demons, spirits, historical personages and allegoric figures. They are usually carved of wood and painted in vivid colours. The masked dances are accompanied by the recitation of prayers and sacred texts.

The laymen see in the masked figures not so much lamas enacting gods and demons, but rather the mystic presence of the divinities and demons represented by the masks. In Tibet it was usual for the spectators to prostrate themselves before the masked figures of gods, and to solicit their blessing. The mystery play here assumes the character of an immediate interaction between man and supernatural powers.

Masked dances on the Indonesian island of Bali are also of ritual nature, but in other Asian countries, such as Sri Lanka, masks originally having religious importance are used in dramatic performances which are given for entertainment by professional dancers. Yet, masks are used there also in rites of exorcism and curing, and in these cases masks represent the disease spirits from which the patient is to be freed.

Where the mask has lost its religious significance it can still survive in a secular role. Typical of this development was the role it assumed in the theatre of ancient Greece. Originally animal masks had been used in the cult of Dionysus and Demeter, the Earth Mother. Later the mask found its way into both the comedies and the tragedies of the classical theatre, where it played an important role. The use of masks enabled actors to double and triple the number of parts they could play during

Singhalese dance mask with grotesque figures.

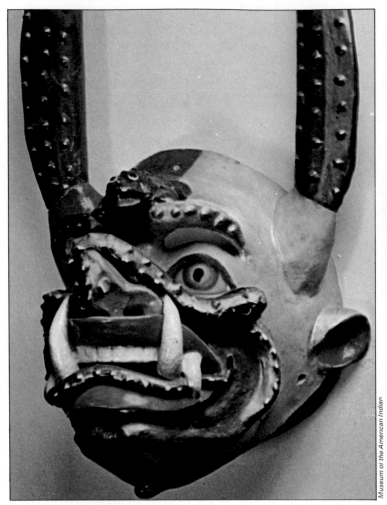

Museum of the American Indian

Put on a mask and you become a different person. In many primitive societies a mask is more than a means of changing your appearance; it is a link with the world of the spirits, a channel by which men can tap the force possessed by supernatural beings.

Above left Horned mask from Bolivia, used in the performance of a devil dance.

Above right Beaked mask from Indonesia.

any one performance, and male actors could convincingly play female roles.

Another example of the transference of the mask's function from the religious to the secular sphere occurs in Japan. There masks were originally widely used in religious ritual, and in the 8th century AD dancers in four-eyed masks were charged with the task of warding off demons from the royal palace. Later there developed the institution of court dancers, and out of this grew the classical drama of the *Noh* theatre, in which all actors appear in painted masks.

In Europe the use of ritual masks persists only in some folk customs observed in some remote valleys of Austria and Switzerland, where pagan practices have coexisted with Christianity in a reinterpreted form. The Carnival, celebrated widely in Europe and Latin America, provides an opportunity for the wearing of masks; that it is a survival of a pagan spring festival is forgotten.

Purpose Behind the Mask

Protection against supernatural dangers is a function of masks worn in certain ritual situations, such as at funerals to avoid

recognition by the souls of the dead. Conversely masks are sometimes worn to enhance a warrior's image and to terrify opponents, and this idea underlies the warmasks and use of war-paint among many primitive peoples. The warrior wearing a mask symbolizing a superior power identifies himself with this force and is thereby fortified. This identification is part of the nature of masks, and it assumes great importance where people wear masks representing gods and other supernatural beings.

Living Solid Face

Of all the masked gods the strangest and most engaging is that kindly, grotesque creation of the Delaware Indians which goes by the name of Misinghalikun – the Living Solid Face. When Egyptian priests appeared, as Apuleius pictured them, masked as Isis or Horus, they represented a deity that had his proper human form as well as his disguise as an animal. But the Living Solid Face is what it says it is – a mask, a living mask. When the Indians first saw Misinghalikun riding a buck, and herding the deer, it was simply a fir-clad figure with a wooden face, the right half red, the left black. Following a disaster, the Living Solid Face taught the Delawares to make a mask like his, and promised that when they wore it his spirit would go into it. Every year Misinghalikun appears at the ceremonies of the tribe, and on the third day sees them off upon a hunt, the twelfth night he dances in the Big House, where his face is carved upon twelve pillars. His mask, his black bearskin clothes, his turtle rattle, and his stick are kept by a family that burns tobacco

before it now and then. The Living Solid Face is a bit of a moralist at the Big House meeting, and, when a parent finds his child weak, sick or disobedient, Misinghalikun is ready to attend. But his main function is general beneficient guidance over the tribe and the hunt.

K. MacGowan and H. Rosse
Masks and Demons

Masks serve also as signs of distinction and classification. Thus all the ritual masks of men's societies have the function of emphasizing the position of the fully initiated members and in some societies distinctive masks are reserved for those who have achieved specific ranks.

The masks of such societies have also the function of concentrating power in the hands of those who are in charge of the sacred objects. Thus they are linked not only with the representation of power, but also with its exercise. The human guardian and wearer of the mask partakes of the power of the divinity or spirit which the mask symbolizes and is thereby elevated above the common mass of the uninitiated. The mask is thus a link with the supernatural world and a channel by which men can tap the force possessed by supernatural beings. Thus masks are and always were primarily means of transformation and identification with the entities of a nonmaterial sphere to which man has access only if he sheds his own identity and enters that of beings existing on a superior plane.

Games

Generally played for entertainment and recreation in the modern West, games have been recorded throughout history, and often reflected the social customs, and sometimes the religious beliefs, of the players. Some of the older games claim a legendary or mythical origin, and, because chance plays a large part in their attraction, divination, fortune telling and magical beliefs are in many cases associated with them.

Distinctions may be drawn between a sport such as archery, once of national importance and the more familiar ball games such as football and hockey. There are also games of chance played mainly with cards and dice, and board games such as chess.

Archery originated in the Stone Age, when small, delicately chipped arrow heads were used for hunting and in war; in Saxon England they were called 'elf darts' and were treasured as charms.

In ancient times arrows were widely regarded as mediums for divination and fortune telling. In Palestine, Chaldea and Arabia the usual method was to shake the quiver in front of an image of the god being addressed, and note which arrows, previously marked, fell out. When Nebuchadnezzar, King of Babylon, was unable to decide whether he should attack Jerusalem or Ammon, he used several methods of divination, one of which was the shaking of arrows (Ezekiel, chapter 21). Also in the Old Testament is the story of how the dying prophet Elisha laid his hands on those of Joash, King of Israel, as the latter shot 'the Lord's arrow of victory over Syria'. He then commanded the King to strike the arrows on the ground, and prophesied that Joash would overcome Syria in battle as many times as he had struck the ground (2 Kings, chapter 13).

In fairy tales the hero often shoots an arrow into the air and follows its path to fortune. Arrow heads are found buried under the foundations of buildings or built into the walls of houses or churches to protect them from evil influences, and they were at one time placed in stables to protect the animals from disease.

Wherever there is anything which may be used as a ball, there is a potential game; ball games have been played through the ages. The balls used may have been 'natural', such as pebbles, a block of wood or a lump of clay, or they may have been fashioned from wood, bone or ivory, made from plaited straw, or from strips of skin or fibres. A skin or woven cover may have been stuffed with hair, wool or other material, or inflated with air. Unfortunately all except those made of stone or bone were perishable, and there is little archeological evidence of their existence, although the remains of balls made from skin filled with grass or hay have been found in early Egyptian tombs.

Rubber balls were used in South America long before rubber was first brought to Europe; in North America red and yellow balls symbolized the sun, and ball games celebrated the conquest of day over night, and light over darkness.

Football is one of the most popular and possibly one of the most sophisticated games in the world today; but in its primitive form, needing nothing more than an object to kick and someone to kick it back, it has been an obvious form of game since unrecorded times. It is not mentioned by name until the 14th century, and then chiefly in prohibitions as, for instance, when Edward III told his sheriffs to suppress football as the game interfered with training in archery.

Medieval football was independent of grounds and of rules. The ball was placed in a neutral place, often the churchyard, and the villagers, perhaps a hundred to a side, hurled themselves on it, and attempted to carry it off to their base.

Games are often mysterious matters, closely linked with social and religious customs. In classical Greece dice were made from bones, and were originally instruments of divination; eventually this method of determining the wishes of the gods developed into a gambling game in which the winner was the player who received the best 'omen' when the dice were cast: Greek statuette in terracotta, 300 BC.

Peter Clayton

Traditionally the game was played on Shrove Tuesday when it symbolized the conquest of spring over winter. As a contest between married and unmarried men, the game appears to have been a relic of a fertility rite. Shrovetide football was also played vigorously by women as well as men until well into the 19th century, a custom that has continued into modern times.

In Chester, football was believed to commemorate kicking the head of a captured Dane; in Derby it was thought to celebrate a local victory over the Romans. At St Ives in Cornwall the Mayor used to throw a ball coated with silver, perhaps a relic of sun-worship, from the pier and crowds fought for it, without limit and without rules.

Hockey, which is known as 'hurling' in Ireland, and 'shinty' in Scotland, possibly originated in Persia; a similar game was played by the Greeks and Romans. In Morocco it appears to have some connection with fertility rites, as it is played in the spring to induce rain and at other times if there is a drought.

The Wichita of Oklahoma believed that the game was handed down to them by a mythical ancestor, and it was played during their spring festival. The team with the green hockey sticks and balls overcame the opposing side, symbolizing the conquest of winter. In the south-western desert region, the Hopi Indians believed they could foretell the maize yield by playing hockey with a buckskin ball filled with seeds. If the seeds spilt out the harvest would be good; if the ball failed to burst, crops would fail.

Princely Pastimes

Chess, one of the oldest and most honoured of board games, originated in Asia and is commonly assumed to have been brought to Europe through the Arabs. 'Checkmate', from *shah mat*, 'the king is dead', is derived from Arabic, but it is not known whether the Arabs were introduced to the game in Persia or in India. Early names for the game, and for some of the pieces, are Indian.

An Indian legend, one of the many concerning the origin of the game, relates how chess was invented by the wife of the giant Ravana, King of Ceylon, to entertain him when Rama, the mythical hero of the *Rama Yana* (which dates from about 500 BC), was besieging him in his palace. But gaming boards and primitive chessmen have been discovered by archeologists in Palestine on sites which date from 1500 BC or even earlier. Boards, with small blue pottery cones and pyramids, were revealed when a large house near Jerusalem was uncovered; and inlaid gaming boards have been discovered in Crete.

The Crusaders are generally credited with bringing chess to England from the East after the Crusades of the early Middle Ages, but there is evidence that the game was known long before then. In Irish folk-tales King Arthur plays chess with the Irish knight Owain, and the chieftain-god Midir the Proud wins the fairest maid in the world by checkmating Eochaid, the King of Ireland.

Playing cards are believed to have descended from the Tarot cards, which are popularly supposed to have been imported into Europe by gypsies, who originally brought them from Egypt. The modern pack of 52 cards came to England from France in the 15th century. These have been used for innocent amusement and for reckless gambling, for divination and for fortune telling ever since.

There are many superstitions connected with playing cards, which the Presbyterians nicknamed the Devil's Picture Book or the Devil's Bible. A player will get up and walk round the table, or he will turn his chair round, to change his luck. A number of cards have their own superstitions such as the Ace of Spades, which is connected with death, and Nine of Diamonds, known as the 'curse of Scotland'. Sailors and thieves regard all cards as unlucky; cards are thrown overboard in a storm and no thief will include a pack in his loot.

Gambling with dice was common in ancient times in Egypt, the Far East, Greece and Rome; and there is possibly even earlier evidence of the use of a form of dice for gambling, or for divination, in the pebbles painted in red ochre, which were found among artefacts dated to about 7000–5000 BC, in the cave of Mas d'Azil in France.

The dice used in classical times were derived from the little cuboid bones known as *astragali* which are found in the joints of many animals, especially sheep, and in human ankles. They have been discovered on the site of Ephesus in Asia Minor, and in Sparta. Bone or wooden dice, their six sides marked with dots or numbers, were commonly used for telling fortunes.

Children's Games

Traditional children's games tend to consist of more-or-less standard movements, often with an accompanying song, or poem or prose dialogue. The most complex are those with song accompaniments. The games are often imitations of adult activity, or contain survivals of activities that once involved the whole community.

The most significant games are those involving death, and sometimes a funeral. In these we are nearest to the supernatural, especially if there is also a reference to resurrection. *Jenny jo* is a game of this kind.

Two children represent Jenny and her Mother. Jenny hides behind her Mother while a line of children, containing one or more suitors, advances singing:

I'm come to court Janet jo,
  Janet jo, Janet jo,
I'm come to court Janet jo,
  How's she the day?

Mother answers, singing:

She's up the stair washin,
  Washin, washin,
She's up the stair washin,
  Ye canna see her the day.

Then the line retreats and the verse is repeated, referring to various household chores – washing, starching, ironing and so on, until finally Janet jo's illness and death are announced. Then Mother steps aside to reveal Janet jo lying dead. She sings:

Janet jo's lying dead,
  Lying dead, lying dead,
Janet jo's lying dead,
  You can't see her the day.

In the following question and answer, the best mourning colour is discussed. Janet jo is carried out, amidst the other children mourning. There are variations on this, with significant local additions, some of which may be very old. One of the questions sometimes asked in Ireland is, 'Shall we come in green?' and the answer is:

Green is for the good people, good
  people, good people,
Green is for the good people, you
  can't come in that

The 'good people' are, of course, the fairies.

One version, in describing Janet jo's funeral, has the couplet:

Ashes to ashes, dust to dust,
If God won't have you the Devil must.

Janet jo rises from the ground and runs after the other children. The one caught becomes Janet jo in the next game. This is significant for it represents resurrection, one of the most ancient of human beliefs. In a Southampton version Janet jo is recognized as a wicked ghost and the other children run from her. An old Irish nurse remembered no more than a fragment, ending:

Pipes and tobacco for Jenny jo, Jenny
  jo, Jenny jo,
Pipes and tobacco for Jenny jo, all
  the day long.

This mention of smoking makes the children's game an adult activity. In former times, children were more closely integrated with adult life, as they still are in the more primitive parts of the world and to some extent still are in the more remote parts of Britain. A rigid distinction between adult rites and children's games is a modern intellectual construction, which must be seen for what it is if the origin and significance of traditional children's games is to be discerned. The children's game of *Jenny jo*, in which there are a wooing, a funeral and a symbolic resurrection bears out the theory that these children's games are relics of adult ceremonies.

Love and Death

A possible adult origin of a game called *Green Grass* can be found in an account written in 1815 by Thomas Wilkie, a friend of Sir Walter Scott. Wilkie recorded that in the south of Scotland when a man died, he was washed, and prepared for burial. One of the oldest women then lighted a special kind of candle and waved it three times

Modern football is one of the most popular and possibly one of the most sophisticated of modern games; in fact, in its primitive form, requiring only an object to kick and someone to return it, it has been played through the centuries. In various parts of the world the game has acquired a symbolic meaning, sometimes as a fertility rite. sometimes portraying the conquest of spring over winter. Football players by Rousseau, 1908.

Played since classical times, hockey has a ritual significance in some parts of the world; in Morocco, for instance, it is played to induce rain. Until comparatively recently hockey in England was a rough game, not suited to 'weakly or timid players': illustration from *The Popular Educator* by F. Wentworth.

round the corpse, which was thus 'sained' or shielded from evil influences. Then she put three handfuls of common salt into a wooden or stoneware plate, which she placed on the dead man's heart to keep him down. Three empty platters or dishes were laid on the hearth near the fire. Everyone walked out of the room, returned backwards, and put his hands in the dishes, repeating a rhyme of saining, the exact wording of which Wilkie was unable to quote. The company then ate some bread and cheese, drank spirits and departed from the house.

Half a century later, Wilkie's rhyme of saining was quoted by William Henderson in his *Folk-lore of the Northern Counties* as:

A dis, a dis, a dis,
A green grass,
A dis, a dis, a dis.

These are, in fact, the first words of *Green Grass*, a game which is very similar in action to *Jenny jo* and which has become more a wooing-marriage game than a death-burial-resurrection game. How is this phenomenon to be interpreted?

There seems to be a general tendency for a death-and-resurrection ceremony, once it

becomes a children's game, to put less and less stress on death and more on wooing and marriage, until only hints of death remain. Love, marriage and the bearing of children provide an alternative link with the future, one closely associated in the mind with concepts of resurrection and immortality, and one which children may find more familiar, more comprehensible, more acceptable and perhaps more interesting as it constitutes an imitation of the everyday world of the adults around them.

A Sacrificial Victim

One children's game from which it is quite possible to draw certain significant conclusions is *London Bridge*:

London Bridge is broken down,
    Dance o'er my lady lee,
London Bridge is broken down,
    With a gay lady.

In this game, there is an implication that a sacrificial victim is needed if the building of the bridge is to be successful. Two children join hands and make an arch with their arms; others run under, holding on in a long line. A prisoner enters the game in the question, 'What has this poor prisoner done?', followed by 'Off to prison you must go'.

This occurred in the Hampshire version, while in Cork children sang, 'Let everyone pass by but the very last one, and catch him if you can,' which is reminiscent of the saying 'Devil take the hindmost'.

In the game, the building of London

Bridge is a very difficult undertaking and the prisoner is introduced, as it were, to resolve the difficulty. This idea of a sacrifice being necessary in connection with bridge-building is one that is encountered extremely widely throughout the world.

Another game which has several significant implications is *Mother, Mother, the Pot Boils Over*. One girl is the Mother, another the Witch. The Mother names her children after the days of the week. A tenth girl is chosen as Guardian, and Mother goes out to wash. The Witch is allowed by the Guardian to light her pipe, if she does not spit on the hearth. She lights her pipe, spits on the hearth, and carries off the child named Sunday. 'Mother, Mother, the pot boils over!' shouts the Guardian. One by one, the children are carried off by the Witch. Finally Mother fetches all her children, except one who is caught by the Witch and becomes the new Witch. There are hints of fire-worship here, the sacredness of the hearth, and the magical pot which in Welsh mythology is the cauldron of Ceridwen. Fouling the hearth was sacrilege, and the borrowing of fire gave power over the inmates who gave the fire.

Leaping for Growth

Oats and Beans and Barley Grows, another ring game, is connected with the growing of grain and the subsequent mystery of growth. The question is asked, 'Do you or I or anyone know how oats and beans and barley grow?' The imitative magic in this game is very ancient. In Jane Harrison's translation of a hymn of the Curetes of ancient Crete (in her book *Themis*), with its theme of fertility and the growth of crops, occur the lines: 'To us also leap for full jars, and leap for fleecy flocks, and leap for fields of fruit, and for hives to bring increase.'

Although they are unaware of the reason, this is what children are doing when they dance, jump and throw up their arms in these games with a fertility significance. The marriage in this game, as in others, is not intrusive; our ancestors quite reasonably connected human fertility with the fertility of the earth.

The story of the Grail has this belief at the centre of it: the impotence of the ruler of the Waste Land is the cause, or is linked with, the failure of the crops. The recovery of the ruler, when the right question is asked, is accompanied by the restoration of the land's fertility.

Sally Water, with its wedding, is another game which turns on the theme of human fertility. The game begins: 'Sally, Sally Water, sprinkle in the pan.' Water in association with fertility rites occurs in the practice of Hindu and Esthonian brides, who have the habit of sprinkling their husbands and their houses with water in order to induce fertility.

The Soul in the Maze

There are many games with action only and no dialogue. One significant game is *Hop Scotch*, which is known as *Peever* in Scotland. It is played within a pattern chalked on the ground. There are various versions of the pattern in which squares are arranged in different ways, two of which are the maze and the basilica – so called because it contains seven squares which are roughly in the shape of a church. The children kick a stone through the squares in a traditional order and their feet must not touch upon any of the lines of the squares.

Hop Scotch has an ancient meaning although the children who still play it in city streets are completely unaware of it. The stone represents the soul which must travel through the maze until it escapes. In the basilica form, the stone – or soul – progresses from the inner squares to the top, and these are taken as representing the altar and hence salvation.

The reason why children who play these games are totally unaware of their supernatural implications is because children's games have become largely divorced from adult life. Children may create little rhymes or add lines to traditional games, but the original ritual was created by adults in a pagan religious setting. It is only by sifting among the childish relics of these ceremonies that we can recognize where they began.

The Olympic Games developed partly because men feared that the earth might never come to life again after winter; the saviour of the harvest was thought to be the man who had the magic of victory in him, and he was chosen through a simple race. Later, the man who was the embodiment of goodness and excellence was sought: scene on a Greek vase, c 525 BC.

The Olympic Games

The first Olympic Games of which there are historical as opposed to mythical records, were held in 776 BC, to mark a truce between the states of Elis and Pisa in western Greece. For the next thousand years they were one of the greatest unifying influences in the Greek world, providing satisfaction in athletic accomplishment for both competitors and spectators, and also pleasing the gods who were thought to look down with favour on the highest achievements of mortals.

The Games had their origin in the myths surrounding the feats of god-like creatures, once mere men, who existed in the heroic age of Greece. Hercules is said to have cleansed the Augean Stables, the sixth of his twelve labours, by diverting a river at Olympia, the site where all later Olympic Games were held.

The ancient Games developed partly as a result of man's desire to predict the unpredictable. There was a primitive anxiety that the earth might never come to life again after winter. With the soil bare and food scarce, who could give an assurance that another year would bring a fresh harvest? The saviour of the harvest was the person with the magic of victory in him, the athlete born of Zeus the sky god. A simple race was the way to choose this man.

Later the man who embodied all the qualities of goodness or excellence was sought. Bronze statues, probably modelled from the victors, overlooked the stadium and were called *zanes*, a word that is derived from Zeus. In this way the athletic heroes of the ancient Games were to become almost deified.

Rule of Nakedness

The Games developed until in the 5th century BC, the poet Pindar described them as 'the Flower of Festivals, excellent as water, bright as gold, brilliant as the noonday sun'. This was a superlative extension of athletics to the world of art, poetry and sculpture, but the importance of the Games still lay in the search for one man, a hero who embodied all this excellence.

It is not known for certain why the Games were held every four years if they were associated with an annual event; but it is probable that the Greeks felt that a complete cycle consisting of a sun cycle and a moon cycle was required. Using their primitive algebra, they calculated this to be four years.

In the early Olympic Games the prize for the Olympic victor was a crown of wild olives, possibly showing that the victor represented vegetation, that is, he was the new life of the year. Alternatively the olive crown could have represented simply the great distinction of the victor, and have been of no value in itself.

The honours were shared fairly equally among the various city-states. Athletes came from all parts of Greece and at the time of the Games there was a general truce to hostilities. The contests were open to all

Metropolitan Museum, New York

National Film Archive

The lighting of the Olympic flame is a recent innovation, but in symbolizing a period of truce for the Games, it perpetuates a tradition that originated in classical Greece, and emphasizes the ideals that are common to both the ancient and modern Olympic Games: scenes from *Olympische Spiele*, directed by Leni Riefenstahl.

men of true Greek descent. The only woman admitted to the Games was the priestess of Demeter, the corn goddess. In fact, this rule acted as a spur to contestants' mothers and sisters, and there are various stories of women obtaining entry disguised as men. In an attempt to restrict entries to men, it is said that the rule of nakedness was extended to trainers as well as contestants.

Apart from the chariot races, the main contests were four running events, boxing, two types of wrestling, and a pentathlon consisting of javelin, discus, long jump, running and wrestling, in each of which the competitors took part. This basic pattern of events remained almost unchanged for a thousand years.

The runners completed distances which were multiples of the *stade*, about 180 yards. The name of any man who achieved a particular combination of victories for the first time was recorded. Our word 'agony' is derived from *agon* which is Greek for an athletic contest.

When Rome inherited the power of Greece the Games became more international, professionalism crept into sport, and the Games eventually became a great tourist attraction. Physical training was carried out in gymnasia which were also known as centres of learning. Intellect and physical fitness were not thought to be mutually exclusive, as has so often been the case in other civilizations.

Sport has never since been held in such esteem, yet at the same time the Greeks had a sense of proportion. For instance, the delicate and skilful art of wrestling was preferred to the more brutal boxing, and was the sport of the common man.

The early Christian Church rejected all athletics, believing that they were a pagan indulgence. By the 4th century AD the Games had become vulgar and discredited, and as a result of this they were finally abolished by the Christian Emperor Theodosius I in 393 AD.

The Olympic Games owe their revival in the 19th century largely to the enthusiasm of Baron Pierre de Coubertin, the French educationalist. The first of the modern series of Games was held in Athens in 1896 and since then they have been held every four years, apart from the intervals caused by the two world wars.

Competitors must take an oath declaring that they are true amateurs, and the winners are awarded silver-gilt medals. In victory ceremonies the flag of the victor's country is raised, and his national anthem is played. The lighting of the Olympic flame, a modern innovation, accompanies the release of pigeons from the stadium, to signify a period of truce for the Games just as, more than 2000 years ago, the city-states of Greece agreed to keep the peace during the ancient Olympic Games.

National Film Archive

Ritual Magic

Textbooks

The European magical textbooks, or grimoires, contain all sorts of processes, including instructions for making love talismans or wax images, but they reserve their most impressive ceremonials for the attempt to summon up a 'spirit', a supernatural force or entity of some kind, which can be subjugated by the magician and forced to carry out his orders or reveal what it knows. It is this type of operation to which, in the European context, the term 'ritual magic' particularly refers.

The ceremonies in the grimoires naturally vary in detail but there is a clear general pattern. The spirit is summoned and dominated in a series of commanding incantations, through which the magician brings all the resources of his will to bear on the operation. But before he can begin the ceremony itself, he must make the necessary preparations.

A magical operation of any difficulty cannot be performed in a normal condition of mind and body, and the magician must begin by 'consecrating' or dedicating himself to the work, in the sense of cutting himself off from his everyday surroundings and concerns, and excluding all distractions from his mind. The methods of doing this, recommended in all the grimoires, are continence and fasting, cleanliness and devout prayer to God. The *Heptameron* or *Magical Elements* (attributed to a 14th century authority on medicine, Peter of Abano, but probably dating from the 16th century) says that: 'The operator should be clean and purified for the space of nine days before beginning the work; he should be confessed also, and should receive the Holy Communion.' Abstinence must be positively reinforced by concentration on the work in hand. *True Black Magic* (an 18th century French derivative of the *Key of Solomon*) says that the magician must fast and be chaste, must 'abstain from every labour of soul and body', and must 'meditate on those things which he is about to put in practice for nine complete days before undertaking the work'.

Detail from an American Masonic Diploma.

The insistence on austerity and the presence of prayers and celebrations of Holy Communion in these rituals, are surprising at first sight but are the result of the principle that magical power works automatically and regardless of motives. God's power can be tapped by the use of his name and through forms of prayer to him. The Mass brings into the magician's body and soul the power of the consecrated host. Confession and abstinence rid him of impurities on which the spirit that is to be summoned might seize, or from a modern point of view rid him of trivial distractions which would weaken his concentration.

Abstinence also helps build up the magician's own powers. By remaining chaste he creates a reservoir of sexual energy, by going short of food and sleep, he weakens his body and gives strange powers to his mind. Some modern magicians have tried to reach the same goal by the opposite route, using drink or drugs or sex, separately or in combination, to put themselves into a state of physical exhaustion combined with a heightened mental condition.

Washing is also recommended, again to banish impurities or distractions. In the *Key of Solomon*, which recommends nine days of austerity before the operation begins, the magician is instructed to immerse himself in water which has been blessed by a priest, saying a prayer in which he states his own divine potential as the earthly image of God and asks for God's grace. 'O Lord Adonai, who hast formed me, thy unworthy servant, in thine image, from plain earth: bless and sanctify this work, for the cleansing of my soul and body, and may no deceit or stupidity be here. O most powerful God, through whose power the people were able to walk through the Red Sea from Egypt: give me this grace, purified and cleansed by this water, pure in thy presence.'

If the novice magician has not been put off by the austerities recommended, he may quail at the list of magical 'weapons' or instruments which he requires. *True Black Magic*, for instance, says he will need a sword, a staff, a wand, a lancet, a hook, a sickle, a poniard, a white-handled knife and a black-handled knife, the last of these being used for drawing the magic circle. Aleister Crowley's list of magical weapons includes swastika, crown, wand, crook, sword, spear, scourge, lamp and girdle, apron, sandals, dagger, tripod, cup, cross and sickle.

These instruments should be made by the magician himself (or as a second-best he may buy them, provided they are brand new) and the directions for manufacturing them and 'consecrating' them to the work are of daunting complexity. A comparatively simple example is *True Black Magic*'s sickle, which must be made of virgin steel and forged on the day and in the hour of Jupiter. It must be doused under moonlight with a mixture of mole's blood and pimpernel juice. A horn handle must be fitted to it in the hour of Jupiter and an incantation 'by the authority of God the Father Almighty' recited over it to infuse it with power. It must be kept until needed in a new wrapping of red silk.

Whether many magicians ever provided themselves with all the accessories or followed all the difficult and taxing directions seems doubtful. The main underlying purpose appears to be psychological. The magician must make his own instruments and follow complicated procedures as a way of totally involving himself and all his faculties in the work, of stretching to the limit his qualities of application and determination. The essential requirement is that his weapons must be 'virgin', not previously owned or used by anyone else. This is partly because a virgin weapon has its full potentiality intact, none of its energies having been dissipated, and partly because it is considered dangerous to use anything second-hand in magic. A previous owner or use may have linked the weapon with undesirable or positively dangerous influences.

The principal weapons of the grimoires are the wand, sword and knife. The wand should be made of hazel wood and, according to the 18th century French *Grand Grimoire* should be $19\frac{1}{2}$ inches long, cut at sunrise with the magic knife and fitted with pointed steel caps at each end. The sword and knife should be forged or bought on the day and in the hour of Jupiter, at a time when the moon is waxing. Incantations are recited over them to give them power.

Robes and Circle

A secluded place should be chosen for the ceremony, so as to avoid interruptions. Somewhere which has a strong atmosphere

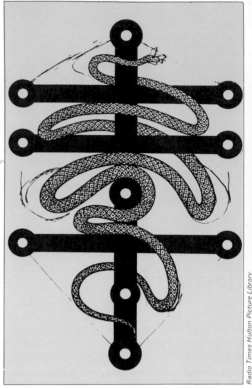

Drawing by Aleister Crowley of the Serpent of Wisdom coiling round the Cabalistic Tree of Life: the Tree is regarded as a diagram of the universe and to follow the serpent's path is to 'rise through the spheres' to supreme power, to command in one's own being all the forces of the world.

Modern magicians have been influenced by Egyptian and Graeco-Egyptian texts, and by Indian beliefs, as in this illustration of 'the mystery of universal equilibrium', by Eliphas Levi.

of its own is desirable, so long as the atmosphere suits the type of ceremony to be performed. Ruins, graveyards, dark woods or crossroads would all be suitable for operations of destruction or communings with evil spirits. If the ceremony is performed indoors, all the windows and doors should be fastened and the room should be hung with drapes of a colour appropriate to the ceremony. Similarly, an appropriate time should be chosen, performing the operation in the hour of the planet to which it corresponds, and using accessories belonging to the planet.

The grimoires recommend white robes, though in black magical operations trappings of black or red would be more suitable. The 'Fourth Book' added to Agrippa's *Occult Philosophy* prescribes a robe of white linen, covering the body from the neck to the feet, fitting closely and tied with a girdle. The *Key of Solomon* recommends white shoes, with magical symbols drawn on them, and a crown of virgin white paper on which names of God are written with 'the pen of the art', one specially made and consecrated for the magician's purposes. So far as possible, buttons, buckles, knots and other fastenings should be avoided because any fastening tends to impede the flowing out of the magician's power.

The colour white represents the purity,

from the magician's point of view at least, of his intentions, and in putting on his robes he is really putting on a suitable frame of mind. In the *Key*, while vesting himself in his robes, he repeats no less than seven psalms and then says, 'Amor, Amator, Amides, Ideodamiach, Amor, Plaior, Amitor. By the powers of those sacred angels I dress myself in these powerful robes. And through them I will bring to a successful conclusion the things that I burn to accomplish: through thee, O most holy Adonai, and thy kingdom and rule is everlasting. Amen.'

Once robed, the magician can proceed to draw the magic circle. This acts as a barrier against all forces outside it and, even more importantly, it focuses and concentrates the forces inside it, the magical energy generated in the ceremony. In the *Key* the circle is drawn with the magic knife, at the end of a rope nine feet long. Names of power, crosses, pentagrams, hexagrams, herbs and bowls of holy water are placed in the rim of the circle, to reinforce it. According to the *Lemegeton*, a triangle should be drawn outside the circle, two feet away from it, and it is into this triangle that the spirit is summoned. The name Michael is inscribed inside and the names of power Anexhexeton, Tetragrammaton, Primematum are written along its edges.

Israel Regardie comments (in *The Tree of Life*) that the triangle is required in evocation, when the magician summons up something from within himself and projects it into the universe outside him, but not in

invocation, when the magician summons something from outside himself, which takes place entirely inside the circle. When Aleister Crowley and his pupil, the poet Victor Neuburg, conjured up the mighty demon Choronzon in a ritual based on the *Lemegeton* and the *Grimoire of Honorius*, Crowley placed himself in the triangle, into which the demon was summoned, so offering himself as the vehicle of its manifestation: according to some, he was possessed by the demon for the rest of his life.

The Perfumes of Venus

Pentagrams and hexagrams, drawn on parchment or engraved on an appropriate metal, may be placed in the circle or outside it, or worn or carried by the magician and his assistants. They protect against evil and they may be used for banishing irrelevant or disruptive influences before the main ceremony begins.

A small brazier is placed inside the circle (or sometimes outside it), on which a fire of charcoal is lit and various substances are burned. The choice of substance depends on the nature of the ceremony. For a work of Venus, for example, ambergris, aloes wood, musk, myrtle, rose, red sandalwood, pigeon's blood or sparrow's brain would create a suitable perfume. Like the colours, metals and other accessories, the perfume brings the appropriate planetary influence to bear on the operation. The fumes also provide material from which the spirit can make itself a visible body. It is likely that this is connected with the alchemical notion that when a substance is burned, the smoke given off is its 'spirit'.

But again the principal use of the fumigations is psychological. Like the whole apparatus of weapons, colours and symbols, the fumes help to intoxicate the magician's senses. It is worth noticing that some of the materials' recommended for burning in black magical operations – henbane, for instance – give off fumes which may cause hallucinations and delirium.

It is important to have a clear mental picture of the spirit that is to be summoned. Its nature, attributes and appearance are formulated so as to build up a vivid image of it, on which the magician and his associates concentrate. The *Lemegeton* describes the appearance of 72 demons, presumably for this purpose. The spirit Orias, for example, who will teach the magician astrology and cause even his enemies to fear him, appears in the form of a lion riding on a great horse. He has a snake for a tail and in his hands he holds two more snakes. The 'Fourth Book' provides descriptions of spirits associated with the planets: a spirit of Mars may show itself as a king riding a wolf and holding a naked sword in his right hand and a severed human head in his left.

In the modern magician's 'assumption of god-forms', a vivid picture of a deity's characteristic appearance, attributes, symbols and myths is built up and concentrated on while the god is invoked. The magician identifies himself with what he has pictured, a 'god' which is a great universal force or current, or 'aspect of cosmic life', which also has its existence in the human mind, and Crowley and other modern magicians have discovered that some of the many deities of ancient Egypt were particularly suitable for this purpose.

In many of the processes in the grimoires an animal, usually a kid, is killed as part of the preliminaries and the magician uses its skin to make parchment, on which he inscribes pentagrams and other magical symbols. But sometimes the slaughtered animal is also a sacrifice. In the *Key* the magician decapitates the kid at one blow, naming the spirit he intends to summon and saying 'O high and powerful being, may this sacrifice be pleasing and acceptable to thee. Serve us faithfully and better sacrifices shall be given thee.'

In modern rituals the sacrifice, if performed at all, is much more closely linked with the main ceremony itself and may occur at the height of it. When the animal is killed, its vital energy is believed to be liberated, so increasing the supply of force inside the circle. The fumes of its blood provide an additional supply of energy on which the spirit can fasten to make itself manifest. And again the killing contributes to the magician's intoxicated but masterful state of consciousness.

A bird or small animal may be slaughtered, or the magician may gash himself or one of his assistants so that the blood runs. If this is combined with the achievement of orgasm, a still greater 'charge' of energy is released into the circle and it is this sexual 'sacrifice' that some modern magicians regard as peculiarly effective.

Martin Weaver

In the Lake of Fire

When all is ready, and the magician and his assistants are in their places in the circle, the summoning of the spirit begins. It is summoned through the magic of language, the use of compelling incantations and 'names of power', which are believed to contain inherent force. There is no single correct formula of incantation, and finding those which work is a matter of trial and error. The incantations begin quietly and gently but as they continue the magician gradually works up his own inner forces until he is in a state of fervid but still controlled ecstasy in which with every fibre of his being he commands and compels the spirit to appear. The most influential of them is the celebrated *Key of Solomon*, on which many of the others are based. Strongly influenced by cabalistic and astrological magic, the *Key* sets out the lengthy preliminaries, the choosing of a suitable time and place, the weapons, robes and 'pentacles' or diagrams which the magician will need, the drawing of the magic circle, the incantations for summoning spirits and for compelling their obedience. As usual in the grimoires, the processes are complicated, elaborate and difficult. E. M. Butler commented that they 'read like the worst sort of obstacle race' and 'are certainly calculated to deal the death-blow to any notions harboured by intending practitioners that magic is a short cut to their desires.'

Infernal Devices

Printed copies of the *Key* are extremely rare (the edition which MacGregor Mathers

Magicians and witches use 'weapons', robes, instruments, perfumes, jewels, which are believed to be occultly linked to natural forces and which also intoxicate the magicians' mind and heighten his powers.

published in 1889 is heavily expurgated) but it exists in numerous manuscripts in various languages. Most of these date from the 16th century or later but a Greek version in the British Museum may date from the 12th or 13th century. Solomon enjoyed a great legendary reputation as a powerful magician and a worshipper of strange gods, and as far back as the 1st century AD the Jewish historian Josephus referred to a book of incantations for conjuring up demons, supposedly written by Solomon. The *Testament of Solomon* (not the same as the *Key*) dating from c 100 to 400 AD, lists the names and powers of demons which Solomon had subdued with his magic ring. In the 13th century Roger Bacon, himself a reputed magician, knew of magical works attributed to Solomon and c 1350 *Le Livre de Salomon*, containing methods of evoking demons, was burned by order of Pope Innocent VI.

The key of the title is the instrument which unlocks the doors of hidden power and wisdom, a symbolism strengthened by the words of Jesus to St Peter which magicians took as a kind of warrant or charter. 'I will give you the keys of the kingdom of heaven, and whatever you bind on earth shall be bound in heaven . . .' (Matthew 16.19).

Also attributed to Solomon is the *Lemegeton* or *Lesser Key of Solomon*, divided into

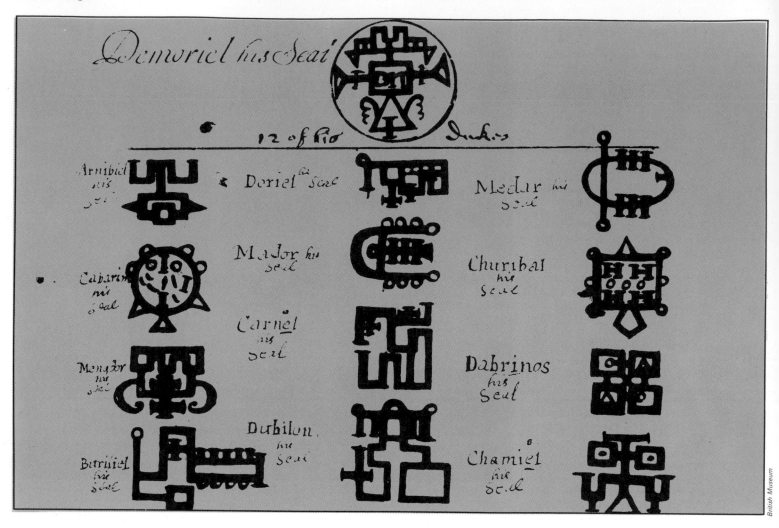

The seal of Demoriel, ruler of the North, from the *Key of Solomon*; below are the seals of 12 of the spirits who serve him.

four sections and dating from the 16th century or earlier.

Of all the grimoires, the *Lemegeton* has perhaps the most formidable armoury of incantations. The magician conjures the spirit by a battery of names of power to 'appear forthwith and show thyself to me, here outside this circle in fair and human shape, without horror or deformity and without delay'. If the spirit does not appear, this opening incantation is repeated a second time and, if necessary, a third, with the magician gradually introducing a more urgent and commanding note into his voice.

If the spirit has still not appeared, a second and stronger incantation is chanted, which may again have to be repeated a second and third time. The spirit is summoned with a great array of names of power, and the incantation ends with: 'By the dreadful Day of Judgement, by the Sea of Glass which is before the face of the Divine Majesty, by the four Beasts before the Throne, having eyes before and behind, by the Fire which is about the Throne, by the Holy Angels of heaven and the Mighty Wisdom of God, by the Seal of Basdathea, by the name Primematum which Moses uttered and the earth opened and swallowed up Corah, Dathan and Abiram, answer all my demands and perform all that I desire. Come peaceably, visibly and without delay.'

The magician is now working himself up to a high pitch of intensity and using a more compelling and dominating tone. If the spirit still fails to appear, he proceeds to a third conjuration, again to be repeated up to three times, in which he commands the spirit by the seven secret names with which Solomon mastered all demons and threatens it with the torments of hell. 'I will bind thee in the depths of the bottomless pit, there to remain till the Day of the Last Judgement. I will chain thee in the Lake of Eternal Fire and Brimstone . . .'

This should certainly force the spirit to appear, and he must be kept firmly in subjection to the magician's will. Once the magician has finished with him, the spirit must be forced to go away with the 'licence to depart'. This final stage of the ceremony is extremely important because the magician and his assistants cannot safely leave the circle until the spirit has been banished. Even if the spirit has apparently refused to answer the magician's summons, the formal licence to depart must be pronounced in case he is invisibly present.

The spirits of the *Lemegeton* are summoned for a variety of purposes, including harming the magician's enemies, gaining money, status and influence for him, and assisting him to slake his lust, but the majority of them are teaching demons. They supply him with knowledge about a large range of subjects, even including ethics, and they reflect the tradition of the Watchers, the rebel angels who first brought knowledge

to men. When a modern magician 'holds conversation' with what he has invoked (as distinct from evoking something from himself and objectifying it), he learns what it has to teach, so to speak, by identifying himself with it.

Three famous French grimoires were based on the *Key* and the *Lemegeton*. The *Grand Grimoire* first printed in the 17th century, contains 'the Infernal Devices of the Great Agrippa for the Discovery of all Hidden Treasures and the Subjugation of every Denomination of Spirits, together with an Abridgement of all the Magical Arts.' Also known as the *Red Dragon*, it explains how to make a pact with the Devil and how to use 'the dreadful Blasting Rod, which causes the spirits to tremble.' *True Black Magic* or 'The Secret of Secrets', published at Rome in 1750, includes a collection of magical symbols and talismans. The *Grimorium Verum* also belongs to the 18th century though characteristically claiming to have been published by Alibeck the Egyptian at Memphis in 1517.

The French *Grimoire of Honorius the Great* probably dates from the late 16th century and is the most laborious and most paradoxically Christian of all. Its array of prayers, psalms and pious sayings of Mass, harnessed to the calling up of the Devil, have given it a particularly black reputation.

Among many other grimoires are the *Arbatel of Magic*, allegedly published at Basle in 1575 and mainly concerned with the summoning of the seven Olympic Spirits which rule the planets. Typically, its aims range from acquiring the supreme knowledge of God to making money and prolonging life. The Fourth Book, added to Agrippa's *Occult Philosophy* but probably not written by him, provides methods of invoking the planetary spirits. The *Heptameron. or Magical Elements* is a sequel to the Fourth Book and gives procedures for summoning the Spirits of the Air and for controlling supernatural beings which will find hidden treasures, cause wars and hatred, nose out secrets, open locked doors and procure the love of women.

The Terrible and Invisible God

Modern magicians have taken much from grimoires but they have also looked back beyond them to ancient Egyptian and Graeco-Egyptian rituals. The Golden Dawn attached great importance to a Graeco-Egyptian magical text on which they based a ritual of invocation of the 'higher genius' or 'holy guardian angel', which is the magician's higher self. The 'angel' is invoked by incantations which declare its names and attributes and its supreme power. Then it is summoned. 'I invoke Thee, the Terrible and Invisible God Who Dwellest in the void place of the Spirit. . . . Hear me and make all Spirits subject unto me, so that every Spirit of the firmament and of the Ether, upon the Earth and under the Earth, on dry land and in the Water, of Whirling Air and of Rushing Fire, and every spell and scourge of God may be made obedient unto me.'

The ritual continues with rising fervour, the magician concentrating all his resources of will and imagination, until the angel itself is felt to be present. In a passion of ecstasy the magician unites himself with it, and cries out, 'I am He, the Truth.' And the command to 'make all Spirits subject unto me' is spoken again, but as if by the angel, for it and the magician are now one.

Magical Obstacle-Race

The almost incredible complications and elaborations of these initial rites and ceremonies . . . read like the worst sort of obstacle-race. They are certainly calculated to deal the death-blow to any notions harboured by intending practitioners that magic is a short cut to their desires. On the contrary it appears here in the light of a severe discipline both on the mystical and the practical side; and those who have ever attended Hindu rites and ceremonies will recognize the similarity of an outlook which transforms all the actions of everyday life into an act of worship. Would-be sorcerers might well pause before embarking on the path traced out for them by 'Solomon'; but could comfort themselves with the reflexion that the results would be in proportion to the effort expended. And when they failed, they would be unlikely to blame their mentor. For they could never be quite sure that they had not deviated at some point or other from his sometimes ambiguous instructions.

E. M. Butler *Ritual Magic*

The seven planets, with the sun at the centre: the planetary gods personify forces which ritual magicians attempt to use in their operations which should be performed in the hour and day of the appropriate planet.

Ritual Incantation

The mixture of prayer and command, the use of solemn and striking language, the confident belief that saying a thing is so makes it so, became part of the European tradition. So did the recitation of the names, characteristics and acts of a god, as a way of capturing the essence of the god and bringing him down into the magician's being and within the magician's control.

Some of the Greeks who settled in Egypt in the time of the Ptolemies (from 323 BC onwards), often influenced by gnostic ideas, adopted Egyptian magical methods with enthusiasm. The results are the Graeco-Egyptian magical texts which appeal to, and sometimes threaten, not only the Egyptian gods but also Greek gods and goddesses – especially Hermes, Hecate and Apollo – and in some cases the god of the Jews and Jesus Christ.

The writers of the grimoires were naturally still more heavily influenced by Christianity, and also by cabalistic speculation about the various names and titles of God in the Old Testament. For example, a threatening incantation in the *Grimoire of Honorius*, for forcing a demon to appear, says:

If you do not obey promptly and without tarrying, I will shortly increase your torments for a thousand years in hell. I constrain you therefore to appear here in comely human shape, by the Most High Names of God, HAIN, LON, HILAY, SABAOTH, HELIM, RADISHA, LEDIEHA, ADONAY, JEHOVAH, YAH, TETRAGRAMMATON, SADAI, MESSIAS, AGIOS, ISCHYROS, EMMANUEL, AGLA, Jesus who is ALPHA and OMEGA, the beginning and the end, that you be justly established in the fire, having no power to reside, habit or abide in this place henceforth; and I require your doom by the virtue of the said Names, that St Michael drive you to the uttermost of the infernal abyss, in the name of the Father, and of the Son, and of the Holy Ghost. So be it.

The words in capital letters are 'names of power', some of them from Hebrew, some from Greek and others of unknown origin. The name of a god is considered effective in magic because it contains the god's power. To pronounce it, automatically brings the god's power into operation – hence the use of the names of God and Jesus in the grimoires, even in operations of a distinctly black magical nature.

The Frenzy

Like poetry, an incantation depends for its effect on the combination of meaning and sound. Though it is a statement of the magician's orders, it is not said flatly but rhythmically chanted, with gradually increasing force as the ritual proceeds and the incantations are repeated over and over again. Through this chanting the magician, as he believes, taps the powers of 'gods' and supernatural forces, and states his commands in forceful words, but he also works himself up into a state of frenzied intoxication in which his own inner energies are raised to their highest pitch and in which he compels the 'spirit' to appear and to obey his commands.

The Weapon of Language

Words are weapons of power in magic because they are weapons of power in ordinary life. We use them to influence each other. Gestures and facial expressions help, and are also used in magic, but to state your wishes with commanding clarity or persuasive charm you usually resort to speech. The magical theory is that just as someone of powerful personality can use forceful words to dominate other people, so the magician armed with the lightning of concentrated will-power and the thunder of overwhelming language can dominate anything in the universe, natural or supernatural. 'In magic,' according to the French magician Eliphas Levi, 'to have said is to have done', and again, 'to affirm and will what ought to be is to create; to affirm and will what ought not to be is to destroy.'

In other words, to assert that something is so makes it so – at least under certain conditions. One condition is that the

In the same way as the poet or orator depends on the power of words to convey impressive ideas and to sway his audience, so the magician with his incantations and sometimes the suppliant with his prayers, although fulfilling different needs, make deliberate use of compelling language, both engaging in sound and clear in meaning. Wall painting on the tomb of Senedjem at Luxor near the ancient Egyptian city of Thebes, showing Senedjem and his wife chanting prayers to the sun.

William MacQuitty

assertion must be made with sufficient strength of will. Another is that the words used must be the right words. They may be 'right' because they are tested and found effective by the magician who uses them or because they are hallowed by time and tradition, which means that they have seemed effective in the past. The Lord's Prayer, for example, has often been turned to magical uses. In the 13th century Arnald of Villanova said that a priest cured him of over 100 warts in 10 days. The priest touched each wart, made the sign of the cross and repeated the Lord's Prayer, but substituting for 'deliver us from evil' the words 'deliver Master Arnald from the wens and warts on his hands'. Then he took three stalks from a plant and put them in the ground in a damp and secluded place. When the stalks began to wither, the warts began to go.

Evidently the priest believed that the words of the prayer contained power which could be used for wart-charming, and Arnald believed it too and it worked. In some societies, among the Maori in New Zealand, for instance, or some of the Pueblo tribes in North America, the words of an incantation or a prayer must never be changed. In others, as in Europe, the magician may experiment with words and phrases until he hits on those which seem to work best for him, though considerable respect is still paid to traditional formulas. This respect is not confined to magicians. In 1963 the Ecumenical Council voted to authorize the saying of Mass in languages other than Latin, provided that Latin was retained for 'the precise verbal formula which is essential to the sacrament', the words spoken by the priest, assuming the person of Christ and using the same ceremonies used by Christ at the Last Supper, which transform the bread and wine into the body and Blood. Inscribed on the wrappings of the mummy of Pharaoh Thothmes III were words intended to make his body imperishable.

Hail to thee, O my father Osiris, I have come and I have embalmed my flesh so that my body may not decay. I am whole, even as my father Khepera was whole, who is to me the type of that which passes not away. Come then, O Form, and give me breath, O lord of breath.

Perhaps long ago, as language developed, the use of words had natural elements of

Far left The magic circle is used to contain the magician's power within a limited area and so concentrate it: ceremonial magician invoking the god Pan (1954).

Left The notorious Aleister Crowley in magician's robes.

awe and magic in it, a feeling that words gave man a grasp of reality which he had previously lacked. This is suggested by the old and persistent belief that everything has a 'real' name, a name which enshrines the essence of the thing, which *is* the thing. To know and pronounce the real name of a god, a man or an animal is to exercise power over it.

Lord of the Gods

For magicians in Europe the great example of the magical use of language was the creation of the world as described in Genesis. 'God said, Let there be light; and there was light.' It was assumed that God brought his creations into existence by pronouncing their names.

Besides knowing the name, knowing and reciting the qualities of a thing gives a man magical power over it. The Semang people of Malaya have a song about a particular species of monkey, which describes its behaviour. It tells how the monkey stamps his feet, drags along, climbs up and away, swarms up the bamboo, hangs down, seizes fruit, bends the bough for a leap, lets the bough fly upwards. This song is not just an expression of delight in Nature (though it is that in part) but a hunting spell. The vivid description of the animal, the clear picture of it in the hunter's mind, gives him power over it, and the moment at the end of the song, when the monkey is about to jump, is the moment when the hunter means to kill it. Similarly, early Greek hymns to a god begin with a recital of the god's

names and attributes, which was probably intended to catch the god in the net of his own nature, and to concentrate the worshipper's mind on him, so as to give some measure of control over the god.

In the same way, in a magical ritual devised by Aleister Crowley and called *Liber Samekh*, the magician recites the names and characteristics of a supremely powerful 'spirit', who created the heavens and the earth, night and day, darkness and light. 'This is the Lord of the Gods: this is the Lord of the Universe: this is He whom the winds fear.' He commands this spirit, 'Come thou forth and follow me: and make all spirits subject unto Me so that every Spirit of the Firmament, and of the Ether, upon the Earth or under the Earth: on dry Land, or in the Water: of Whirling Air or of rushing Fire, and every Spell and Scourge of God, may be obedient unto me.'

The spirit is the divine being who is the magician's own inner self, and he announces his identity with it at the climax of the ritual by repeatedly proclaiming, 'I am He'. By describing the spirit, by vividly imagining it, the magician summons it up and controls it. He commands it to come forth and with every ounce of energy in his being he asserts that he and it are one. Finally the command 'Come thou forth' is repeated as if by the spirit itself, which has now taken possession of the magician.

Sound and Fury

This ritual was adapted from a Graeco-Egyptian magical text, itself descended

Above This Buddhist pilgrim to a temple in Katmandu, Nepal, although silent, makes pious avowals of faith by repeatedly turning a prayer wheel.

Right Illustration to *On the Ascent* by the 13th century Spanish occultist Raymond Lull, showing the steps through knowledge and mastery of which the magician will ascend to reach the knowledge and power of God.

from ancient Egyptian spells and incantations, like those in the Book of the Dead which identify the dead man as Osiris, or protect him from dangers in the afterlife, or give him power over his enemies. Here again, the belief that saying a thing is so makes it so is fundamental. The dead man's identification with Osiris depends heavily on the solemn assertion that he is, as in the spell identifying the dead Pharaoh Unas with Osiris.

Crowley's *Liber Samekh* also illustrates another essential principle of incantation, the use of sonorous, rhythmical, rhetorical language which is not spoken flatly but chanted, with steadily rising intensity as the ritual proceeds. This contributes to a rising state of intense excitement and self-intoxication, in which the magician convinces himself that the words he utters are charged with invincible power and are actually taking effect.

Because the chanting is an aid to self-intoxication, a magical operation of high importance and difficulty is likely to involve repeating several incantations several times over. A short spell or charm is usually applied only to comparatively minor and simple acts of magic. This is not always the case: a grimoire called *The Black Pullet* says that you can open any lock at a touch by reciting the words Saritap Pernisox Ottarim, but you can equally call up all the powers of heaven and hell by chanting the magic words Siras Etar Besanar. But it is doubtful whether many magicians would take this seriously.

The words 'incantation' and 'enchant' are both derived from Latin *cantare*, 'to sing' (and 'charm' is from Latin *carmen*, 'song'). The element of singing or chanting is magically important because it means that the words are put together deliberately – not in the slapdash hurry of most everyday speech – and are rhythmical. Not only do they build up the magician's own excitement but their impressive sound and beat influences the supernatural forces which he attempts to control. These forces are believed to be swayed by compelling sound in the same way that human beings are moved by poetry, oratory, preaching or honeyed words of love – all of which depend for their effectiveness on their combination of meaning and sound.

In *The Anatomy of Puck*, Katharine Briggs quotes an incantation in which the magician appeals to the judge of hell to discipline an obstinate demon. Part of it runs:

O thou most puissant prince Rhadamanthus, which dost punish in thy prison of perpetual perplexity the disobedient devils of hell, and also the grisly ghosts of men dying in dreadful despair, I conjure, bind and charge thee by Lucifer, Belsabub, Sathanas, Jauconill and by their power, and by the homage thou owest unto them, and also I charge thee by the triple crown of Cerberus his head, by Stix and Phlegiton, by your fellow and private devil Baranter, that you do torment and punish this disobedient N. (naming him) until you make him come corporally to my sight and obey my will and commandments in whatsoever I shall charge or command him to do. Fiat, fiat, fiat. Amen.

This incantation uses language which is impressive in sound, evocative and atmospheric, and clear in meaning, a combination which, with all his own inner powers concentrated on his object, the magician believes will exert an irresistible force on the lords of hell.

There is an obvious basic difference between a magical incantation and a prayer. The essence of incantation is command and the magician orders supernatural forces to do his bidding. A prayer is not a command but a request: the worshipper begs for help (though prayer can be turned to many other purposes, including thanksgiving, praise, confession of sin, and repentance). The prayer of Jesus in the garden of Gethsemane, in horror of his approaching torment, makes the difference between incantation and prayer quite clear: 'Abba, Father, all things are possible to thee: remove this cup from me; yet not what I will, but what thou wilt' (Mark 14.36).

Oaths

The idea that truth – or for that matter, virtue – can be its own reward is a relatively modern principle of morality. In the past it was taken almost for granted that no individual in his right senses would be likely to act in a manner contrary to his own interests, and for this reason a man's solemn word was not considered an acceptable token of his intentions unless it had been reinforced by supernatural sanctions. An oath consisted of a form of words capable of invoking punishment from the supernatural powers, should the obligation contained in them not be carried out. The oath has been described as 'essentially a conditional self-imprecation, a curse by which a person calls down upon himself some evil in the event of what he says not being true.' In its original form the oath was a magical formula, arising from the power inherent in the cursing words.

Oaths take a wide variety of forms. They involve calling upon a god or gods, or upon the psychic force contained in some ritual object or symbol of power, but they can also be self-imprecatory as in the familiar children's declaration: 'Cross my heart and hope to die.'

The oath which is sworn by or on some sacred, divine or even dangerous authority is intended to establish contact with its power, which can then be turned against the one who violates his given word. Developments of this are the oaths sworn upon Yahweh or Allah, or that in which the Comanche Indian calls upon the Great Spirit as witness to the truth.

In other cases it is not so much the god who is invoked as the sacred object with which he is associated, and this is reverently touched at the time that it is sworn upon. The particular object varies in accordance with whatever happens to be considered of psychic importance in a particular community. The early Hebrews, for example, swore upon their genitalia, the symbols of procreative power, while in the modern courtroom the witness takes the oath upon the Bible. Despite the identification of this principle with the higher forms of religion, it represents a clear relic of the older system of magic by touch, the punishment arising not so much from the outraged god as from the inherent power of the object itself.

One example of this type of oath is the Gold Coast ordeal in which the accused is given an article of food 'in some way appertains to a deity, who is then invoked to visit a breach of faith with punishment'.

The same principle underlays the medieval custom in which an accused person would eat the host, praying at the same time that it might choke him if he were not telling the truth. In one medieval form of ordeal a piece of consecrated bread made from unleavened barley was swallowed by the suspect and any violation of the truth was supposed to choke the perjurer or to rack his body with convulsions.

This form of oath depended upon the transmission of a curse into the body of the bread so that it would work upon the perjurer. A well-known English example of the practice was that involving the witch Joan Flower, who strove to defend herself from hanging by calling for the ordeal of bread and butter, wishing that 'it might never go through her if she were guilty'. In the event she 'fell down and died as she was carried to Lincoln Jail.'

Trial by Ordeal

The Emperor Charlemagne was strongly in favour of the Judgement of the Cross, a ceremony in which the accused, having declared his innocence upon oath, took up one of two sticks wrapped in fine wool from the altar, one bearing the concealed mark of a cross while the other was unmarked. If he picked up the stick marked with the cross his innocence was established beyond all doubt in the sight of God and man, but if he took

Left Albert Einstein takes the oath of allegiance on becoming an American citizen.

Below An accused witch, tried by ordeal in Kenya: if the frog refuses to slip down the man's throat, he is proved innocent, but if it is swallowed, he is judged guilty.

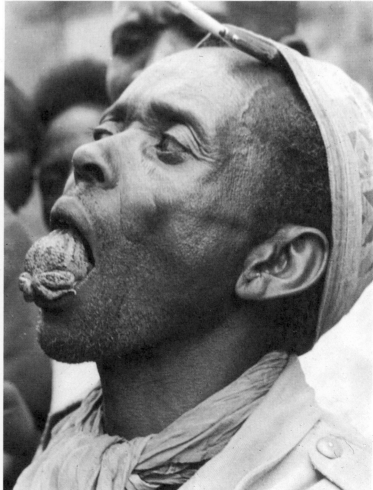

An accused man takes his oath at the court of King's Bench; various forms of trial by ordeal, to test the truth of a prisoner's oath, were accepted features of medieval law.

the other he was judged guilty and punished accordingly.

The legal theorists of medieval Europe made a clear distinction between the spoken and the written oath and that which had been ratified by contact with a sacred object, such as a holy relic. To use the words of one historian: 'So little respect was felt for the simple oath that the adjuncts came to be looked upon as the essential features and the imprecation itself to be divested of binding force without them.'

The older magical principles continued to manifest themselves in medieval jurisprudence. A well-known example was the judgement of trial by ordeal, in which the accused was made to immerse his arm up to the elbow in boiling water to supplement the oath of innocence, in the expectation that God would protect him from the injury if he really was innocent. At an earlier period the accused would be blindfolded and compelled to walk barefooted over nine red-hot ploughshares; if unhurt he would be adjudged as having told the truth. A further expression of the same principle was trial by combat or wager by battle, in which the accused, having taken his oath of innocence, fought out the issue fully armed in the lists and if triumphant was regarded as comply vindicated. On the other hand, to be defeated was evidence of guilt.

Blood Covenant

The covenant is another form of oath-taking, consisting of a mutual oath or a mutual conditional curse: each party conveys the curse to the other should he violate the conditions of the engagement. The binding effect of the covenanting oath is familiar in the rites of secret societies, the best known modern example being that of the Mau Mau movement in Kenya. This type of oath-taking is often reinforced by the most fearful ceremonies and includes the blood covenant, which demands either the drinking or sharing of blood. According to Herodotus (c 485–425 BC) the Medes and the Lydians, when taking an oath, made flesh wounds in their arms, following which they drank each other's blood. The signed contract is the modern equivalent of the ancient oath-bound compact or covenant between the parties.

At all times and among most peoples the oath has played an immense part in binding communities together for the achievement of a common purpose. Sometimes an oath involves the allegiance of the subject to his monarch, while the coronation oath, on the other hand, compels the monarch to honour certain obligations towards the state.

The binding effect of an oath was never more apparent than in Nazi Germany, when it secured the allegiance of the officer caste to the Nazi regime. Its power is also demonstrated in the solemn pact sworn by the desperate English naval mutineers at the Nore in 1797, which was so seriously regarded that the same year a repressive

Mansell Collection

A medieval king takes the coronation oath:
14th century manuscript in the British Museum.

law made it an offence punishable by transportation to administer an unlawful oath. This later resulted in the trial and conviction of the Tolpuddle martyrs, who in 1834 were found guilty of swearing men into a trade union lodge at a time when trade unionism was in itself perfectly legal.

So frightening were the imagined consequences of violating an oath that had been made upon some sacred or magical object, that in the past certain individuals were denied the privilege of oath-taking, since any perjury on their part could have severe repercussions upon the community. Among those exempted in Roman society were the priest of Jupiter and the Vestal Virgins.

An example of a primitive legal oath is that of the Samoan who, when accused of theft, solemnly swears: 'In the presence of the chiefs now assembled I lay my hands on the stone. If I stole the thing may I speedily die.' Such a device has often been quite sufficient to bring a culprit to light. Where this technique fails, however, the unknown thief may well become the target of that ancillary to the oath, the solemn curse, of which the following is an example: 'May fire burn the eyes of the one who stole my bananas. May fire burn his eyes and the eyes of his god also.'

Opposition to oath-taking played a not inconsiderable part in the development of legal and social practices. Certain religious

groups, like the Quakers, have always contended that the word of truth requires no reinforcement, submitting also that the taking of an oath weakens rather than strengthens any declaration or promise. For support the religious man could turn to the precept of Christ: 'Do not swear at all.' At the other end of the ethical scale the free-thinking Charles Bradlaugh was prepared to stand his ground in the House of Commons and even to be ejected from the House by force rather than take an oath in the name of a deity in which he had no belief. The right to affirm instead of swearing upon the Bible has now been established.

Within the legal system the oath now exists as an appeal to God as witness to the truth of the evidence given, for it must be declared on oath that what is to be said shall be 'the truth, the whole truth and nothing but the truth'. Cross-examination of the witness has now taken the place of the primitive ordeal, while the pains of imprisonment have replaced the divine punishment once meted out by an enraged deity.

There is no difference in essence between the oath of the old-time Khond who stood upon his tiger skin and demanded death if he failed to speak the truth, and that of the medieval Englishman with his 'By God!', 'By Jesus!' and 'By the saints above!' Each called upon the supernatural powers as witness to the truth of a declared intention or statement, demanding to be punished if his word were broken. The extent to which the once reverent oath has degenerated into

sheer profanity is a reflection of the debasement of old spiritual values as much as of the misuse of words.

Signed in Blood

'Now look-a-here, Tom, less take and swear to one another – that's what we got to do – swear to keep mum.'

'I'm agreed, Huck. It's the best thing. Would you just hold hands and swear that we –'

'Oh, no, that wouldn't do for this. That's good enough for little rubbishy common things – specially with gals, cuz they go back on you any way, and blab if they get into a huff – but there orter be writing 'bout a big thing like this. And blood.'

Tom's whole being applauded this idea. It was deep, and dark, and awful; the hour, the circumstances, the surroundings, were in keeping with it. He picked up a clean pine shingle that lay in the moonlight, took a little fragment of 'red keel' out of his pocket, got the moon on his work, and painfully scrawled these lines . . . "Huck Finn and Tom Sawyer swears they will kep mum about this and they wish they may Drop down dead in their Tracks if they ever tell and Rot."

. . . Tom unwound the thread from one of his needles, and each boy pricked the ball of his thumb and squeezed out a drop of blood.

In time, after many squeezes, Tom managed to sign his initials, using the ball of his little finger for a pen. Then he showed Huckleberry how to make an H and an F, and the oath was complete.

Mark Twain *The Adventures of Tom Sawyer*

Gestures

To convey meaning without words, attitudes of the body and especially movements of arms and hands are employed. The effect is to give a dramatic charge to meaning by acting it out in a universal sign language, for good gestures, except for certain specialist ones, are immediately comprehensible.

In fact everyone without realizing it knows a great many ritual gestures. There is the Fascist salute of the open hand flung up, which was taken from the ancient Roman salute; it showed that a man held no weapon and therefore came in peace. The corresponding Communist clenched fist implies determination and even a threat, and seems to say: 'But I do have a weapon!' In medieval religious art God is shown with open hand, and rays are often represented coming from his fingers. The open hand was a sign of victory in Phoenicia, and the Roman legions used it in a similar sense, putting it at the tops of their standards as shown in Trajan's column in Rome.

Fingers are crossed 'for luck'. The original intention was the ceremonial stoppage of evil influences, and legs or arms were crossed for the same reason. Three fingers closed, leaving the thumb and little finger erect, gives the sign of the Horned God or 'Devil'. This sign has a long history: called the *mano cornuta* in Italy, it was earlier a general sign for the moon goddess, and used in the cults both of Dagon in the Near East and of Brahma in India. The hand turned sideways, with first and little fingers only extended, is popularly supposed to avert the Evil Eye and is in wide use in Italy and the Near East.

The Devil has much to do with luck, and lucky charms are often sold showing the Devil with his fingers to his nose, in vulgar parlance 'cocking a snook'. The gesture appears to be sexual in origin, nose and thumb being reckoned as phallic symbols.

The most famous popular gesture of recent years, the V for Victory sign popularized by Sir Winston Churchill, seems to be a horns-up sign, implying the power of a horned animal. Another version of this gesture is the old sign of Tudor and earlier times 'Horns to you,' used for telling someone that his wife is being unfaithful. This hoary jest, which never failed to amuse on the Elizabethan stage however often it appeared, was based on the idea that the wronged husband was supposed to be sprouting horns on his brow.

The thumb appearing between the first and second fingers is the common Italian gesture *fica*, 'I don't care a fig,' called *manus obscaena* in late Roman times. It showed contempt to the highest degree. But the thumb has a more noble significance: extended, in Christian baptism it is used for making the sign of the cross in water on children, following the Old Testament custom of using the thumb to apply blood in the ritual of ordination (Leviticus 8, 23–4; Exodus 29.20). Thumbs up or down was the sign whereby the Roman Emperor signified

life or death to the defeated one in the gladiatorial shows of the ancient world.

A Catholic priest celebrating Mass makes use of gesture to indicate to the congregation the point of the service which is being reached. For the most part these gestures arise naturally from the action. When the priest is offering prayer on behalf of the people, he holds the hands open and upward and facing towards the altar. Facing away from the altar, the priest raises one open hand to bless the people. The pope, and later a bishop as well, could bless instead with the third and little fingers closed, so that the thumb, first and second fingers were left to represent the Trinity. This is the ancient *mano pantea* represented at Pompeii, and also well known in India.

To express penitence the right hand bent inwards strikes the breast. Rather more distinctive is the gesture commonly used whilst holding the Host. The priest holds the hands together with thumbs parallel and first fingers bent, having the tips joined upon the tips of the thumbs; the Host is held between the four tips, while the three other fingers are extended joined.

Christianity and Islam share the gesture of joining the thumb and first finger in a circle, leaving the other three fingers extended. The Greek Orthodox Church used it in blessing, and with hands in this position the Moslem recites his creed. A certain threat is implied if the hand is held horizontally; when elevated it means love.

The common ritual gestures of the Buddha are in effect four. The seated Buddha calls the earth to witness with the downward pointing right hand, whilst he receives from above with the upward turned left hand laid in his lap. When the Buddha's hands are together they are holding the begging bowl. When one hand is held up, palm outward, this is known as 'turning the wheel of the law', as this is the gesture which would be used to spin a real wheel.

The Movements of Magic

Ceremonial magic naturally employs many gestures. In one of the more intelligible the arms are outstretched to form a cross with the body, expressing suffering and death, applied in Egyptian magic usually to Osiris; this action also occurs in the Christian Mass. In another gesture the forearms may be held up in a St Andrew's cross, making the pentagram and signifying a rising from the dead. The gesture of the Egyptian god Shu, supporting the heavens with uplifted hands, also occurs in the Mass as a gesture of offering thanks and prayer.

Magical gestures can be traced back to Neolithic and even to Paleolithic times. At St Duzac, Brittany, is a menhir (ancient monumental stone), one of whose carvings shows a god with arms held up supporting a goddess. This bell-skirted lady has her arms crossed, but her hands are held up in a gesture that may mean the union of true hearts or possibly signifies the stopping of

birth. At the top is a pre-Christian figure with the arms extended upon an equal-armed cross.

The ceremonial gestures of ancient Egypt may be deduced from pyramid and tomb reliefs and paintings. In funeral ceremonies the first thought was perhaps to raise the soul. This idea is expressed by holding the hands, palms upwards, above the head. Actual mourning was a matter of holding the arms in a gesture of throwing dust upon the head, and uttering the cries of the professional mourner. Intercession with the gods for the dead is shown by the arms held directly upward. To send away the threatening evil spirits from the dead a pushing movement was made. The ceremony of making offerings to the gods involved specific gestures such as the picking up of the offering and making the offering in the sign of the lotus, which was the most usual flower to be offered.

Some of the most striking examples of the use of ritual gesture appear in dance forms. Of the fully developed systems the greatest are those of India and Bali.

Language of Signs

Of great antiquity, the Hindu dance is generally considered to be based on the 108 poses carved in the Gopurams (terrace passages) of the temple of Shiva Nataraja – (Shiva as lord of the dance) at Cidambaram in southern India. The Hindu word *Natya* means both acting and dancing; that is, gesture with meaning is recognized as an essential part of the dance. Thus there are 108 standard *mudras* or hand gestures in the classical Hindu sacred dance, single or double-handed – the most complete gesture language in the world.

The meaning is essentially mythological; its elements came, it is said, from the basic four sacred books of the *Vedas*. The main centre of action and movement is in the upper body rather than the legs. Poses are prescribed for features and head: there are 52 types of glances, 13 positions for the mouth and 20 for the head and neck. There are also numerous prescribed postures for the hands.

Perhaps the most significant and easily recognized positionings are those that portray a god, of which there are some 16. Five positions represent various manifestations of Shiva: the three-eyed god, the cobra-crowned one, he who wears the moon in his tresses, he who rides the bull, and the Creator of earth and heaven. The monkey god Hanuman has two earthly hands pointing down. The popular Krishna and his milk-girl mate Radha are shown by five gestures. A goddess in general has a mudra of protection – hand up – and of bestowal – hand down; the particular goddess is shown by attaching to the general mudra the gesture depicting her mate.

Seated Bodhisattva 'receiving from above' with hand turned upward. A Buddha's hand pointing down is 'calling the earth to witness', if the hands are together they are holding the begging bowl, if one hand is held up with the palm outward it is called 'turning the wheel of the law'.

William MacQuitty

118

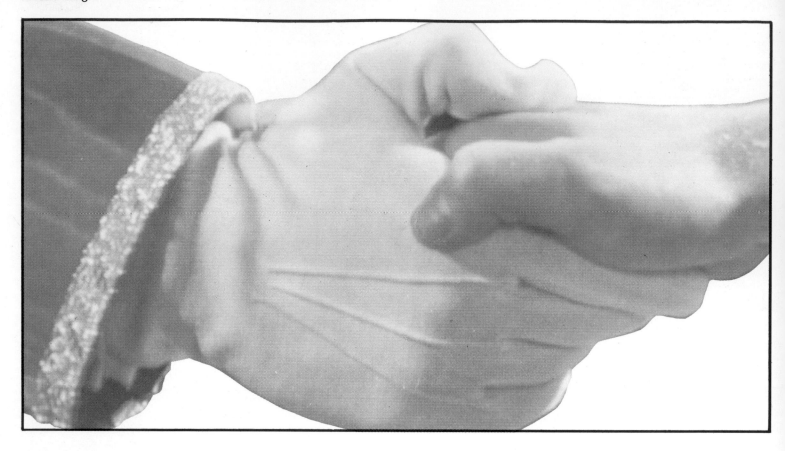

Freemasonry

One definition of Freemasonry is that it is 'a system of morality veiled in allegory and illustrated by symbols'. Freemasons are members of a so-called secret society but membership is freely available to any man of good repute. There is no question of recruitment or invitation to join: individuals simply find their way to the Craft, mostly through a friend who is already a member.

Any brief attempt to explain Freemasonry's inner meaning, its historical development and its place in modern society, presents formidable difficulties. It is not that information is difficult to obtain. On the contrary, anyone sufficiently curious can learn a great deal from the available literature, which is enormous. A Masonic bibliography published in Germany in 1912 contains no fewer than 40,000 titles. It seems, however, that to begin to understand the inner meaning of Freemasonry one must belong to it, if only because the actual experience is more important and significant than merely 'academic' knowledge.

For the outsider the perplexing factors are Freemasonry's status as a secret society and the significance of the secrets that it allegedly so jealously guards. Again, it is often asked why so many adult and presumably sensible men should practise rituals that include secret words and signs. However, on the basis of any merely superficial assessment or, even worse, complete ignorance, it would be unwise to dismiss an international sociological phenomenon as nonsense.

The Craft, which is banned in all Communist countries, in Roman Catholic Spain and Portugal, although not in Italy, continues to attract members on a worldwide scale. Its appeal clearly operates on two different levels. For some the attraction is obviously social. The Lodge is an exclusive club and the business of 'working' a ritual is the prelude to a convivial meal. For others, however, Freemasonry's rituals, teachings and symbolism have a deeper and more spiritual content. In this context we encounter the Craft at its most attractive and significant level.

Band of Brothers

Freemasonry is neither a religion nor a substitute for religion. It embraces all forms of religious belief which conceive of a Supreme Being and in a Lodge men of all creeds meet in complete amity. Its rituals, which in some respects resemble short Morality Plays or moral charades, simply reflect in symbolic terms concepts of idealism, humanity, charity and fraternity.

But why the necessity for secrecy? This, too, has a symbolical meaning. The tradition was inherited from the old Operative or Working Masons, who because of the mobility of their profession, were denied the advantages of a static guild organization. The Lodges arose wherever masons were assembled for large scale building works, such as a cathedral, and formed a flexible network throughout the country. The masons required proof of professional skill before accepting an itinerant colleague as a master craftsman. If the newcomer knew the answers in their correct form to certain veiled questions, also certain passwords and signs, it conveyed to his interrogator that he really was a Master Mason, a master of his craft, and hence qualified to accept employment and if need be help from a fellow craftsman. In other words it was a form of primitive trade unionism.

Later the Speculative (Non-operative) Freemasons took over the traditional questions, passwords and signs, not as an antiquarian mumbo-jumbo, but simply to emphasize that oaths of fidelity, fraternity and the like must never be taken lightly. Hence even Freemasonry's 'secrets' are symbolic. That they contain nothing incompatible with conventional religious beliefs is reflected by the fact that so many Anglican and Nonconformist clergy are Freemasons.

Secrets of Initiation

Freemasons meet in a specially furnished Lodge room. The Worshipful Master, the Wardens and other officers of the Lodge sit in their appointed places. In the anteroom adjoining the Lodge room a functionary known as the Tyler keeps guard to forbid the entry of strangers. First it is necessary to 'open' the Lodge in whichever degree is being 'worked'. A dialogue is held, in the form of questions and answers, between the Worshipful Master and various officers of the Lodge. Its time-honoured purpose is to remind the participants of the symbolical or allegorical nature of the ceremony they are performing.

When an initiation ceremony takes place the Lodge is opened in the First Degree. Outside in the ante-room the candidate

Left The Masonic grip of the raised thumb, initially enabled members to recognize each other without openly revealing themselves.

Right In the 18th century some Masonic groups in France and Germany dabbled in occultism: 18th century engravings of a French initiation ceremony. *Above* The candidate is symbolically lowered into the grave. *Centre* His head is covered with a bloody cloth and the members of the Lodge point their swords at him. *Below* The Grand Master raises the newly received Apprentice with the mason's grip.

is prepared by the Tyler. His collar, tie and jacket are removed and he lays aside his money: with this demonstration that the Lodge accepts him even in penury, he accepts the same obligation towards his fellow Masons. He is then led into the room blindfolded. The Tyler presents him to the Master and in reply to the question 'Whom have you there?' replies: 'A poor Candidate in a state of darkness.' The implication is that the darkness is spiritual but that he will be shown Light.

In the course of the ceremony the candidate swears a solemn oath not to reveal Freemasonry's secrets which, once again, are all symbolical. The blindfold is then removed. He is also shown certain grips and signs, a survival of the old Operative Masonry, and told certain words which refer to the symbolical building of King Solomon's temple.

He is presented with the First Degree Mason's working tools, and the Master explains their significance: the 24-inch gauge represents the 24 hours of the day, to be divided between prayer, work, refreshment and helping a friend; the gavel represents the power of conscience; the chisel represents the advantages of education. Finally the Master explains the symbolism of the First Degree tracing board, a rectangular plank containing a painted representation of the symbols appropriate to the First Degree. The Lodge is then 'closed' in the First Degree according to the appropriate ritual.

In due course the Entered Apprentice will be advanced, normally at intervals of about three months in each case, to the Second Degree (Fellow Craft) and finally to the Third Degree (Master Mason). In each case there is a specific ritual and the disclosure of more information. As a Master Mason the new Brother has nominally reached the end of the road although he can proceed further to the Royal Arch, which can roughly be described as an extension of Craft Masonry, and may later elect to ask for membership of the other available degrees and Orders. This is entirely a matter of choice.

It is possible to buy printed editions of the three Craft rituals but some material will be omitted. Any outsider can obtain at least a notion of the structure of these rituals. It appears however that nothing short of personal experience of participation in the rituals will serve to convey an understanding of what the Craft means to so many men. This means, in effect, that no outsider can ever really grasp Freemasonry's inner meaning.

Chris Barker

Index

Index

Acknowledgments: *Front of jacket:* Studio Patellani; *back of jacket:* Michael Holford; *endpapers:* Breughel's *Children's Games* (Kunsthistorisches Museum, Vienna); *page 5* Harald Schultz; *pages 6–7* Inca ceremony in Cuzco (John Moss); *pages 8–9, left to right:* Frederico and Aldo Patellani, John Moss, British Museum/C. M. Dixon, William Sargant, Camera Press, Library of Congress/Syndication International; *background picture:* Nick Maddren.